Materials and Techniques
of Post-Tonal Music

Materials and Techniques of Post-Tonal Music, Fifth Edition provides the most comprehensive introduction to post-tonal music and its analysis available. Covering music from the end of the nineteenth century through the beginning of the twenty-first, it offers students a clear guide to understanding the diverse and innovative compositional strategies that emerged in the post-tonal era, from Impressionism to computer music.
This updated fifth edition features:

- chapters revised throughout to include new examples from recent music and insights from the latest scholarship;
- the introduction of several new concepts and topics, including parsimonius voice-leading, scalar transformations, the New Complexity, and set theory in less chromatic contexts;
- expanded discussions of spectralism and electronic music;
- timelines in each chapter, grounding the music discussed in its chronological context;
- a companion website that provides students with links to recordings of musical examples discussed in the text and provides instructors with an instructor's manual that covers all of the exercises in each chapter.

Offering accessible explanations of complex concepts, *Materials and Techniques of Post-Tonal Music*, Fifth Edition is an essential text for all students of post-tonal music theory.

Stefan Kostka is Professor Emeritus of Music Theory at the Butler School of Music at The University of Texas at Austin.

Matthew Santa is Professor of Theory and Chair of the Music Theory and Composition Area at the Texas Tech University School of Music.

Materials and Techniques of Post-Tonal Music

FIFTH EDITION

Stefan Kostka

The University of Texas at Austin

Matthew Santa

Texas Tech University

Routledge
Taylor & Francis Group

NEW YORK AND LONDON

Fifth edition published 2018
by Routledge
711 Third Avenue, New York, NY 10017

and by Routledge
2 Park Square, Milton Park, Abingdon, Oxon, OX14 4RN

Routledge is an imprint of the Taylor & Francis Group, an informa business

First edition published by Prentice Hall 1989

Fourth edition published by Prentice Hall 2011

Library of Congress Cataloging-in-Publication Data
Names: Kostka, Stefan M., author. | Santa, Matthew, author.
Title: Materials and techniques of post-tonal music / Stefan Kostka,
Matthew Santa.
Description: Fifth edition. | New York, NY : Routledge, 2018. |
Includes bibliographical references and index.
Identifiers: LCCN 2017044195 (print) | LCCN 2017046370
(ebook) | ISBN 9781315229485 (ebook) | ISBN 9781138714168
(hardback) | ISBN 9781138714199 (pbk.)
Subjects: LCSH: Composition (Music) | Music—19th century—
Analysis, appreciation. | Music—20th century—Analysis,
appreciation.
Classification: LCC MT40 (ebook) | LCC MT40 .K8 2018 (print)
| DDC 781.309/04—dc23LC record available at
https://lccn.loc.gov/2017044195

ISBN: 978-1-138-71416-8 (hbk)
ISBN: 978-1-138-71419-9 (pbk)
ISBN: 978-1-315-22948-5 (ebk)

Typeset in Bembo & Helvetica Neue
by Florence Production Limited, Stoodleigh, Devon, UK

Visit the companion website: www.routledge.com/cw/kostka

Printed and bound in the United States of America by Sheridan

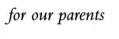

Contents

Preface

Instruction in music theory at the college level has long been concerned primarily with the music of the tonal era, spanning roughly some 300 years and including the Baroque, Classical, and Romantic periods. The reasons for this are not hard to imagine. After all, most of the masterworks that are our steady diet as concertgoers and performers were composed during that time, some significant exceptions such as concert-band music notwithstanding. And probably no one who has studied the tonal system in depth has failed to be impressed with what must surely rank as one of the greatest of humanity's artistic achievements.

But musical achievements since 1900 have also been of great significance, and theorists in recent decades have shown interest in devoting more instructional time to the music of that century. One problem, however, has been the lack of appropriate instructional materials. Although several fine books available on music after 1900 are available, few of them deal with the topic in a way that seems appropriate for the general music student, and it is this need that the present text is intended to meet.

Materials and Techniques of Post-Tonal Music is organized primarily by compositional technique and only partly chronologically. Most chapters deal with some aspect of music (rhythm, for instance) throughout the period, but there is a quasi-chronological method in the ordering of the chapters. No attempt is made in the text to teach music history per se or to explore in detail the style of individual composers. Instead, the emphasis is on musical materials and compositional techniques. Each chapter includes an introduction, several subheaded sections, and a summary. The discussions are illustrated by a large number of musical examples drawn from music literature since 1900. With few exceptions, the examples are currently available in audio format, and as many of them as possible should be listened to. The last part of each chapter consists of exercise material that in most cases is divided into four subsections: Fundamentals, Analysis, Composition, and Further Reading. (See the Bibliography for complete bibliographical references for notes and Further Reading assignments.) Most teachers will find that there are more exercises than they can make use of profitably.

Materials and Techniques of Post-Tonal Music is appropriate for a unit as short as several weeks or as long as a year. In the former case, we suggest omitting some of the chapters that are less vital for a short overview—perhaps Chapters 1, 7, 8, 11, 13, and 15, for example, depending on the interests of the instructor and students. A short course would also have to omit most of the exercise material, but the usefulness of these exercises for class drills and discussion should not be overlooked. Few teaching situations would allow the thorough study of every chapter and the completion of all of the exercises. Some of the Further Reading exercises, in particular, are appropriate only for the more advanced and highly motivated student. Another point to keep in mind is that some chapters (9 and 10, for instance) require more time than the average to complete successfully, while others (such as 8 and 15) require less.

To a certain extent, the chapters in this book are freestanding because they do not follow a chronological sequence, but there are exceptions. Chapters 9, 10, and 13 should be taken up in that order, although other chapters may be interspersed between them. Also, some instructors assign Chapter 9 very early in the sequence so that students can have longer to practice with the concepts that it presents. Finally, Chapters 2 through 6 form the core foundation for many of the chapters to follow, so it would not be advisable to omit any of them.

NEW TO THE FIFTH EDITION

Most of the chapters have been revised to some extent, and a number of new examples have been added. Various new concepts and topics have been introduced: parsimonious voice-leading, scalar transformations, the New Complexity, and set theory in less chromatic contexts. The discussions of spectralism and of electronic music have both been expanded.

The most dramatic change has been the addition of a supporting website (www.rouledge.com/cw/kostka) that includes both links to audio recordings of the musical examples for students and an instructor's manual for instructors.

Acknowledgments

We benefited substantially in the development of this book from the critiques provided by our students at the University of Texas at Austin and at Texas Tech University, and we are grateful for their sympathetic and helpful evaluations. David Rains was generous in sharing his expertise in the area of electronic music, while Mary Blackman applied her considerable organizational skills to the task of obtaining permissions. Thanks go as well to the staff of the Fine Arts Library of the University of Texas, and especially to Olga Buth and Karl Miller, for their expertise and assistance.

Many of the changes found in the second edition were suggested by Kent Kennan, whose close reading of the text was most valuable. Other helpful ideas came from James Bennighof of Baylor University, Joseph DiStephano of East Carolina University, William Dougherty of Drake University, and James O'Donnell of Indiana State University. The revision of Chapter 12 was done with a great deal of assistance from Charles Menoche, also of the University of Texas at Austin and a true authority on music technology.

A number of people made helpful suggestions that were incorporated into the third edition, and I am grateful to them all but especially to Robert Fleisher of Northern Illinois University, Timothy McKinney of Baylor University, and Kip Wile of the Peabody Conservatory. The revision of Chapter 12 was largely done by Keith Kothman of Ball State University, whose expertise was most appreciated. Other helpful ideas came from William Lake (Bowling Green University), Per F. Broman (Bowling Green University), and Robert Maggio (West Chester University).

The planning for the fourth edition was aided enormously by the input of various colleagues across the country, including L. Christine Amos (The University of Texas at San Antonio), Christopher Bartlette (Binghamton University), Michael Boyd (University of Toledo), Andrew Davis (University of Houston), Stefan Eckert (University of Northern Colorado), Cynthia Folio (Temple University), Patricia Julien (University of Vermont), Robert Peck (Louisiana State University), Kevin Puts (Peabody Institute), Steven Rosenhaus (New York University), Elizabeth Sayrs (Ohio University), Phillip Tolbert (Penn State University), Ryan Virgil (Yale University), and Dan Welcher (University of Texas at Austin). Ryan Beavers (University of Texas at Austin) did fine work putting nearly all of the excerpts into Finale notation and into MIDI format.

The fifth edition has benefitted from suggestions by numerous colleagues across the country, many of whom were listed above, but also to Michael Berry (University of Washington), David Forrest (Texas Tech University), Jake Rundall (University of

Illinois), and Michael Stoune (Texas Tech University), but especially from Mei-Fang Lin (Texas Tech University), whose experience teaching and performing new music and whose willingness to share her course materials and her sage advice proved to be invaluable. The fifth edition also owes much to all of the people at Routledge who worked on the book, but especially to Genevieve Aoki, who served as our main contact and helped to keep the project on track in many different ways.

Finally, we would like to express our gratitude to our wives, Mary Robertson and Lisa Garner Santa, for their encouragement and for their inspiring love of music.

Stefan Kostka
University of Texas at Austin

Matthew Santa
Texas Tech University

CHAPTER 1

The Twilight of the Tonal System

INTRODUCTION

Before beginning our study of the materials of music since 1900, we will first look back briefly at what happened to the system of triadic tonality, the primary organizing force in the music of the preceding three centuries. In the course of doing this, we will find it convenient to introduce a few terms that may be new to you. Throughout this book, new terms will appear in **boldface** type the first time they are used in the text.

Tonal music and the principles that govern it did not develop overnight, of course, nor did they decline overnight. In fact, tonal music still thrives today in music for television and film, commercials, jazz, and some popular music, and it has even seen a limited revival in the past few decades in the "serious" music of some postmodern composers. Nevertheless, it is safe to say that by around 1900 the tonal system had become so strained by chromaticism and by the desire for originality that further development of the system seemed impossible.

We will use the term **post-tonal** in this book to refer to music that does not follow the traditional conventions of tonal harmony. This does not necessarily mean, however, that the music being referred to is without a tonal center. The whole issue of tonality in post-tonal music will be discussed more thoroughly in Chapter 5.

DIATONIC TONAL MUSIC

Almost all of the music of the seventeenth and eighteenth centuries is essentially diatonic on all levels.[1] Of course, diatonic tonal music does not lack accidentals or altered tones; after all, a tonal piece of almost any length will almost certainly contain altered tones. But in diatonic tonal music the difference between diatonic and altered tones is always clear, and seldom do we lose our tonal bearings, our sense of key and scale, and our immediate understanding of the function of the altered tones.

Diatonic relationships also prevail at the background levels of a diatonic tonal composition. Think of the keys that Bach is apt to reach in the course of a fugue, or the traditional key schemes for sonata forms and rondos. All represent diatonic relationships because in all cases the secondary tonalities are closely related to the primary tonality of the movement.

Even at the highest level—key relationships between movements—diatonicism prevails. For example, all of the movements of a Baroque suite were in a single key, whereas in multiple-movement works of the Classical and Romantic periods the first and last movements are always in the same tonality (although sometimes in a different mode), and this is considered the tonal center of the composition as a whole.

CHROMATIC TONAL MUSIC

The point at which the organization of tonal music becomes chromatic instead of diatonic is not an absolute one. Much of the harmony of chromatic tonal music can be analyzed by using the same vocabulary for altered chords, modulations, chromatic nonchord tones, and so forth, that we use in the analysis of diatonic music. It is partly a matter of emphasis. Instead of a texture in which diatonic tones predominate over nondiatonic tones, both in number and in significance, we are dealing here with music that is so saturated with chromaticism that the diatonic basis of the music is no longer apparent to the listener. One writer puts it this way: "The critical distinction between the two styles lies in the transformation of the diatonic scalar material of the classical tonal system into the equally-tempered twelve note chromatic complex of the diatonic tonal system."[2] In the next few pages we will look at some features of chromatic tonal music that will have particular relevance to our study of the music of the twentieth and twenty-first centuries.

SOME ASPECTS OF CHROMATIC HARMONY

Two fundamental root movements in diatonic tonal harmony are the circle-of-5ths progression, as in vi–ii–V–I, and the diatonic mediant progression, as in I–vi–IV–ii. Though these progressions by no means disappear in chromatic harmony, another relationship, the **chromatic mediant relationship**, finds a popularity that it did not have in earlier styles. Two triads or keys are in a chromatic mediant relationship if they are of the same quality (major or minor) and their roots are a major 3rd or minor 3rd apart. These relationships are illustrated in Example 1-1 (lowercase indicates minor).

EXAMPLE 1-1 Chromatic Medium Relationships

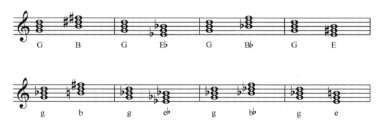

The term **pitch class** is used to refer to any of the 12 notes of the equal-tempered scale regardless of spelling or octave placement. For example, every C, every B♯, and every D♭♭ belongs to the same pitch class. (We will often number the 12 pitch classes from 0 to 11, with 0 usually representing the pitch class to which C belongs.) Notice that in Example 1-1 each of the pairs of triads shares exactly one pitch class. Third-related triads of opposite quality (major and minor) sharing no pitch classes at all are said to be in a **doubly chromatic mediant relationship**, as in Example 1-2. Sometimes chords in chromatic or doubly chromatic mediant relationships are spelled enharmonically (as in G–d♯), but the spelling does not alter the relationship because the pitch classes are unchanged by the spelling.

EXAMPLE 1-2 Doubly Chromatic Mediant Relationships

Chromatic mediant relationships between triads contribute to the color and excitement of Example 1-3. The excerpt is clearly in C major, and it uses the following progression:

C–a–F–d–B♭–G–C–A♭–F–C

Certainly both the circle-of-5ths and diatonic mediant progressions are important here, but the three chromatic mediant relationships (indicated by the "<m>" symbols in the example) add a certain freshness and unpredictability to the harmony of the passage. Incidentally, this simplified piano reduction gives only a hint of what this music is really like; try to listen to a recording with the full score.

EXAMPLE 1-3 Liszt: *Les Préludes* (1854), mm. 35–42 (simplified texture)

Example 1-4 provides a further illustration of chromatic mediants, and several other things besides. Chord roots, inversions, and qualities are indicated below the example. The progression contains two circle-of-5ths progressions (D–G and C–f) and three chromatic mediants. It also contains two **tritone relationships** (indicated by the "<t>" symbols in the example), a root movement commonly found in earlier music in only a few progressions (such as VI–ii° in minor and N⁶–V). A listener could interpret Example 1-4 as a IV⁶–N⁶–V–I⁶ progression in G, followed by an identical progression in F, ending on a minor tonic. Except for the last chord, the excerpt illustrates a **real sequence**, a sequence in which the pattern is transposed exactly, as opposed to a diatonic sequence, in which only the notes of a single diatonic scale are used, thus reproducing the pattern only approximately. A real sequence has the effect of quickly throwing the music out of one key and into another, even if only for the duration of a few chords. Real sequences contribute a good deal to the **brief tonicizations** that are typical of much chromatic harmony.

EXAMPLE 1-4 Wagner: *Siegfried* (1871), Act II, Scene 1, mm. 238–245

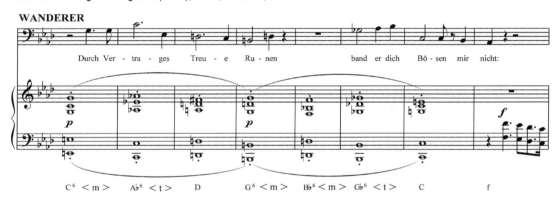

A real sequence begins Example 1-5 (mm. 1–4), using only dominant 7th chords (the last one enharmonically spelled) from the keys of D♭, B♭, E, and D♭ again. The root movements involve two chromatic mediant relationships and one tritone. Notice that in each case the dominant 7th chords share exactly two pitch classes. This is true only of dominant 7th chords whose roots are separated by a minor 3rd or a tritone. Example 1-5 illustrates two more characteristics of chromatic harmony—suspended tonality and nonfunctional chord successions. The first term is used to refer to passages that are tonally ambiguous. The dominant 7th chords in Example 1-5 do little to establish any key, because they are both unexpected and unresolved, and the A♭7–C–A♭ progression that ends the excerpt is of little help. Presumably Liszt had the tonality of A♭ in mind, since the piece ends similarly to mm. 5–6. Play through the example and see what you think. To say that the chords in Example 1-5 form a nonfunctional chord succession does not imply that it is useless, but rather that the chords do not "progress" in any of the ways commonly found in diatonic tonal harmony.

Nonfunctional chord successions are often the result of what is commonly called **parsimonious voice leading**, which simply means voice leading that is as smooth as possible. The logic of chord progressions based on parsimonious voice leading depends

EXAMPLE 1-5 Liszt: "Blume und Duft" ("Flower and Fragrance") (1862), mm. 1–6

upon the consistency of the smooth voice leading, in which most voices either move by half step or not at all, rather than on the familiar root motions that drive traditional harmonic progressions. (While parsimonious voice leading such as augmented-6th chord resolutions and the so-called omnibus progression[3] also may be found on occasion in traditional harmony, they are the exceptions that prove the rule.) The resulting verticalities are usually tertian (triads and 7th chords), but the chords form nonfunctional successions or brief tonicizations. For instance, play through Example 1-6. The essential elements are a chromatic descent from B4 to E4 in the top voice and B2 to E2 in the bass to make a convincing cadence.[4] The soprano and alto move in parallel major thirds until the last two beats, the alto stopping its descent on reaching the leading tone, which eventually resolves. The tenor enters on a C4 and moves in parallel motion with the upper voices for three beats, stops momentarily on B♭/A♯3, and then moves to the 7th of the dominant chord before resolving to G3. The bass enters last, doubling the soprano momentarily before moving into its cadential figure. On a higher level, the progression in this excerpt is simply tonic–dominant–tonic, beginning with the incomplete tonic triad at the opening of the phrase. But on the surface, the chords created by the various voices, beginning with beat 2 of the first measure, are as follows (the c°7 and the F7 are enharmonically spelled):

F–E–E♭–c°7–F7–B7(♭5)–e

Although there is a IV6–ii°7–V$_3^4$ progression in B♭ here, it is doubtful that anyone would hear it that way. The only traditional harmonic progression in the excerpt is the final authentic cadence (with a lowered 5th in the dominant 7th creating a French 6th sonority). The music preceding the cadence makes use of parsimonious voice leading and creates a nonfunctional chord succession.

EXAMPLE 1-6 Grieg: "Gone," Op. 71 , No. 6 (1901), mm. 1–2

From Edition Peters.

The chords in Example 1-6 were created primarily by parallel or similar motion. Three independent gestures combine to produce the chords in Example 1-7. The first gesture is a chromatic ascent in the melody from F♯4 to G5 (doubled at the octave above). The second element is an augmented triad in the inner voices (beginning in the third measure of the excerpt), which moves, more slowly than the soprano, chromatically downward through a minor 3rd. The final element is the ostinato in the bass, swaying back and forth from B♭2 to A2, finally settling on A. The nonfunctional voice-leading chords created by the combination of these three gestures are sometimes tertian and sometimes not; some of them are highly dissonant (mm. 38–39, for example). Suspended tonality is the result, even at the end, where the final sonority does little to confirm the presumed tonality of G.

EXAMPLE 1-7 Liszt: "Gray Clouds" ("Nuages gris") (1881), mm. 33–48

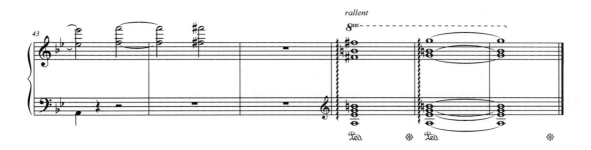

Unresolved dissonances, as in the Liszt example, are typical of some late nineteenth-century music. In many cases they come about through the juxtaposition of apparently independent musical ideas (melodies, sequences, and so on) with no attempt being made to put those dissonances into any traditional context, and they often contribute to a feeling of suspended tonality.

Augmented triads and diminished 7th chords are both examples of **equal division of the octave**. Real sequences frequently divide the octave into equal parts, usually by transposing the pattern by a minor 3rd or a major 3rd. This is closely related to the concept of the **interval cycle**, which is the transposition of a pitch class two or more times by the exact same interval. We mentioned earlier that pitch classes are sometimes represented by the numbers 0 through 11, with 0 usually representing C. The other numbers[4] are assigned chromatically upward, so that C♯/D♭ is represented by 1, D by 2, and so on:

0 = C   1 = C♯   2 = D   3 = D♯   4 = E   5 = F

6 = F♯   7 = G   8 = G♯   9 = A   10 = A♯   11 = B

The chromatic scale can be created by an interval cycle that moves by ascending a half step, which we will call a **C1 cycle**: 0 1 2 3 4 5 6 7 8 9 10 11. An augmented triad results from a **C4 cycle**, as in 0 4 8 or 1 5 9 and so forth, and a diminished 7th chord results from a **C3 cycle**, as in 0 3 6 9 or 1 4 7 10, etc. All of these divide the octave into equal parts. We will learn about other interval cycles in the next chapter.

SUSPENDED TONALITY AND ATONALITY

Earlier in this chapter we used the term "suspended tonality" to describe a passage with a momentarily unclear or ambiguous tonality. This term is appropriate only when used in the context of a tonal composition. It is not the same as **atonality**, a term that will appear frequently in this text, and that needs to be defined at this point.[5]

In a very general way, atonality means music without a tonal center. More specifically, it refers to the systematic avoidance of most of those musical materials and devices that traditionally have been used to define a tonal center. Those materials and devices would include, among others, the following:

Diatonic pitch material
Tertian harmonies
Dominant–tonic harmonic progressions
Dominant–tonic bass lines
Resolution of leading tones to tonics
Resolution of dissonant sonorities to more consonant ones
Pedal points

Although chromaticism led historically to atonality, chromatic tonal music is not the same as atonal music. A more thorough study of atonality will have to be postponed until later chapters, although the term will come up from time to time throughout this text.

SUMMARY

The decline of the tonal system as the primary organizing force in music coincided with and was largely due to the ascendancy of chromaticism. Diatonic tonal music is essentially diatonic on all levels, whereas chromatic tonal music is based to a much greater extent on the chromatic scale. Some of the characteristics of chromatic tonal harmony are listed here in the order in which they are introduced in the chapter:

Chromatic (and double chromatic) mediant relationship
Tritone relationships
Real sequences
Brief tonicizations
Suspended tonality
Nonfunctional chord successions
Parsimonious voice leading
Unresolved dissonances
Equal division of the octave (interval cycles)

Atonality is not a characteristic of music of the nineteenth century. Atonal music avoids the use of most of those musical materials and devices that traditionally have been used to define a tonal center.

MUSIC FROM THE CHAPTER IN CHRONOLOGICAL CONTEXT

Year	Composer	Work	Reference
1854	**Liszt**	*Les Préludes*	**p. 3**
1862	**Liszt**	**"Blume und Duft"**	**p. 5**
1871	**Wagner**	*Siegfried*	**p. 4**
1881	**Liszt**	**"Nuages Gris"**	**p. 6**
1894	Debussy	*Prelude to the Afternoon of a Faun*	Impressionism
1901	**Grieg**	**"Gone," Op. 71, No. 6**	**p. 6**
1912	Schoenberg	*Pierrot Lunaire*	Expressionism
1913	Stravinsky	*Rite of Spring*	Primitivism

Works in **bold** are from the chapter; those not in bold are landmark pieces written around the same time.

NOTES

1. "Diatonic" here simply refers to the notes in a given key. The notes and chords diatonic to C major are all drawn from the scale C–D–E–F–G–A–B–C.

2. Gregory Proctor, "Technical Bases of Nineteenth-Century Chromatic Harmony: A Study in Chromaticism," p. 131. (See the Bibliography at the end of the book for complete citations.)

3. The omnibus progression is discussed in Robert Gauldin's *Harmonic Practice in Tonal Music*, pp. 599–602, and Stefan Kostka and Dorothy Payne's *Tonal Harmony with an Introduction to Twentieth-Century Music*, pp. 477–480.

4. Some prefer to use T and E (or t and e) for 10 and 11.

5. There are various well-founded objections to this term. Nevertheless, it has by now attained a permanent place in our theoretical vocabulary, whereas possible improvements, such as "pantonality," have not. Also, though "atonal" is used by some writers only in reference to the preserial works of the second Viennese school, it is used in this book in its broader meaning of "not tonal."

★

EXERCISES

Part A: Fundamentals

1. For each triad below, list the four triads that are in a chromatic mediant relationship to it.

    Bb major   C minor   F major   D minor   E major

2. Name several traditional chord progressions in tonal harmony that make use of chromatic mediant relationships. Use Roman numerals.

    Example: IV–V/V

3. Which of the following progressions involves dominant 7th chords that share two pitch classes?

    V7–V7/vi   V7/ii–V7/V   V7/IV–V7/V

4. For each dominant 7th chord below, list the three dominant 7th chords that share two pitch classes with it.

    E♭7   G7   F7   C♯7

5. Complete this C3 cycle: *2* ___ ___ ___

    Show the same cycle with letter names: *D* ___ ___ ___

    And this C4 cycle: *2* ___ ___

    Show the same cycle with letter names: *D* ___ ___

Part B: Analysis

1. Berlioz: *Requiem* (1837), mm. 66–78.

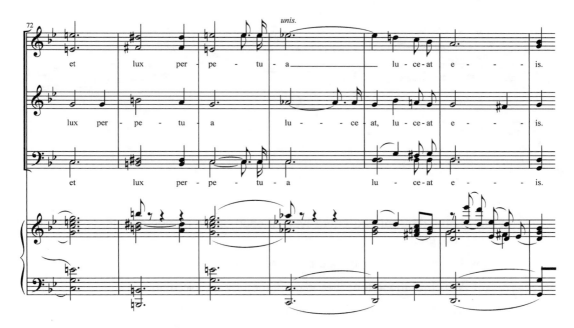

This passage modulates from B♭ major to G minor.

(a) Are the keys of B♭ major and G minor in a chromatic mediant relationship?

(b) Still another tonality is implied in mm. 71–74. What is it, and what is the relationship between that key and G minor?

(c) Explain the construction of mm. 66–68.

(d) Provide a Roman-numeral analysis in G minor of mm. 68–70 and mm. 75–78.

2. Grieg: "Summer's Eve," Op. 71, No. 2 (1901), mm. 9–19.

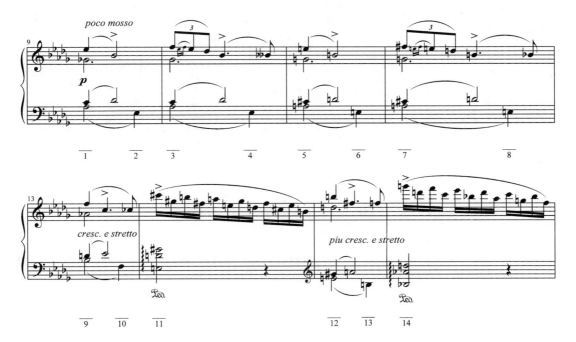

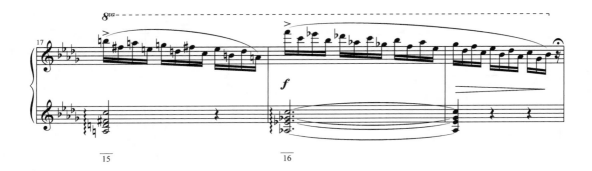

(a) Label the root and chord type of each of the numbered chords (e.g., "G7," "f♯," etc.).

(b) List the tonalities implied by these chords.

(c) Which of those tonalities is confirmed by a tonic triad?

(d) The 16th-note figures use pitches from what tonalities?

(e) What single tonality is the most important in this passage?

(f) How many pitch classes are shared by chords 9 and 11? Chords 12 and 14? Chords 15 and 16?

(g) Do these shared pitch classes appear in the same register?

(h) Discuss the use of sequence in this passage.

3. Brahms: "Der Tod, das ist die kühle Nacht," Op. 96, No.1 (1884), mm. 7–10.

(a) Analyze the first and last chords in the key of C.

(b) Label the roots and qualities of all of the others chords.

(c) Assuming that second-inversion triads tend to be heard as tonic $\frac{6}{4}$ chords, list all of the keys implied by dominant 7th chords or $\frac{6}{4}$ chords.

(d) The tonalities other than C are weakly implied, at best. Explain in your own words what is really going on in this passage.

4. Wagner: *Siegfried*, Act I, Scene 1, mm. 193–200.

Explain this passage as best you can in your own words, following the approaches used in the previous exercises and in the chapter text. Incidentally, would there be any justification for hearing the B♭ in chord no. 7 as an A♯?

Part C: Composition

1. Continue this example, using chromatic mediants above the asterisks and employing conventional voice leading.

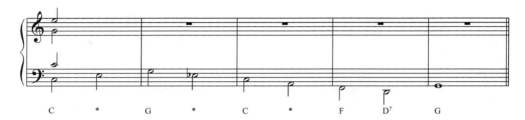

2. Wagner: *Siegfried*, Act I, Scene 2.

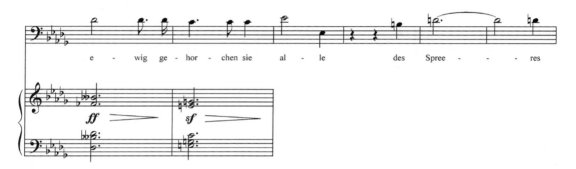

Use the first two measures of this accompaniment as the first part of a three-part real sequence, moving down a minor 2nd each time. Place an <m> between each pair of chords in a chromatic mediant relationship.

3. Using only augmented triads in a four-voice texture, see if you can combine a chromatically ascending soprano line with a circle-of-5th sequence in the bass. Continue for several chords.

4. Compose a passage similar to Example 1-7, using a chromatically descending melody with chromatically ascending half-diminished-7th chords as an accompaniment. The accompaniment chords should be in second inversion and should ascend faster than the melody descends. Let the dissonances fall where they may.

5. Compose an example in four-part texture using a conventional harmonic progression and employing mostly stepwise motion in all of the voices. Then elaborate with a generous application of stepwise nonchord tones, especially chromatic passing tones, neighbors, and suspensions. The added tones, in most cases, should not create sharp dissonances (minor 2nds, major 7ths) with the chords tones or with each other. Be sure to do this work at a piano! The excerpt below can serve as an example.

6. Maximally smooth voice leading is the most extreme form of parsimonious voice leading, in which only one part moves by half step while the other parts hold common tones. Write a series of quarter-note chords for three upper voices that is maximally smooth. It should begin and end with the same chord, and the top voice should move exclusively by descending half step or by common tone. All chords in the series should be one of the four triad types (major, minor, diminished, or augmented), but inversion may be used freely. Label all chords using chord symbols (C, Cm, Co, etc.), but not with Roman numerals. Then add a bass line that moves exclusively by common tone or by leap, and is composed solely of notes from the chords above. Hint: Compose the upper parts at the same time while playing them with your right hand on the piano. The excerpt below can serve as an example.

FURTHER READING

The suggested reading assignments are intended to help you obtain a broader exposure to the subject of this chapter. The approach and terminology used in the texts will probably differ from each other as well as from this text. Complete bibliographical information is provided in the Bibliography at the end of this book.

Aldwell, Edward, and Carl Schachter. *Harmony and Voice Leading.* See Chapter 31, Chromatic Voice-Leading Techniques, and Chapter 32, Chromaticism in Larger Contexts.

Benward, Bruce, and Marilyn Saker. *Music in Theory and Practice,* Vol. 2. See Chapter 12, Chromatic Mediants.

Kostka, Stefan, and Dorothy Payne. *Tonal Harmony with an Introduction to Twentieth-Century Music.* See Chapter 27, Tonal Harmony in the Late Nineteenth Century.

Samson, Jim. *Music in Transition.* See Chapter 1, The Nineteenth-Century Background.

Simms, Bryan R. *Music of the Twentieth Century.* See Chapter 1, Tonality in Transition.

Steinke, Greg A., and Paul O. Harder. *Bridge to 20th-Century Music.* See Chapter 4, Expanded Tonality; Chapter 5, Ultrachromaticism I; Chapter 6, Ultrachromaticism II; and Chapter 7, Denial of Harmonic Function.

CHAPTER 2

Scale Formations in Post-Tonal Music

INTRODUCTION

The music of the Baroque, Classical, and Romantic periods was based almost exclusively on the major and minor scales with which we are all familiar. Though these scales have not been discarded altogether, composers since the early twentieth century have also made use of a large number of other scale formations. Not all of these scale formations are new—in fact, some of them had been used long before the tonal era and had since fallen out of fashion. But new or old, these scales were all unfamiliar to audiences accustomed to major/minor tonality, and so they helped composers to distance themselves from the older style.

It is unusual in post-tonal music to find an entire piece that uses only a single scale (with the exception of chromatic and microtonal scales). Instead, one typically finds that only a few measures will use a particular scale, or the melody may conform to the scale while the accompaniment does not, or the music may include only a few notes that seem to imply the scale.

The organization of this chapter is based on the number of notes in the scale; that is, five–note scales are discussed first, then six-note, and so on. (In counting the number of notes, we do not include the octave, so the major scale, for instance, is a seven-note scale.) Examples have been chosen to illustrate clearly the scales being discussed, but the reader should be aware that in much music it would be difficult to say with certainty what scale formation is the basis of a given passage.

FIVE-NOTE SCALES

"Pentatonic" is a generic term for all five-note scales, but when one refers to *the* pentatonic scale, the scale in Example 2-1 is usually the one that is meant. Notice that the intervals between adjacent notes of the scale are all major 2nds and minor 3rds. Because this version of the scale contains no half steps, it is sometimes called the **anhemitonic pentatonic scale**. One could think of it as a diatonic scale with the notes that form its dissonant tritone (scale-degrees 4 and 7 in major) removed.

EXAMPLE 2-1 The Anhemitonic Pentatonic Scale

Five steps through any C5 cycle will generate an anhemitonic pentatonic scale. In the case of Example 2-1, the steps would be E–A–D–G–C or, in pitch-class numbers, 4–9–2–7–0. Pitch-class arithmetic may be easier for you to understand if you visualize it on a clock diagram, substituting 0 for 12, as in Example 2-2. From that diagram you can see, for example, that for a C5 cycle to move past 9, one has to move clockwise five steps from 9 to 2.

EXAMPLE 2-2 A Clock Diagram

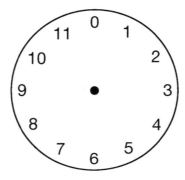

Any member of a pentatonic scale can serve as the tonal center; thus, five "modes," or rotations, are available.

EXAMPLE 2-3 Modes of the Pentatonic Scale

And, of course, the pentatonic scale can be transposed.

EXAMPLE 2-4 Transpositions of the Pentatonic Scale

The pentatonic scale is obviously a limited source of melodic pitch material, and it is also limited in its tertian harmonies. The only tertian chords that could be constructed from Example 2-1 are triads on C and A and a minor 7th chord on A. This means that the accompaniment to a pentatonic melody will probably be either nontertian or nonpentatonic or both. In Example 2-5 Bartók harmonizes a pentatonic melody (top line in the example) with major triads, using the melody note as the root of the triad in each case. The accompaniment here uses no particular scale, although the tonality is certainly C. A few measures later, the same melody is harmonized again with major triads, but this time each melody note is the 5th of its triad. The last melody note is changed to a D, resulting in a "half-cadence" on a G chord.

EXAMPLE 2-5 Bartók: *Bluebeard's Castle* (1911) (piano reduction), mm. 765–770

Other versions of the pentatonic scale are possible—versions employing minor 2nds and major 3rds—but they occur less often in Western music. One example is the scale sometimes known as the **Hirajoshi pentatonic**—as in A–B–C–E–F—which occurs in the closing section of George Rochberg's *Slow Fires of Autumn* (1979) and in the second movement of Janice Giteck's *Om Shanti* (1986); another, sometimes called the **Kumoi pentatonic**—as in D–E–F–A–B, was used by Ralph Vaughan Williams for the opening theme of his Concerto for Bass Tuba (1954) and by Jonathan Kramer in his *Moving Music* (1976).

SIX-NOTE SCALES

The only six-note scale to see much use in post-tonal music is the **whole-tone scale**. It is constructed entirely from major 2nds (although one of them has to be notated as a diminished 3rd). In terms of pitch-class content, only two whole-tone scales are possible; any other transposition or "mode" will simply duplicate the pitch-class content of one of the scales in Example 2-6. Whole-tone scales may be labeled according to a convention that identifies the whole-tone scale that contains C (pitch class 0) as WT–0 and the scale that contains C♯/D♭ (pitch class 1) as WT–1. Enharmonic spelling of the scales is common. For instance, WT–0 might be spelled as C–D–E–G♭–A♭–B♭–C.

EXAMPLE 2-6 Whole-Tone Scales

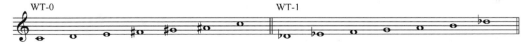

Whole-tone scales can be generated by any C2 cycle.

The whole-tone scale is often associated with Impressionism, and especially with Debussy, but it is also found in the music of many other composers. Interestingly, it is even more limited than the pentatonic scale, both melodically and harmonically. No triads other than augmented ones are possible, and the only complete 7th chords available are the major-minor 7th chord with the 5th lowered (the traditional French augmented-6th sonority) or raised.

Example 2-7 begins with three measures using WT–0 followed by two measures using WT–1. The tonality or tonalities of the passage would be open to some interpretation.

EXAMPLE 2-7 Paul Dukas: *Ariadne and Bluebeard* (1906), Act III

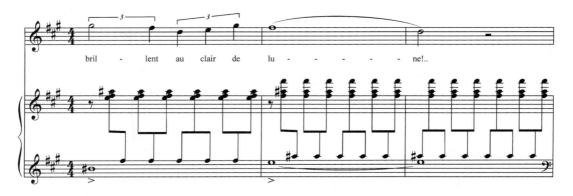

A more recent use of the whole-tone scale is seen in Example 2-8. Here the whole-tone scale (WT–0) is in the vocal duet, except for the A at the end of Toni's melody. Notice that the pitch class G♯/A♭ is spelled one way in Hilda's part in m. 984 and another way in m. 986. The tonal center of this excerpt, if there is one, would be difficult to determine. The accompaniment will be discussed in more detail later in this chapter.

EXAMPLE 2-8 Hans Werner Henze: *Elegy for Young Lovers* (1961), Act I, Scene 12, mm. 984–986

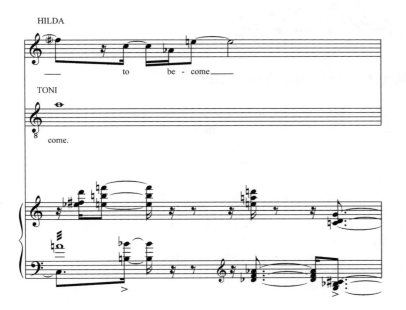

The **augmented scale** (also called the "hexatonic scale"), which has been used in both concert music and jazz, consists of alternating half steps and minor 3rds (perhaps spelled enharmonically). Two related instances are seen in Example 2-9, in both of which four-note figures are transposed down a minor 6th to create an augmented scale. Notice that the pitch-class content of the two scales is the same: 0–1–4–5–8–9.

EXAMPLE 2-9 Ellen Taaffe Zwilich: Piano Trio (1987), III (piano only)

Copyright © Theodore Presser Co.

SEVEN-NOTE SCALES: THE DIATONIC MODES

Seven steps through a C5 cycle will result in a seven-note diatonic collection. For example, the pitch classes of the C major scale can be produced by this C5 cycle: B–E–A–D–G–C–F. Rotations of the major scale produce the seven diatonic modes.

Modal scales had been largely out of favor with composers since the beginning of the Baroque period, although interesting exceptions, such as the Phrygian opening of Chopin's *Mazurka* in C♯ Minor, Op. 41, No. 1 (1839), do occur. But modality was enthusiastically rediscovered by a number of early twentieth-century composers. Though the modal theory of the Renaissance recognized both authentic and plagal modes, the distinction is not important in modern usage. One way to present the modes is to notate them using the pitches of the C major scale (Example 2-10).

The Ionian mode is the same as the major scale, although some writers find it useful to use "Ionian" to refer to major-mode passages that do not employ traditional harmonic progressions. The Locrian mode has rarely been used, probably because it lacks a consonant tonic triad and a perfect fifth between scale degrees $\hat{1}$ and $\hat{5}$. (Here and elsewhere a caret over a number indicates that the number represents a scale degree). An unusually clear use of the Locrian mode occurs in the opening of Shostakovich's String Quartet No. 10, Op. 118 (1964), second movement.

EXAMPLE 2-10 The Diatonic Modes

It is most efficient to learn the modes in relation to the major and natural-minor scale patterns. The following information should be memorized:

Major Modal Patterns

Lydian: same as major with raised $\hat{4}$.
Mixolydian: same as major with lowered $\hat{7}$.

Minor Modal Patterns

Aeolian: same as natural minor.
Dorian: same as natural minor with raised $\hat{6}$.
Phrygian: same as natural minor with lowered $\hat{2}$.
Locrian: same as natural minor with lowered $\hat{2}$ and lowered $\hat{5}$.

You will not always be able to identify the scale being used just by determining the tonal center and looking at the key signature because not all composers use modal key signatures. Instead, a composer might use the conventional major or minor key signature and add the accidentals necessary to produce the modal scale desired. This is the case in Example 2-11, where we see a G minor key signature used for a G Phrygian theme. Notice the leading-tone F♯ in the viola part. Such nonscale tones are as common in modal music as they are in major/minor music, and we should not let them confuse us in our analysis.

EXAMPLE 2-11 Debussy: String Quartet, Op. 10 (1893), I, mm. 1–3

There is no key signature at all for Example 2-12, the opening theme of a movement in A. The accompaniment to this Lydian tune consists only of A major triads in second inversion.

EXAMPLE 2-12 Bartók: Music for Strings, Percussion, and Celesta (1936), IV, mm. 5–9 (melody only)

Copyright © 1937 in the USA by Boosey & Hawkes, Inc. Copyright renewed. Reprinted by permission.

In Example 2-13 the music drifts easily from D Aeolian (mm. 1–4) into D Dorian (mm. 5–7). A change in modal flavor such as we find here is a frequently encountered device. Note that this is *not* a modulation, because the tonal center is unchanged.

EXAMPLE 2-13 Debussy: Preludes, Book I (1910), "Footprints in the Snow" ("Des pas sur la neige"), mm. 1–7

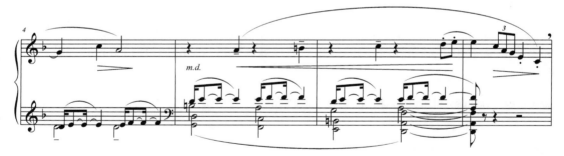

OTHER SEVEN-NOTE SCALES

Many other seven-note scales are possible, although none of them have been used as frequently as the diatonic modes. Fourteen modes can be derived from the scales shown in Example 2–14. All of them use major and minor 2nds exclusively, yet none of them is identical to any of the diatonic modes. These two scale systems, along with our familiar diatonic modal system, exhaust the possibilities for seven-note scales using only major and minor 2nds.

EXAMPLE 2-14 Two Seven-Note Scale Systems

You may expect to encounter these scale formations occasionally in post-tonal music. The scale in Example 2-14a (a mode of the melodic minor scale) was used several times by Bartók, and it has acquired the name Lydian-Mixolydian because of its combination of raised 4th and lowered 7th scale degrees (it is also sometimes called the lydian–dominant scale or the acoustic scale). Debussy makes momentary use of this scale on C in the first three measures of Example 2-15. Then the G and A are replaced by A♭ in m. 148, resulting in the WT–0 whole-tone scale.

EXAMPLE 2-15 Debussy: *The Joyous Isle* (*L'isle joyeuse*) (1904), mm. 145–151

Some seven-note scales make use of one or more augmented 2nds. A familiar example is the harmonic minor scale. Example 2-16 would seem to be constructed from a G Aeolian scale with a raised fourth scale degree.

EXAMPLE 2-16 Grieg: "Shepherd Boy," Op. 54, No.1 (1891), mm. 1–8

From Edition Peters.

To list all of the possibilities would be impractical.[1] It is enough to be aware that a particular passage must be approached on its own terms, not with the assumption that only certain scales are allowed.

EIGHT-NOTE SCALES

Octatonic, like pentatonic, is a generic term that has nevertheless come to refer to a specific scale. This scale, illustrated in Example 2-17, consists of alternating whole and half steps (or half and whole steps), so another name for this scale is the **whole-step-half-step scale**. Yet another name for it is the **diminished scale** because it can be partitioned into two diminished-7th chords. In terms of pitch-class content, there are only three transpositions of the octatonic scale—the three shown in Example 2-17—but they can begin with either a half step or a whole step, and they may be spelled enharmonically.

EXAMPLE 2-17 The Octatonic Scale

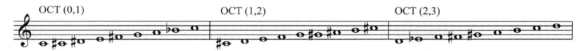

By convention we label the three transpositions of the octatonic scale as shown above Example 2-17. For instance, if the scale contains the pitch classes 0 and 1, no matter where they occur in the scale, we label it as OCT(0,1).

The octatonic scale is a rich source of melodic and harmonic material. It contains all of the intervals, from minor 2nd up to major 7th. All of the tertian triads except for the augmented triad can be extracted from this scale, as can four of the five common 7th chord types (the major-7th chord cannot). If it has a weakness, it is its symmetrical construction, a characteristic it shares with the whole-tone scale, which can make establishment of a tonal center more difficult.

Certain nineteenth-century Russian composers, notably Rimsky-Korsakov, were among the first to make use of the octatonic scale. An excerpt from a twentieth-century Russian work appears as Example 2-18. In this passage Scriabin uses OCT(0,1). The tonal center here, if there is one, would seem to be E♭.

EXAMPLE 2-18 Alexander Scriabin: Prelude, Op. 74, No. 5 (1914), mm. 14–17

Excerpted from the International Music Co. edition, New York, NY 10018.

In Example 2-19 Messiaen is using OCT(1,2). The passage is headed toward a cadence on F♯, so these measures may be functioning as a kind of dominant on C♯.

2-19 Messiaen: *Vingt regards sur l'enfant Jésus* (1944), "Le baiser de l'enfant Jésus," mm. 54–57

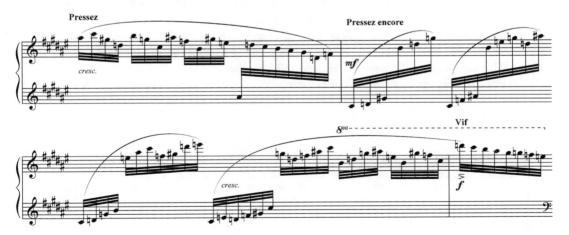

While the use of whole-tone and modal scales declined as the twentieth century progressed, the opposite seems to have been true of the octatonic scale. The octatonic scale has also found a home in contemporary jazz, where it is especially useful in improvisation over diminished 7th chords and altered dominants.

THE CHROMATIC SCALE

Many passages in post-tonal music avail themselves of all or nearly all of the tones of the chromatic scale. In some cases it is only the harmony or only the melody that is chromatic, while in other cases both are. In Example 2-20 Hindemith omits only the pitch class D in the course of an 18-note melody. Hindemith's melody is obviously a tonal one, beginning strongly on F and ending with a convincing melodic cadence on A. We could even "explain" the chromaticism in terms of diatonic scales—F major (notes 1–6), Gb major (notes 7–14), and A minor (notes 14–18)—but such explanations of chromatic passages are not always helpful. Turn back to Example 2-8 and consider the accompaniment. The voices, you will recall, are confined almost entirely to a whole-tone scale, but the accompaniment uses the chromatic scale as its pitch source. All 12 notes of the chromatic scale are used in the first one and a half measures of the accompaniment, and though there are some conventional sonorities (an A major triad in m. 984 and a Db major triad in m. 986), it makes no sense to attempt to discuss the accompaniment in terms of any scale other than the chromatic.

EXAMPLE 2-20 Paul Hindemith: Sonata for Trombone and Piano (1941), I, mm. 1–5 (trombone only)

MICROTONAL SCALES

In modern usage, **microtone** means any interval smaller than a minor 2nd. Though we might assume that microtones are a very recent discovery, they actually were used in the music of ancient Greece and were mathematically defined by the theorists of that time. Nevertheless, microtones, like the diatonic modes, were rediscovered in the twentieth century by composers who used them in new and varied ways.[2] Though in most cases the microtones employed have been quarter-tones—that is, an interval half the size of a minor 2nd—other microtonal intervals have been used as well.

A number of methods have been derived for specifying microtones in musical notation. In his Chamber Concerto (1925), Alban Berg notated quarter-tones by placing a "Z" (for "Zwischenton") on the stem. The "Z" means the performer must raise the tone if the musical line is ascending chromatically and lower it if it is descending. Julián Carrillo, in his *Dos Bosquejos* for String Quartet (1926), used a slanted line after the notehead to indicate a quarter-tone alteration up or down, whereas Bartók used ascending and descending arrows above the notes in his Violin Concerto No. 2 (1937).

Other methods have typically involved variants of the traditional system of accidentals. György Ligeti used microtones of various sizes in his String Quartet No. 2 (1968). In his system, an arrow is attached to a flat, sharp, or natural sign, pointing up or down. The resulting intervals are no larger than quarter-tones and may be smaller, the precise size being determined partly by context and partly by the choice of the performer. Krzysztof Penderecki in several works uses variants of the traditional sharp sign to indicate tones a quarter-tone and three quarter-tones higher, and variants of the flat for a quarter-tone and three quarter-tones lower. Traditional accidentals are used for half-step intervals.

A method used by Witold Lutoslawski is seen in Example 2-21. In this work he employs four special accidentals:

ↄ = lower the note by a quarter-tone
♭ = lower the note by three quarter-tones
↑ = raise the note by a quarter-tone
♯ = raise the note by three quarter-tones.

In each of the two phrases in Example 2-21, Lutoslawski fills in the quarter-tone chromatic space between A4 and E5, cadencing first on C, then on D♭. The midpoint, of course, would be the quarter-tone between these two pitches.

EXAMPLE 2-21 Witold Lutoslawski: *Livre pour orchestre* (1968), mm. 1–4 (first half of violin I only)

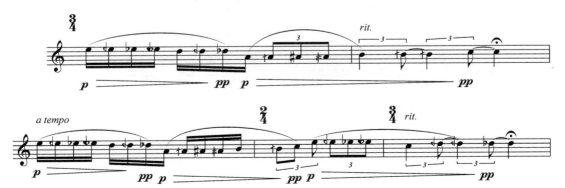

Microtones smaller than a quarter-tone have been used on occasion. One example by Ligeti was mentioned above; another is Ben Johnston's String Quartet No. 2 (1964), employing a scale with 53 tones to the octave. Harry Partch advocated microtones of various sizes, especially a 43-tone scale using unequal intervals, and he designed instruments to play them.[3] In her *Acrostic Wordplay* (1991), Unsuk Chin leaves the details of the microtones to five of the ten instrumentalists, instructing them to tune anywhere between a sixth of a tone and a quarter-tone sharp.

Stringed instruments would seem to be the most suited of all traditional instruments for playing microtones, pianos and organs the least. Nevertheless, microtonal works for specially tuned pianos have been composed. Examples include *Three Quarter-Tone Pieces for Two Pianos* (1923–24) by Charles Ives, Henri Pousseur's *Prospection* (1952) for three pianos, using sixth tones, and Johnston's Sonata for Microtonal Piano (1965). The most natural environment of all for microtones is the electronic medium, where the entire pitch spectrum can be precisely partitioned into intervals of any size or combination of sizes; however, a discussion of electronic music will have to be postponed until a later chapter.

SCALAR TRANSFORMATIONS

With the post-tonal addition of scales beyond the major and minor scales of common-practice tonality came the exciting possibility of transforming melodic material from one scale to another, often a very different one. Presenting a theme in major first and then later presenting it in the minor mode (or vice versa) was common in tonal music, but in post-tonal contexts, it became possible to transform a theme from a scale of one size to a scale of another. Example 2-22 shows the transformations of two melodic ideas in the music of Bartók, the first from a chromatic scale to a diatonic scale, and the second from a chromatic scale to an octatonic scale. Example 2-23 shows the transformation of a melodic idea in Debussy's *Three Nocturnes* from a Dorian scale to a whole-tone scale, and then to a Mixolydian scale. Debussy's melodic idea uses seven scale degrees, but the whole-tone scale only has six, so in Example 2-23, the Dorian seventh scale degree maps onto the whole-tone's first scale degree in the upper octave and onto its sixth scale degree in the lower one.

EXAMPLE 2-22 Bartók: two melodic ideas and their scalar transformations

a) Bartók, Music for Strings, Percussion, and Celesta, I; transformation from chromatic to diatonic

b) Bartók, String Quartet No. 4, I; transformation from chromatic to octatonic

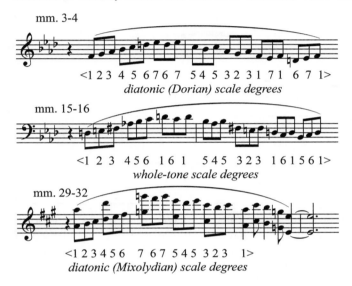

EXAMPLE 2-23 Debussy: melodic idea from *Three Nocturnes*, "Fêtes" and its subsequent transformations

OTHER POSSIBILITIES

The reader should not assume that everything there is to know about scales in post-tonal music has been discussed in this chapter. There are always other possibilities. Olivier Messiaen, for example, was interested in what he called "modes of limited transposition." These are scales of from six to ten notes that have fewer than 12 transpositions without duplication of pitch–class content.[4] He identified seven such scales, including the whole-tone and octatonic scales, and used them in various compositions (as in Example 2-19). This quality, known as "transpositional symmetry," will be discussed in Chapter 9.

Another possibility is the simultaneous use of more than one scale type. We have already seen this in connection with Example 2-8, where a whole-tone vocal duet was provided with a chromatic accompaniment. In Example 2-24 an E Phrygian melody is set over an E major ostinato.

EXAMPLE 2-24 Bartók: *Mikrokosmos* (1926–37), No. 148, "Six Dances in Bulgarian Rhythm, No. 1," mm. 4–8

SUMMARY

Though the major and minor scales of the tonal era have by no means become extinct since the nineteenth century, they have to some extent been supplanted by a variety of other scales, some of them quite old, others recently devised, using from five to dozens of notes within the octave. The scales most often encountered in post-tonal music are included in this chapter, but you should not be surprised to encounter still others, some of which may not even have names.[5] The scales discussed in this chapter include the following:

Pentatonic scale (with modes and variants)
Whole-tone scale
Augmented scale
Diatonic modes
Other seven-note scales using only major and minor 2nds
Seven-note scales using augmented 2nds
Octatonic (diminished) scale
Chromatic scale
Microtonal scales
Modes of limited transposition

The distinctive character of a particular phrase or melodic figure may often be explained by reference to some scale type that is only hinted at. For instance, Example 2-13 was seen to conform entirely to the Aeolian and Dorian modes, but Debussy chose to begin the melody in a manner that reminds us of yet another scale, the whole-tone scale: Bb–C–D–E–D–C–Bb.

MUSIC FROM THE CHAPTER IN CHRONOLOGICAL CONTEXT

Year	Composer	Work	Reference
1891	**Grieg**	**"Shepherd Boy"**	**p. 25**
1894	Debussy	*Prelude to the Afternoon of a Faun*	Impressionism
1906	**Paul Dukas**	***Ariadne and Bluebeard***	**p. 20**
1911	**Bartók**	***Bluebeard's Castle***	**p. 19**
1912	Schoenberg	*Pierrot Lunaire*	Expressionism
1913	Stravinsky	*Rite of Spring*	Primitivism
1914	**Alexander Scriabin**	**Prelude, Op. 74, No. 5**	**p. 27**
1930	Stravinsky	*Symphony of Psalms*	Neoclassicism
1935	Berg	Violin Concerto	Serialism
1936	**Bartók**	**Music for Strings, Percussion and Celesta**	**p. 24**
1941	**Paul Hindemith**	**Sonata for Trombone and Piano**	**p. 28**
1944	**Messiaen**	***Vingt regards sur l'enfant Jésus***	**p. 27**
1961	**Hans Werner Henze**	***Elegy for Young Lovers***	**p. 21**
1968	**Witold Lutoslawski**	***Livre pour orchestre***	**p. 29**
1987	**Ellen Taaffe Zwilich**	**Piano Trio**	**p. 22**

Works in **bold** are from the chapter; those not in bold are landmark pieces written around the same time.

NOTES

1. Vincent Persichetti illustrates and names several on p. 44 of his *Twentieth-Century Harmony*.

2. Joseph Yasser, in *A Theory of Evolving Tonality*, attempted to show that a 19-tone scale would be the logical historical successor to the chromatic scale.

3. Harry Partch, *Genesis of a Music*.

4. Olivier Messiaen, *The Technique of My Musical Language*, pp. 58–62.

5. Several dozen scales are named and defined by Robert Fink and Robert Ricci in *The Language of Twentieth Century Music*; see especially the list on p. 114.

★

EXERCISES

Part A: Fundamentals

1. Taking the pattern C–D–E–G–A–C as the model, notate pentatonic scales starting on the following notes:

    G F♯ B E♭

2. Notate whole-tone scales starting on the following notes, and label each one as WT–0 or WT–1:

    E C♯ A♭ F

3. Notate the following modal scales:

    (a) Dorian on F   (g) Aeolian on G

    (b) Mixolydian on E   (h) Locrian on F♯

    (c) Lydian on E♭   (i) Lydian on D♭

    (d) Mixolydian on D   (j) Dorian on C

    (e) Phrygian on A   (k) Phrygian on B

    (f) Aeolian on A♭   (l) Ionian on B♭

4. Notate the following octatonic (diminished) scales, and label each as OCT(0,1), etc:

    (a) One beginning F♯–G   (d) One combining a°7 with b°7

    (b) One beginning A♭–B♭   (e) One combining d♯°7 with e°7

    (c) One beginning D–E♭   (f) One combining a♯°7 with e♯°7

5. Notate and label every major, minor, augmented, or diminished triad available in the following scales:

    (a) Pentatonic on A   (d) Mixolydian on A♭

    (b) Whole-tone on B   (e) Octatonic beginning E–F

    (c) Phrygian on C♯   (f) Augmented beginning B–C

6. Of the scales listed in the Summary section:

    (a) Which one(s) consist of two augmented triads?

    (b) Which one(s) contain no whole steps between adjacent notes?

Part B: Analysis

1. Puccini: *Turandot* (1926), Act I, Rehearsal 42, mm. 1–7 (voice only).

   The tonal center of this excerpt is G♭. Name the scale.

2. Debussy: *Six Antique Epigraphs* (1914), I, mm. 4–7.

   (a) Name the scale found in the melody.

   (b) The melody at the beginning of the excerpt suggests G as a tonal center. If it is, the melody combined with its accompaniment uses what G scale?

   (c) The cadence at the end of the excerpt suggests C as a tonal center. In that case, the melody combined with its accompaniment uses what C scale?

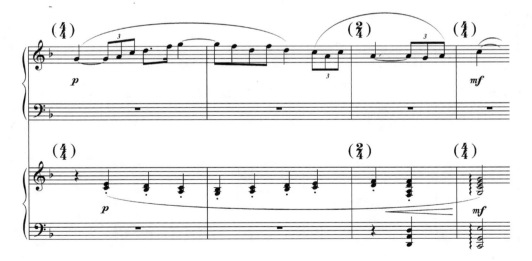

3. Anton Webern: Symphony, Op. 21 (1928), I, mm. 1–14.

This is a "concert score"—all of the instruments sound as notated. What scale is being used?

4. Alfredo Casella: *Eleven Children's Pieces* (1920), "Siciliana," mm. 1–19.

    This excerpt suggests several scales, all with D as a tonal center. Be sure to consider the accompaniment when answering the following questions:

    (a) What scale is used in mm. 1–9 of this excerpt?

    (b) And in mm. 9–11?

    (c) What scale is hinted at in m. 12?

    (d) And what scale is used in mm. 13–17?

    (e) There are eight pitch classes in mm. 18–19. Do they form a diminished scale?

5. Joan Tower: *Island Prelude* (1988), m. 135 (oboe cadenza).

The first note in this excerpt is a D#, held over from the previous measure, and all of the Bs in the second system are B♭s. Given that information, what scale is used here?

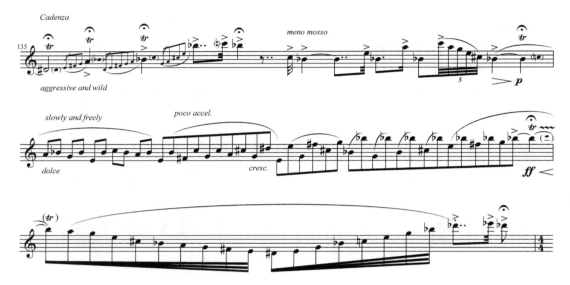

Music by Joan Tower. Copyright © 1989 by Associated Music Publishers, Inc. (BMI) International Copyright Secured. All Rights Reserved. Reprinted by permission.

6. Ravel: *Valses nobles et sentimentales* (1911), II, mm. 1–15.

(a) What scale is used in m. 1 of this excerpt?

(b) And in m. 2?

(c) What scale would account for mm. 1–2 combined?

(d) After a transitional cadence in mm. 6–7, a new scale is introduced with G as a tonal center in mm. 8–15. What scale is it?

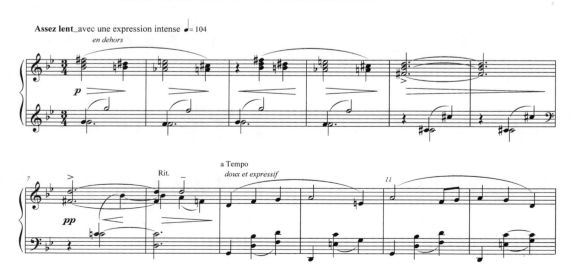

7. Debussy: Preludes, Book I (1910), "Sails" ("Voiles"), mm. 38–44.

   (a) Two scales are used in this excerpt. The first is in mm. 38–41. What is it?

   (b) The second scale is found in mm. 42–44. Name it.

Part C: Composition

1. Compose short melodies illustrating the pentatonic, whole-tone, octatonic, and chromatic scales.

2. Compose short melodies illustrating the Dorian, Phrygian, Lydian, Mixolydian, and Aeolian modes. In each melody, try to emphasize the tonic note as well as those notes that are especially characteristic of that scale.

3. Continue this example, using the G Mixolydian mode.

4. Continue this example, using the F Dorian mode.

5. Compose an example that makes use of several different scales, using the Casella excerpt as a model (Example 2-B-4, that is, the excerpt from Chapter 2 exercises, Part B, Exercise 4; please make note of this format because it will be used throughout the book). Label each scale you use, and use scalar transformation to move between them.

6. Compose an example of two-voice counterpoint using the octatonic scale. Start with a slow, rather simple tune, unaccompanied, and bring in the second voice after a measure or two. Continue to a cadence on an octave. Compose for instruments in your class, or be able to play it at the piano.

FURTHER READING

Dallin, Leon. *Techniques of Twentieth Century Composition*. See Chapter 3, Modal Melodic Resources, the section titled "Additional Scale Resources" in Chapter 4, and Chapter 16, Microtones.

Day-O'Connell, Jeremy. *Pentatonicism from the Eighteenth Century to Debussy*.

Kostka, Stefan, and Dorothy Payne. *Tonal Harmony with an Introduction to Twentieth-Century Music*. See the section titled "Scale Materials" in Chapter 28.

Persichetti, Vincent. *Twentieth-Century Harmony*. See Chapter 2, Scale Materials.

Piston, Walter. *Harmony*. See the section titled "Modal Scales and Modal Harmony" in Chapter 30 and the sections titled "The Pentatonic Scale," "The Whole-Tone Scale," and "Artificial Scales" in Chapter 31.

Slonimsky, Nicolas. *Thesaurus of Scales and Melodic Patterns*.

Steinke, Greg A., and Paul O. Harder. *Bridge to 20th-Century Music*. See Chapters 9 and 10, Enlarged Scale Resources I and II.

Vincent, John. *The Diatonic Modes in Modern Music*. See Chapter 30, The Modes in the Contemporary Period.

CHAPTER 3

The Vertical Dimension:
Chords and Simultaneities

INTRODUCTION

The music of the tonal era is almost exclusively tertian in its harmonic orientation. That is, its harmonies can generally be thought of as being constructed of stacked 3rds, the only exceptions being "voice-leading chords" such as the family of augmented-6th chords and the chords produced by the omnibus progression. That tonal music used tertian harmony was not the result of a conscious decision on anyone's part but instead was the result of classifications of consonance and dissonance and the development over centuries of various voice-leading procedures. The fact that the underlying harmonies in the tonal style are known to be tertian makes the labeling of chords and the identification of nonchord tones in tonal music a relatively simple task.

Much music since 1900 is also basically tertian, but there is in addition a good deal of music using chords built from 2nds, from 4ths, and from combinations of various intervals. Even the tertian music frequently uses new kinds of tertian sonorities, as we shall see. One result of this unlimited array of harmonic material is that the distinction between chord tones and nonchord tones is often difficult or impossible to make. Also, chords sometimes seem to result more or less accidentally from the combination of harmonically independent lines. For these reasons, many writers prefer at times to use terms such as "verticality," "simultaneity," "sonority," or "note complex" instead of "chord." In this text, however, "chord" will be used freely along with the other terms to refer to any vertical collection of pitches, no matter how it originates.

The present chapter surveys in an organized way the chords found in music since 1900. The *contexts* in which these chords are used is a subject that involves both voice leading and harmonic progression. These topics will be taken up in Chapters 4 and 5.

CONVENTIONAL TERTIAN SONORITIES

Tertian triads and 7th chords have remained an important, if less preponderant, part of the harmonic vocabulary of music since 1900. Certain composers make more use of these sounds than do others. Some of the works by composers such as Sergei Rachmaninoff, Gian Carlo Menotti, and Aaron Copland, for example, might be expected to contain a high proportion of triads and 7th chords, whereas other composers, such as Paul Hindemith, tend to reserve the pure sound of a triad for important cadences or even for the end of a movement. Still other composers rarely make use of these more traditional sounds. Examples of the use of triads and 7th chords will be found in Chapters 4 and 5, where voice leading and harmonic progression are discussed.

Tertian sonorities "taller" than the 7th chord—9th chords, 11th chords, and 13th chords—are not an important part of the harmonic vocabulary before the late nineteenth or early twentieth century. In theory, any diatonic triad can be extended to a 13th chord before its root is duplicated (see Example 3-1). In practice, however, it is the dominant and secondary dominant chords, and to a lesser extent the supertonic and submediant chords, that tend to be singled out for this treatment. Chromatic alterations, especially of chords with a dominant function, are often used. Example 3-2 illustrates some of the possibilities.

EXAMPLE 3-1 Diatonic 13th Chords

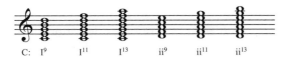

EXAMPLE 3-2 Altered Dominants

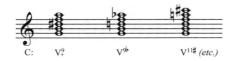

Chords taller than a 7th are frequently incomplete, posing certain problems in analysis. In Example 3-3, for instance, the first chord would probably best be analyzed as an incomplete supertonic 11th chord because of the $\hat{2}$-$\hat{5}$-$\hat{1}$ bass line, but one could also argue that it is a V_3^4. And is the second chord an incomplete dominant 9th or an incomplete dominant 13th? The answer depends on whether one hears the C5 in the melody as a chord tone or as an appoggiatura, and either reading is defensible. The final chord is a tonic triad, the F3 in the tenor being an ornamented suspension.

EXAMPLE 3-3 Debussy: Preludes, Book II (1913), "Heaths" ("Bruyères"), mm. 1-5

Ninths and other tall chords can be inverted, of course, but inversions can be problematical, as we just saw with the ii¹¹ chord in Example 3-3. Referring back to Example 3-1, notice that the pitch-class content of every diatonic 13th chord is identical, meaning that every diatonic 13th chord could be analyzed as an inversion of every other diatonic 13th chord. The situation is only slightly less ambiguous with 9th and 11th chords, as Example 3-4 illustrates.

EXAMPLE 3-4 Inverted 9th and 11th Chords

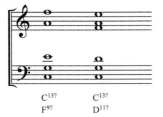

A typically ambiguous example is seen in Example 3-5. The excerpt begins with a tonic triad in D major, but the next chord is open to some interpretation (remember to include the flute part in your analysis). The pitch classes, in alphabetical order, are A, C, D, E♭, F♯, G. Bass notes usually want to be roots, if they can, and the high D in the flute on the fourth beat reinforces the notion that this might be some sort of G chord. On the other hand, the G could be the 11th of a complete D 11th chord: D–F♯–A–C–E♭–G, and the A5 to D6 in the flute seems to support that. Or perhaps it should be analyzed as a D 9th chord presented simultaneously with G, its note of resolution. The uncertainty is not resolved by the B♭ major 7th chord that follows, because neither G–B♭ nor D–B♭ seems particularly compelling as a progression. The remainder of the excerpt is more straightforward: A minor 7th to D minor 7th in m. 3, both slightly ornamented, to a more lavishly ornamented G major triad in m. 4.

EXAMPLE 3-5 Prokofiev: Sonata for Flute and Piano, Op. 94 (1943), I, mm. 1–4

Music by Sergei Prokofiev. Edited by Jean-Pierre Rampal. Copyright © 1986 International Music Co. Copyright renewed. International copyright secured. All rights reserved. Used by permission.

TERTIAN CHORDS WITH ADDED NOTES

Though the possibility of adding to a triad a note that is a 6th above the root was recognized by theorists as early as the eighteenth century, chords with added notes (sometimes called *chords of addition*) did not become an accepted part of the harmonic vocabulary until the twentieth century, when they appeared more or less simultaneously in concert music, popular music, and jazz. The basic chords are usually triads, and the added notes (always figured above the root) are usually 2nds or 6ths, less frequently 4ths. Any triad with an added 6th could also be analyzed as an inverted 7th chord, but the context will usually settle the issue, as Example 3-6 illustrates.

EXAMPLE 3-6 Added 6th and Inverted 7th Chords

Similarly, a triad with an added 2nd or 4th could be interpreted as an incomplete 9th or 11th chord, especially if voiced with the added note above the triad. Because the root is the same in either case, the distinction is not a crucial one. For all practical purposes, a chord with an added 2nd or 4th can be considered the same as one with an added 9th or 11th. See Example 3-7.

EXAMPLE 3-7 Chords with Added 2nds and 4ths

The situation is unambiguous in Example 3-8, where the cadential chords are the dominant 7th and the tonic with an added 6th in G♭ major. And in Example 3-9, the final chord is clearly a C triad with an added 9th. But Example 3-10 is more involved. In the first phrase (mm. 1–2) a double pedal point on G4 and B4 (in the middle of the texture) adds bite to a conventional progression. Though several of the sonorities could be analyzed as added-note chords, the pedal-point analysis is just as good, explaining all the dissonances except the added 4th in the passing tonic $^6_4$. The second phrase (mm. 3–4) keeps the B as a pedal point, shifting it down an octave in m. 4. Again, the pedal point accounts for most of the dissonances, but the tonic triads are probably best analyzed as added-note chords.

EXAMPLE 3-8 Debussy: Preludes, Book I (1910), "The Girl with the Flaxen Hair" ("La fille aux cheveux de lin"), mm. 23–24

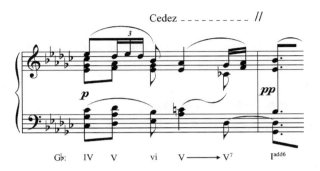

EXAMPLE 3-9 Debussy: Preludes, Book II (1913), "Canope," mm. 29–33

EXAMPLE 3-10 Stravinsky: Suite Italienne (1932), "Introduction," mm. 1–4

Copyright © 1934 by Boosey & Hawkes (London) Ltd. Copyright renewed. Reprinted by permission of Boosey & Hawkes, Inc.

Added notes are a feature of what is sometimes called "wrong-note style," in which the listener's conventional expectations are almost met, but not quite. This was the case in Example 3-10, where Stravinsky is *almost* quoting Pergolesi, an early eighteenth-century composer. The result is often humorous, as in Example 3-11, where the melody heads toward a G4 but lands a half-step too high (m. 41), then a half-step too low (m. 42), before finally succeeding (m. 43).

EXAMPLE 3-11 Gian Carlo Menotti: *The Telephone* (1946), mm. 41–43 (piano vocal score)

TERTIAN CHORDS WITH SPLIT CHORD MEMBERS

A special kind of added-note chord features one or more chord members that are "split" by adding a note a minor 2nd away. Common examples are triads and 7th chords with split 3rds, but split roots, 5ths, and 7ths also occur. Some of the possibilities are shown in Example 3-12. There is no standard analytical symbol for split chord members. In this text an exclamation point will be used, as in the example.

EXAMPLE 3-12 Chords with Split Chord Members

Arpeggiated triads with split thirds occur in Example 3-13, in some cases with enharmonic spellings. For instance, the first four notes outline an A♭(3!), but the minor 3rd is spelled as B instead of as C♭. This is followed in the next seven notes by a B♭(3!) triad. Notice also that Bartók has arranged the triads in such a way that their intersections form diminished 7th chords, as with the b°7 chord in m. 6.

In Example 3-14 Ravel uses a series of major triads with split roots. The effect is not as dissonant as you might expect because of the speed at which the chords are played.

EXAMPLE 3-13 Bartók: *Mikrokosmos* (1926–37), No. 143, "Divided Arpeggios," mm. 6–13

EXAMPLE 3-14 Ravel: *Miroirs* (1905), "Oiseaux tristes," m. 15

Aaron Copland uses split-3rd chords on C and E in Example 3-15. The effect is intensified by the violin and cello, which play Es that are a quarter-tone flat and Gs that are a quarter-tone sharp. Notice the notation that Copland uses here for the quarter-tones, a system used also by Alois Hàba, among others.

EXAMPLE 3-15 Copland: *Vitebsk* (1929), mm. 1–2

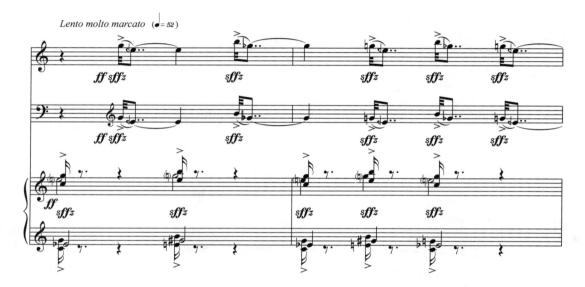

A more complex example was contained in Example 2-8 (p. 21). The accompaniment in m. 984 clearly contains an A major triad on beat 3, accented. Below and above it are C♮s (a split 3rd), the higher C leaping up to an F (a split 5th), while an inner voice sustains an E♭ (another split 5th). Meanwhile, the singers produce B♭ (split root) and G♯ (adding a major 7th to the chord). The listener cannot follow all of this, of course; the aural effect is one of extreme dissonance competing with the sound of a pure triad.[1]

OPEN-5TH CHORDS

Although a large number of added-note chords are possible, there is only one important "chord of omission"—that is, a traditional sonority that is transformed into something unusual by leaving out a note—and this is the triad without a 3rd. Omitting the root or the 5th, or omitting anything from a 7th chord, only results in yet another traditional sonority. But the sound of an open 5th had been out of style for centuries, except for its occasional use in two-part counterpoint or for special effect.

EXAMPLE 3-16 Carl Orff: *Carmina Burana* (1936), "Veris leta facies," mm. 4–6

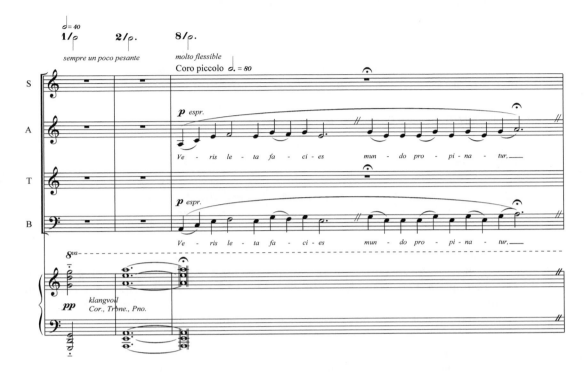

The sound of open 5ths rapidly becomes tiresome, so extended passages based on this chord are rare. Typically they are used to create an impression of the Orient or of the distant past. In Example 3-16 open 5ths on G and A are used to introduce a chant melody in the chorus. The notation of the time signatures in Example 3-16 is a very practical one that a number of post-tonal composers adopted.

QUARTAL AND QUINTAL CHORDS

Post-tonal composers have not restricted themselves to tertian sonorities—that is, to chordal formations based on stacked 3rds. There are essentially only four possibilities:

Chords built from 2nds (7ths)
Chords built from 3rds (6ths)
Chords built from 4ths (5ths)
Chords built from mixed intervals.

In this section we will explore quartal and quintal chords—those built from 4ths and 5ths. Later sections will deal with chords constructed from 2nds and with mixed-interval chords.

A **quartal chord** can have as few as three pitch classes (as in Example 3–17a) or it can have several (Example 3–17b). It is sometimes possible to omit a member of a quartal or quintal chord (the E4 in Example 3–17b, for instance) without losing its character. Various voicings and octave duplications are also used (as in Example 3–17c), but some arrangements could destroy the quartal character of the sonority. **Quintal chords** work the same way (as in Example 3–17d), but they have a more open and stable sound and, of course, occupy more vertical space per chord member. Surely a near-record for range must be held by the ten-note quintal chord that occurs near the end of György Ligeti's orchestral *Melodien* (1971), spanning a range of more than five octaves, from A♭1 to B6.

EXAMPLE 3-17 Quartal and Quintal Chords

A convenient way to describe quartal and quintal chords is to use, for example, "3 × 4 on B" to mean a three-pitch-class quartal chord with B as the bottom pitch class, as in Example 3–17a. Example 3–17b would be a "7 × 4 on C♯." All of the chords in Example 3–17c would be "4 × 4 on E," and "5 × 5 on G" would describe Example 3–17d. A static 6 × 4 chord on A is the basis for Example 3–18.

EXAMPLE 3-18 Howard Hanson: Symphony No. 2, Op. 30 (1930), I, rehearsal J (strings only)

EXAMPLE 3-19 Copland: Piano Fantasy (1957), mm.20–24

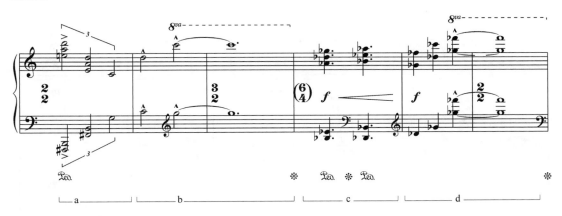

The chords in Example 3–19 are almost exclusively quartal, but the analysis is complicated by arpeggiations and voicings. One possibility is to analyze the harmony as four quartal chords, as marked on the score:

a = 5 × 4 on F♯
b = 3 × 4 on D ("inverted")
c = 5 × 4 on B♭
d = 4 × 4 on D♭

A second approach (and still others are possible) would be to combine a and b into a single 7 × 4 chord on F♯ and to combine c and d into a single 7 × 4 chord on B♭. Both of these analyses are supported by the pedal markings. Notice that the a/b chord contains all of the pitch classes of the G major scale, and the pitch classes from C♭ major make up the c/d chord. Notice also the oversize time signatures Copland employs here. Presumably these are seen more readily than are the traditional time signatures, certainly when used in a conductor's score, as in Example 3-20.

The last 21 measures of the movement from which Example 3-20 is taken are static harmonically, consisting for the most part of embellishments of a quintal chord on D♭. At the very end, shown here, the chord turns out to be a 5 × 5 chord on D♭.

Quartal and quintal chords are most often made up of perfect intervals, but augmented and diminished 4ths and 5ths may be included. In Example 3-21 each of the arpeggiated triplet chords, as well as the 8th-note chords beneath them, is a 3 × 4 chord, with the lower 4th augmented.

The use of diminished 4ths and augmented 5ths in quartal and quintal chords can lead to perplexing questions because they are enharmonic with major 3rds and minor 6ths. An example is Scriabin's **mystic chord**, a sonority that flavors much of his music, although he seldom uses it in a literal fashion. This chord is found in at least the two forms shown in Example 3-22. One °4 occurs in Example 3-22a (F♯/B♭), and two are found in Example 3-22b (F♯/B♭ and A/D♭). Both chords also contain two augmented

EXAMPLE 3-20 Percy Grainger: *Lincolnshire Posy* (1937), III, "Rufford Park Poachers," mm. 99–103

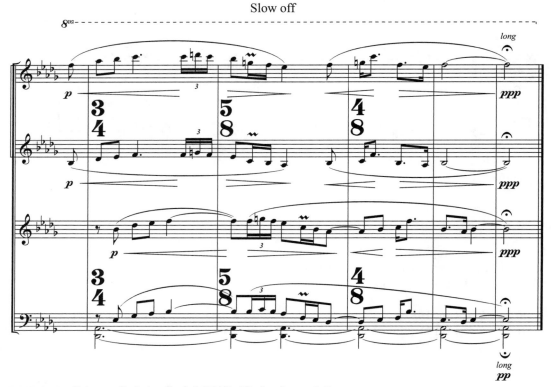

EXAMPLE 3-21 Debussy: Preludes, Book II (1913), "Ondine," mm. 4–7

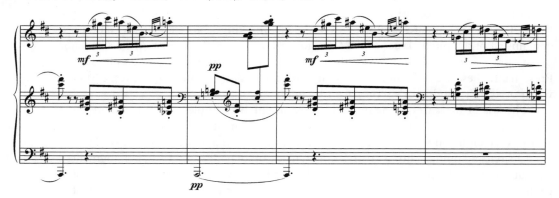

EXAMPLE 3-22 Scriabin's Mystic Chord

4ths (C/F♯ and B♭/E). As long as the voicing is predominantly quartal, as it is here, it is probably correct to analyze both chords as altered 6 × 4 chords, but other voicings might lead to other analyses. The octatonic scale can serve as the source for the chord in Example 3-22b. If you turn back to Example 2-18 (p. 27), you will see that this chord is strongly suggested in various transpositions and voicings in that excerpt.

Ginastera made frequent use of a mostly quartal chord derived from the open strings of the guitar: E2–A2–D3–G3–B3–E4. An example can be found at the beginning of the third movement of his String Quartet No. 1 (1948).[2]

SECUNDAL CHORDS

The third possibility for chord construction is the **secundal chord**, a sonority built from major or minor 2nds or from a combination of the two. Such chords may be voiced as 7ths rather than as 2nds, but this is the exception. More often the notes of a secundal chord are placed adjacent to each other, an arrangement sometimes referred to by the terms **cluster** and **tone cluster**.

The secundal chord in the second measure of Example 3-21 above is voiced as a cluster, but the arpeggiations obscure this somewhat (the chord is F♯–G–A–B–C♯). Example 3-23 provides a clearer illustration of clusters.

EXAMPLE 3-23 Charles Ives: Piano Sonata No. 2 (*Concord*) (1915), II

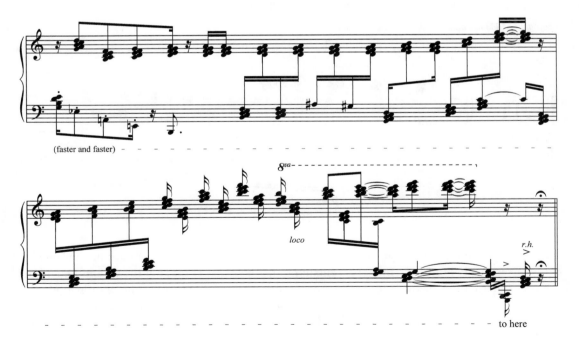

In some keyboard works, special notation is used to indicate whether or not the black keys are to be included in the cluster. Others require that the cluster be performed with the forearm or with a board. In Example 3-24, the pianist plays black keys with the left hand (as indicated by the **I** symbol) and white keys with the right, resulting in nearly chromatic clusters of eight or nine pitches each.

EXAMPLE 3-24 Sofia Gubaidulina: *Lamento* for Tuba and Piano (1977)

Copyright © 1991 by Musikverlag Hans Sikorski, Hamburg.

In Example 3–25a, the composer suggests two ways of playing a "lateral tremolo" between white and black keys, shown in Example 3–25b.

EXAMPLE 3-25 William Bolcom: *12 New Etudes for Piano* (1986), No. 5, m.11

Copyright © 1988 by Edward B. Marks Music Company.

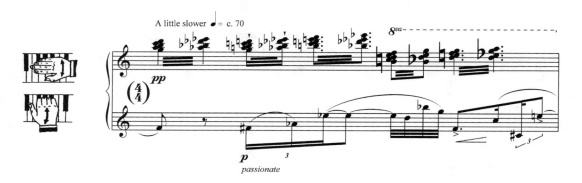

The chords that accompany the first violin in Example 3-26 might be explained as secundal chords, the first one containing the pitch classes G♭, A♭, B♭, C, and D, and the other chords being transpositions of the first one. The voicing of the chords, however, is not as clusters, but as alternating major thirds and tritones, resulting in what sounds like incomplete 13th chords. A reduction of the first chord is shown below the example.

EXAMPLE 3-26 Paul Hindemith: String Quartet No. 4, Op. 22 (1921), V, mm. 64–66

MIXED-INTERVAL CHORDS

A **mixed-interval chord**[3] is one that did not originate as a series of 2nds, 3rds, or 4ths, but instead combines two or more of those interval types (with their inversions and compounds, of course) to form a more complex sonority. The possibilities are numerous.

Most mixed-interval chords are subject to other interpretations—that is, they could, on closer inspection, be arranged to look like secundal, tertian, or quartal chords. The mixed-interval chord in Example 3-27 will be used to illustrate this. It could be arranged, although incorrectly, as:

A secundal chord	D–E–G♯–A♯–B
A tertian chord	E–G♯–B–D–F–A♯
A quartal chord	F–B–E–A♯–D–G♯

EXAMPLE 3-27 George Walker: Piano Sonata No. 4 (1985), II, m. 58

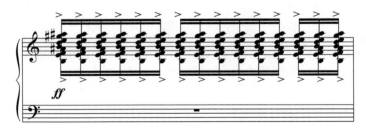

In most cases the context will suggest the best analytical approach. For instance, the sonata from which Example 3-27 comes is an atonal work with few, if any, secundal, tertian, or quartal chords, so it is appropriate to call this a mixed-interval chord, even if that term is too broad to be very descriptive.

This brings us to the question of just how one goes about analyzing and labeling these sonorities, a complicated problem that has been tackled by various composers and theorists—notably Paul Hindemith, Howard Hanson, and Allen Forte. Because so many combinations of intervals are possible, a completely new system of chord classification had to be devised, and this system is the subject of much of Chapter 9.

WHOLE-TONE CHORDS

Any chord whose members could be obtained from a single whole-tone scale is a **whole-tone chord**.[4] A number of such chords are possible, of course. A few of them are illustrated in Example 3-28. Such sonorities for the most part appeared rarely in classical tonal harmony, but some whole-tone chords, including those in Example 3-28, are at least reminiscent of traditional chords. Example 3-28b, for instance, is an incomplete dominant 7th chord, and Example 3-28d is a French augmented-6th chord, but Examples 3-28c and e would have to be explained as altered versions of simpler chords.

EXAMPLE 3-28 Whole-Tone Chords

(a)   (b)   (c)   (d)   (e)

Whole-tone chords will naturally occur in any music that is based on the whole-tone scale. For an illustration, turn back to Example 2-7 (p. 20), a whole-tone excerpt by Dukas. The first measure uses a French augmented-6th sonority (B♯–E–F♯–A♯). When the B♯ moves to E in the next measure, we are left with only the notes of an incomplete dominant 7th chord (E–F♯–A♯). Neither of these chords is used in a traditional manner. The last two measures are based on a different whole-tone scale, and the whole-tone chords, though present, are more difficult to characterize.

More interesting, perhaps, is the use of whole-tone chords in passages that are not based primarily on the whole-tone scale, because here they provide an unexpected harmonic color. Again an earlier example, Example 2-11 (p. 23), can provide an illustration. In this case the pitch environment is Phrygian, except for the last chord of the second measure (A♭–F♯–C–D). The altered tone, F♯, produces a whole-tone chord that could be explained as a French augmented-6th chord moving directly to the tonic G, or as a second-inversion dominant 7th in G with a flatted 5th (A♭). More whole-tone chords are seen in Example 3-29, the first phrase of a work that is atonal until a suggestion of a G♭ tonal center in the final cadence. In this phrase the measures alternate between WT–1 and WT–0, although each measure includes a passing tone that is out of the scale.

EXAMPLE 3-29 Scriabin: Etude, Op. 56, No. 4 (1907), mm. 1–4

Finally, look once more at the Hindemith excerpt, Example 3-26. We have analyzed the chords in this excerpt as secundal chords, as mixed-interval chords, and as 13th chords; we can see now that they are also whole-tone chords, each one being derived from one of the two whole-tone scales.

POLYCHORDS

A **polychord** combines two or more chords into a more complex sonority, but it is crucial that the listener be able to perceive that separate harmonic entities are being juxtaposed if the result is to be a true polychord. Any 11th or 13th chord could be explained as a combination of two simpler sonorities, but this would be an incorrect analysis if we do not hear them that way.

EXAMPLE 3-30 Apparent Polychords

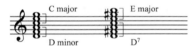

To be heard as a polychord, the individual sonorities must be separated by some means such as register or timbre. In Example 3-31 the first and last chords could easily be heard as 11th chords, but in the rest of the phrase the different registers and the pervading contrary motion between the two chord streams results in an unambiguous polychordal texture. Persichetti concludes another of his works, the Symphony for Band, Op. 69 (1956), with a spectacular polychord that combines four registrally distinct sonorities: Bb major, A major 7th, B major 7th, and F major with an added 9th. The resulting polychord contains all 12 pitch classes.

EXAMPLE 3-31 Vincent Persichetti: Little Piano Book, Op. 60 (1953), "Prologue," mm. 1–4

Reprinted by permission of Carl Fischer, Inc.

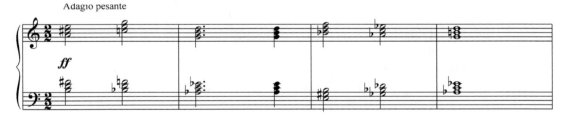

Stravinsky's famous **Petrushka chord** combines two triads a tritone apart: C major and F♯ major. This polychord is seen in Example 3-32, along with another polychord: F♯ major/G major. In the orchestral version, the ascending figures are played on a piano, the descending ones on clarinets.

EXAMPLE 3-32 Stravinsky: *Petrushka* (1911), Second Tableau, mm. 17–20

Copyright © 1912 by Hawkes & Son (London) Ltd. Copyright renewed. Reprinted by permission of Boosey & Hawkes, Inc.

The constituents of polychords are usually tertian triads or 7th chords, but all of the other kinds of sonorities discussed in this chapter could also conceivably be susceptible to polychordal treatment. For instance, near the end of Example 2-8 (p. 21) there is a 3 × 4 chord on E in the upper staff of the accompaniment and a D♭ major triad in the lower staff. The only requirement for a polychord is that the listener be able to perceive the chords as separate entities. There will inevitably be ambiguous cases, however, where one listener hears a polychord and another hears a single complex sonority.

SUMMARY

The harmonies of tonal music were limited for the most part to tertian triads and 7th chords. In contrast, composers, since the nineteenth century, have felt free to make use of any conceivable combination of pitches. In the simplest terms, there are four possibilities for chord construction:

Secundal chords (also tone clusters)
Tertian chords (including 9th, etc.)
Quartal chords (also quintal chords)
Mixed-interval chords.

Tertian chords, the most traditional of the four types, have been subjected to some new variations:

Added notes
Split chord members
Open 5ths.

One special case, especially important in the early part of the twentieth century:

Whole-tone chords.

Finally, the possibility of juxtaposing two or more aurally distinguishable sonorities:

Polychords.

It is frequently the case that a particular sonority is open to more than one interpretation. This is particularly true with mixed-interval chords, many of which can be arranged to resemble secundal, tertian, or quartal chords. The student must be sensitive to the context and the voicing when attempting to choose the best analytical approach. The three chords in Example 3-33, though containing the same pitch classes, obviously must be analyzed differently.

EXAMPLE 3-33 Three Different Chords Containing the Same Pitch Classes

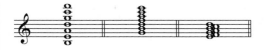

MUSIC FROM THE CHAPTER IN CHRONOLOGICAL CONTEXT

Year	Composer	Work	Reference
1894	Debussy	*Prelude to the Afternoon of a Faun*	Impressionism
1905	**Ravel**	***Miroirs*, "Oiseaux tristes"**	**p. 49**
1907	**Scriabin**	**Etude, Op. 56, No. 4**	**p. 59**
1912	Schoenberg	*Pierrot Lunaire*	Expressionism
1913	Stravinsky	*Rite of Spring*	Primitivism
1915	**Charles Ives**	**Piano Sonata No. 2 *"Concord"***	**p. 55**
1929	**Copland**	*Vitebsk*	**p. 50**
1930	Stravinsky	*Symphony of Psalms*	Neoclassicism
1930	**Howard Hanson**	**Symphony No. 2**	**p. 52**
1935	Berg	Violin Concerto	Serialism
1936	**Carl Orff**	*Carmina Burana*	**p. 51**
1937	**Percy Grainger**	*Lincolnshire Posy*	**p. 54**
1943	**Prokofiev**	**Sonata for Flute and Piano**	**p. 45**
1946	**Gian Carlo Menotti**	*The Telephone*	**p. 48**

1953	Vincent Persichetti	Little Piano Book, Op. 60	p. 59
1957	Copland	Piano Fantasy	p. 53
1977	Sofia Gubaidulina	*Lamento* for Tuba and Piano	p. 56
1985	George Walker	Piano Sonata No. 4	p. 57
1986	William Bolcom	*12 New Etudes for Piano*	p. 56

Works in **bold** are from the chapter; those not in bold are landmark pieces written around the same time.

NOTES

1. Another approach to chords with added notes and split chord members is taken by Bryan Simms in *Music of the Twentieth Century*, pp. 55–58. He identifies nine pairs of "triadic tetrachords"—that is, four-note chords that contain a major or minor triad. The first chord of each pair is a major triad plus one of the other nine notes of the chromatic scale, while the second chord of each pair is the mirror inversion of the first.

2. Thanks to David Sommerville for this reference.

3. Some writers use the term *compound chord*.

4. Some theorists use the term *whole-tone dominant* for whole-tone chords that have a traditional dominant function.

★

EXERCISES

Part A: Fundamentals

1. Review the nine chord types listed in the Summary section. Then find one example of each type in the example below.

2. Make up one example of each of the nine chord types and notate them on staff paper. Try not to duplicate any of those found in the text. Label each chord.

3. Find the doubly chromatic mediant relationship in Example 3-9.

4. Name the scales used in the following excerpts:

   (a) Example 3-3, treble-clef melody

   (b) Example 3-9, last four measures (without the E♭; C is tonic)

   (c) Example 3-15

   (d) Example 3-21

   (e) Example 3-22b OCT(__,__)

   (f) Example 3-26, cello only (missing an A)

   (g) Example 3-27 (missing C♯ and G)

Part B: Analysis

1. Two different types of tetrachords are used in Example 2-9 (p. 22), one in 2-9a and one in 2-9b. Identify these chord types.

2. Debussy: Preludes, Book I (1910), "The Engulfed Cathedral," m. 1–5.

   There are three planes to the texture of this excerpt. One is the static three-note chord in the highest register, another is the quarter-note chords, and the third is the three-note chords in the lowest register. What kind of chord do all three planes make use of? To what scale do the quarter-note chords belong?

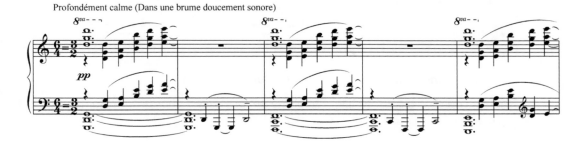

3. Stravinsky: *The Rake's Progress* (1951), Act III, Scene 2.

   What kind of sonority predominates in this passage?

4. Debussy: *The Joyous Isle (L'isle joyeuse)* (1904), mm. 152–155.

And in this one?

5. Ravel: *Menuet sur le nom d'Haydn* (1909), mm. 50–54.

The chords here are tertian. Label the six bracketed chords with Roman numerals.

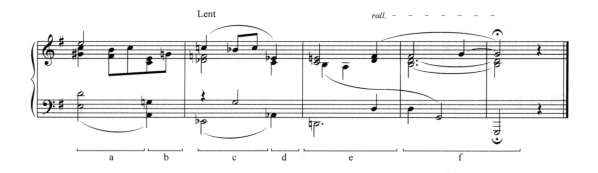

6. Ravel: Sonatina (1905), I, mm. 79–84.

This excerpt contains several sonorities that could be analyzed as added-note chords. Find them, as well as an unconventional German augmented-6th chord.

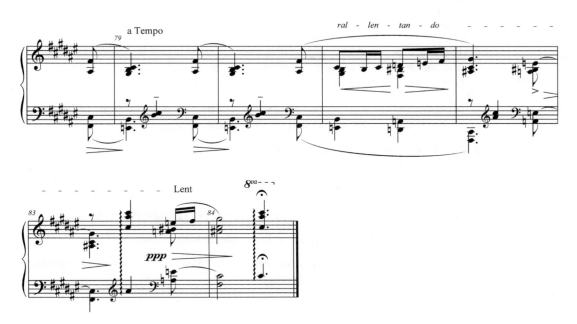

7. Charles Ives: Violin Sonata No. 4 (1915), II.

Explain or discuss each of the five labeled chords.

8. Alban Berg: "Warm Is the Air" ("Warm die Lüfte"), Op. 2, No. 4 (1910), mm. 20–25.

This is a complicated and intriguing excerpt from early in Berg's compositional output. Our analysis will be concerned only with the piano part, while recognizing that the relationship between the voice and the accompaniment would have to be considered in a complete analysis.

(a) There are at least two ways to approach chords a–f analytically. One is to understand how they are "generated"—that is, how they come about. What sort of pattern does the bass line under chords a–f follow?

(b) Meanwhile, the right hand in chords a–f moves a three-note chord down chromatically. How would you classify that chord?

(c) The second way of dealing with chords a–f is to analyze each individually. The last of them could be analyzed as a dominant 7th with a split 3rd: B7(3!). The others appear to be mixed-interval chords, but closer inspection reveals that they could also be analyzed as tertian chords. Which chords out of a–e could be analyzed as incomplete dominant 7th chords with split 3rds?

(d) And which could be analyzed as incomplete 13th chords?

(e) Of the remaining chords (g–l), list any that are identical to or are transpositions of one of the earlier chords (a–f).

(f) What single category would best describe chords g, i, and k?

(g) What pattern seems to emerge in chords g and i?

(h) Considering your answer to the preceding question, what note seems to be missing from chord k?

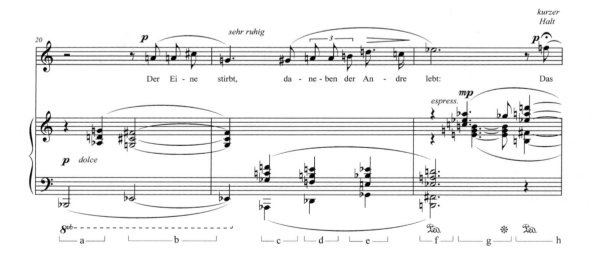

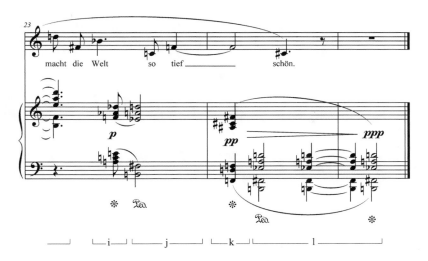

macht die Welt   so   tief_____   schön.

Reprinted by permission of the original publisher, Robert Lienau, Berlin.

FURTHER READING

Dallin, Leon. *Techniques of Twentieth Century Composition.* See Chapter 6, Chord Structure.

Kostka, Stefan, and Dorothy Payne. *Tonal Harmony with an Introduction to Twentieth Century Music.* See pp. 507–515.

Persichetti, Vincent. *Twentieth-Century Harmony.* See Chapter 3, Chords by Thirds; Chapter 4, Chords by Fourths; Chapter 5, Added-Note Chords; Chapter 6, Chords by Seconds; Chapter 7, Polychords; and Chapter 8, Compound and Mirror Harmony.

Piston, Walter. *Harmony.* See pp. 499–507 in Chapter 31, Scalar and Chordal Types.

Reisberg, Horace. "The Vertical Dimension in Twentieth-Century Music," in Gary Wittlich, Ed., *Aspects of Twentieth-Century Music.* See pp. 322–372.

Simms, Bryan R. *Music of the Twentieth Century.* Sec the section titled "Triads and Triadic Extensions" in Chapter 3.

Steinke, Greg A., and Paul O. Harder. *Bridge to 20th-Century Music.* See Chapters 11 and 12, Expanded Chord Vocabulary I and II.

CHAPTER 4

The Horizontal Dimension: Melody and Voice Leading

INTRODUCTION

Voice leading—how chords are created by the motion of individual voices—is one of the main concerns of conventional tonal theory.[1] Even today the voice-leading conventions followed by composers of the tonal era occupy an important part of the course of study in colleges and universities around the world. But a glance at the table of contents of this book will reveal that voice-leading conventions are not a central issue in post-tonal music. In fact, as we shall see later in this chapter, one of the most hallowed principles of voice leading was an early casualty of the assault on musical conventions made by a number of composers around the beginning of the twentieth century.

Melody, on the other hand, is usually slighted in courses in music theory, perhaps because we tend to think of such courses as dealing with tonal *harmony* rather than with tonal *music*. Nevertheless, all of us probably have a pretty good notion of what conventional tonal melodies are like, even if we have never actually tried to analyze one. The first part of this chapter will examine some of the new melodic techniques that have been used by composers since around 1900.

SOME NEW STYLISTIC FEATURES OF POST-TONAL MELODY

It is safe to say that since 1900 melodic lines have tended to become **more disjunct**. Consider, for example, the Hindemith theme in Example 2-20 (p. 28). In this theme leaps dominate over steps by a two to one ratio, and the leaps range from fourths to a ninth. Two even more extreme instances of disjunct melodies are seen in Example 4-1 (the flute in G sounds a P4 lower than written), and this excerpt illustrates two more tendencies in melodies since 1900: **wider range** and **unconventional rhythms**. Beginning with the flute part, notice the extreme range of almost three octaves, with most of that occurring within m. 2 alone, and the overwhelming preponderance of leaps, especially wide ones, over stepwise motion. The vocal range is not as extreme, but the voice part is equally disjunct and difficult to perform. Both parts draw their pitch material from the **chromatic scale** and employ unconventional rhythmic techniques. Both parts also use **more expression marks** (dynamics, articulation) than was customary in earlier styles.

EXAMPLE 4-1 Pierre Boulez: *Le marteau sans maître* (*The Hammer without a Master*) (1955), III, mm. 1–15

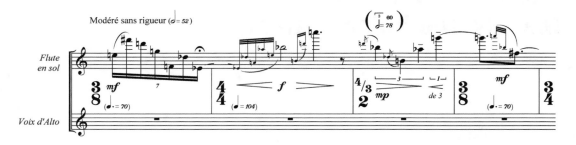

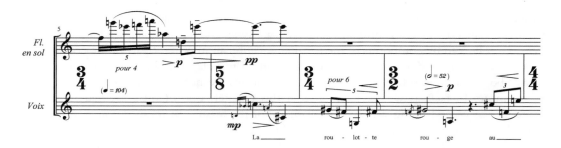

It would be misleading to imply that all post-tonal melodies span a wide range and use a large number of leaps. Though this would be true of many melodies, others do just the opposite. The range of the melody in Example 4-2 is only a perfect 5th, and the largest interval is a minor 3rd. One aspect that gives this melody its post-tonal sound is its **chromaticism**. Each phrase (if we take each slurred segment as a phrase) spans some segment of the chromatic scale:

Phrase 1	M3	(A–C♯)
Phrase 2	tt	(A–E♭)
Phrase 3	P4	(B–E)
Phrase 4	P4	(B♭–E♭)

In each case, the second part of the phrase fills in chromatic notes missing from the first part (sometimes called "gap-fill technique"). Another feature of this melody is its unconventional rhythm. While details of rhythm in post-tonal music are discussed in a later chapter, we can observe here that, in spite of the carefully notated changes in time signature, the listener perceives only an unpredictable mixture of eighths and quarters, with stressed notes coming at irregular intervals.

EXAMPLE 4-2 Bartók: Music for Strings, Percussion, and Celesta (1936), I, mm. 1–4

Copyright © 1937 in the USA by Boosey & Hawkes, Inc. Copyright renewed. Reprinted by permission.

Music since 1900 has tended toward using **less lyrical** melodies than in the tonal era, and this is supported by the examples (Hindemith, Boulez, Bartók) that we have discussed so far—that is, many melodies seem inherently less vocal, less flowing, more angular, and frequently more fragmented than we might expect in a tonal melody. In fact, we might observe that the music of many composers became **less concerned with melody** in general after the tonal era. There are a great many exceptions to these generalizations, of course. A fine twentieth-century example of a long, flowing melody in the lyrical tradition is the opening theme of William Walton's Violin Concerto (see Example 4-3). This melody contains the numerous leaps so characteristic of many post-tonal melodies, but its implied tertian harmonies, its straightforward tonality (with some modal flavor), and above all its mode of expression are obviously more Romantic than modern in conception. Some composers in more recent years have shown a renewed interest in melodicism in the traditional sense, either through the quotation of melodies from earlier times or through the composition of new, more lyrical melodies. Both of these aspects will be discussed in later chapters.

EXAMPLE 4-3 William Walton: Violin Concerto (1939), I, mm. 1–18 (solo violin only)

Copyright © 1939 by Oxford University Press. Reproduced with permission.

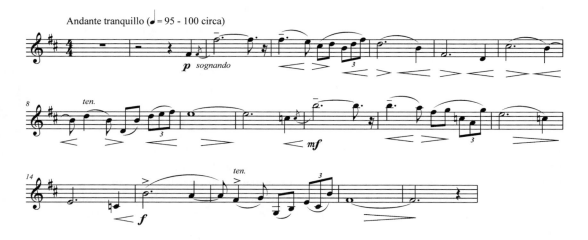

SOME ASPECTS OF MELODIC ORGANIZATION

The motivic devices found in tonal melodies—devices such as repetition, return, sequence, and inversion—also occur in melodies after the tonal era. Surely the melodies in this chapter by Bartók and Walton could be discussed in those terms. Repetition and sequence were also seen in previous examples by Lutoslawski (Example 2-21, p. 29), Bartók (Example 3-13, p. 49), Debussy (Example 3-21, p. 54), Hindemith (Example 3-26, p. 57), and Scriabin (Example 3-29, p. 59). Other melodic devices have also come into use since the end of the tonal era. Study Example 4-4, paying special attention to the three phrase marks. The three segments that occur under the phrase marks, though not related in traditional ways, are related nevertheless. The segments are:

1. A–C–C♯
2. D♯–F♯–D
3. C♯–B♭–D–C♯.

Each of these segments contains three pitch classes. If we rearrange them, we see that each segment spans a major 3rd and the interval content of each segment is identical:

1. A–C–C♯ = m3 + m2
2. D–D♯–F♯ = m2 + m3 (same intervals in reverse order)
3. B♭–C♯–D =m3 + m2.

This kind of motive, really a collection of intervals that can be rearranged and inverted, is often called a **pitch–class cell**. The use of cells, usually of three or four notes each, is an important unifying factor in some post-tonal music, so important that a special terminology has been developed to deal with it. This terminology will be introduced in Chapter 9.

EXAMPLE 4-4 Anton Webern: 5 Canons, Op. 16 (1924), I, mm. 2–5 (voice only)

Another significant factor in the organization of melody has been the development of **twelve-tone melody**. This term does not refer to just any melody employing the whole chromatic scale, but instead to a melody in which each and every pitch class is used once and only once (tremolo figures and immediate repetitions excepted). The horn melody in Example 4–5 is such a melody. Once the 12 pitch classes have been presented, another series of 12 pitch classes, related to the first one, can begin. This procedure is discussed in more detail in Chapter 10.

EXAMPLE 4-5 Arnold Schoenberg: Wind Quintet, Op. 26 (1924), III, mm. 1–7

Two points about the notation of Example 4–5 should be made here. One is that this is a "C score," meaning that all of the instruments sound where written, a development that has no doubt met with the approval of students of music everywhere. The second point concerns the boldface "H" and "N" that appear at the beginning of the excerpt. Schoenberg and others used these letters to designate the *Hauptstimme* (primary voice) and the *Nebenstimme* (secondary voice). The end of the *Nebenstimme* in

Example 4–5 is marked in the bassoon at the end of m. 7. In a more complex texture, the *Hauptstimme* and the *Nebenstimme* would be the two most important parts, and it would be up to the conductor and performers to bring them out.

Many melodies are arranged so that there is a single high point in each phrase or in the melody as a whole, an approach that has been followed more or less faithfully for centuries. If you look back at the melodies presented in this chapter so far, you will find that this holds true for every one of them.

In more general terms, one could say that melodic organization in post-tonal music tends to be less apparent at the surface level and that the progress of such melodies is less predictable than that of tonal melodies. We find also that melodies use **less regular phrase structures** than in the tonal era, with clear period forms often avoided. Repetition and sequence, while still found, are frequently abandoned in favor of other techniques.

VOICE LEADING IN POST-TONAL MUSIC

In the traditional study of tonal harmony, a great deal of attention is paid to the subject of voice leading, or part-writing, and with good reason. Throughout the tonal era and for centuries prior to its beginning, certain voice-leading conventions were followed by all composers that did much to contribute to the homogeneity of their styles. This homogeneity was most pronounced among composers who lived during the same period, such as Haydn and Mozart, but some elements are shared by all composers of the tonal era.

Some of the "rules" that we learn in harmony courses are not actually all that general, even when they are tested against tonal music. These include those procedures gleaned from the study of the works of a particular composer (usually Bach) or that are really valid only for a particular medium (usually choral). We learn them in order to begin the study of tonal composition in a controlled and uncomplicated environment. Two conventions that do seem to be applicable throughout the tonal era, however, are the following:

1. Parallel 5ths and octaves, especially the former, should be avoided.[2]
2. Any chordal 7th should resolve down by step.

It is, of course, possible to find passages of post-tonal music that still adhere to these conventions. This seems to be the case in Example 4–6, from a work that may be more familiar to you under the title "Adagio for Strings." The harmonic vocabulary here is tertian, simplifying the task of sorting out the nonchord tones, but there are several places where more than one interpretation is possible. A suggested chordal analysis is included in the example. There are four 7th chords in the excerpt, with the 7th in each case resolving down by step into the next chord; the voice leading in the other instruments follows for the most part the traditional preference for smooth chord connection. Although Example 4–6 exhibits smooth voice leading, very disjunct voice leading is a characteristic of much post-tonal music. Examples of disjunct voice leading from earlier in this text include Example 2–8 (p. 21) and Example 2–B–3 (p. 36).

Closer examination of Example 4-6 reveals two sets of parallel 5ths and the same number of parallel octaves. One of the sets of 5ths involves a nonchord tone (mm. 3–4, violin II and cello), so it might conceivably be allowed, and both sets of octaves involve temporary octave doubling between an ornamented melody and its slower-moving accompaniment (mm. 4–5 and 7–8), also possibly acceptable. But the parallel 5ths between violin I and the cello in mm. 5–6 cannot be explained at all satisfactorily in traditional terms. This, of course, is not an error on the part of the composer, but instead indicates that one of the most sacred rules of counterpoint no longer has the validity that it once had.

EXAMPLE 4-6 Samuel Barber: String Quartet No. 1, Op. 11 (1936), II, mm. 1–8

PARALLELISM

Parallel 5ths and octaves may occur incidentally in an otherwise traditional texture, as in Example 4-6, but they frequently play a more significant role. For instance, in Example 3-B-6 (p. 65) Ravel makes consistent use of parallel 5ths in the lowest register. Parallel 5ths also occur in **chordal parallelism,** a very important development in twentieth-century music. In tonal music the use of first-inversion triads moving in parallel motion was an accepted compositional device, serving in many cases as a connection between two more important chords and in others as a means of thickening a melodic line. The use of a three-part texture resulted in parallel 3rds, 4ths, and 6ths, but no parallel 5ths or octaves occurred. Other uses of harmonic parallelism included parallel °7 chords and, less frequently, parallel °7 chords. Though parallel 5ths might occur on rare occasion, their use was exceptional.

One reason for the traditional avoidance of parallel 5ths and octaves was that these intervals, more than any other consonant interval, when used in parallel motion imply a breakdown of counterpoint—that is, of relatively independent musical lines. We tend to think of counterpoint as something found in fugues, but counterpoint of some kind was the basis of most tonal music, which in fact evolved the way it did largely because of contrapuntal procedures. In post-tonal music, however, composers have been unrestrained in their use of harmonic parallelism and have shown no aversion to the use of parallel intervals of all kinds. This has led to a redefining of some aspects of counterpoint and to new developments in texture. If we can compare a single melodic line to a line drawn on a canvas with a pen, then the analogy used earlier comparing harmonic parallelism to painting with a broad brush may prove helpful. In Example 4-7 for instance, ascending scales in both hands of the piano part are broadened into root-position triads with roots doubled, resulting in parallel 5ths and octaves.

Harmonic parallelism, so typical of much twentieth-century music, is often referred to as **planing.**[3] Parallelism may be **diatonic,** meaning that it uses only the white keys of the piano or some transposition of them (see Example 4-7); **real,** meaning that the sonority is exactly transposed (see the piano in mm. 1–2 of Example 4-8); or **mixed,** meaning that the parallelism is not consistently diatonic or real (see the cellos in m. 4 of Example 4-8). Though there are lots of "parts" sounding in Example 4-8, it is really an example of three-part counterpoint, twentieth-century style. The three parts are:

1. *Violins and violas.* Use of diatonic planing in m. 1 and real planing in mm. 2–4;
2. *Cellos and piano.* Real planing until m. 4, where two minor triads are employed. The planing in this measure is mixed;
3. Basses.

Notice that the three parts have their own contours and, to some extent, their own rhythms, fulfilling the essential requirements of counterpoint.

EXAMPLE 4-7 Bartók: Piano Concerto No. 2 (1931), I, mm. 295–304

EXAMPLE 4-8 Roger Sessions: Symphony No. 2 (1946), IV, mm. 1–4 (piano and strings only)

International copyright secured. All rights reserved. Reprinted by permission of G. Schirmer, Inc. (ASCAP).

Triads are not the only sonorities that can be planed. Example 4-9 begins with five inverted 9th chords, followed by five inverted 7th chords, then by 7th chords in root position, and, finally, by four root-position triads. Real planing is employed within each group. The progression from complex sounds to simple ones is aurally obvious and effective.

EXAMPLE 4-9 Roy Harris: Symphony No. 7 (1952) (strings only)

Nontertian sonorities are frequently planed as well. Real planing of quartal chords occurs in Example 3-21 (p. 54), and there is diatonic planing of clusters in Example 3-23 (p. 55).

DISSONANCE TREATMENT

We have seen that the tradition that forbade certain parallels is no longer followed in much post-tonal music, but what about the other convention that we discussed, the one about dissonance treatment? In tonal music we sometimes use the term "essential dissonance" to refer to dissonances between members of the same chord (such as between the root and the 7th) as opposed to "nonessential dissonances" involving ornamentation (passing tones and so forth). It is usually not difficult when analyzing tonal music to separate the essential dissonances from the ornaments, and the essential dissonances generally resolve in predictable fashion. Neither of these is necessarily true in post-tonal music. For instance, turn back to Example 4-5 and play it on a piano or listen to a recording. At the beginning, the E♭ in the horn is sustained against G–A–B–C♯ in the bassoon, after which the C♯ is sustained against E♭–C–B♭ in the horn. In neither case is it possible to distinguish essential from nonessential dissonances, since there is no way of identifying the "chords," and the dissonances appear to be approached and left freely.

Example 4-10 looks at first glance like a traditional chorale harmonization. In a number of places a tertian triad or 7th chord is clearly presented. In spite of the key signature, the key seems to be G major, with a half cadence at the first fermata and a cadence on the major submediant at the second. When you look (and listen) closely, however, you find many places where dissonances do not resolve as they would in a tonal piece. See, for instance, the parallel 9ths between bass and tenor in m. 1 or the leap in the alto in m. 2—from a 9th above the bass down to a 7th above the bass!

EXAMPLE 4-10 Stravinsky: *The Soldier's Tale* (1918), "Great Chorale," mm. 1–4

This free treatment of dissonance, called "emancipation of the dissonance" by Schoenberg,[4] is the norm in a large proportion of post-tonal works. Many of the examples already used in this text also illustrate free treatment of dissonance, including those listed below. In some of these excerpts the chords are not difficult to identify, but in none of them are dissonances consistently handled in a traditional fashion.

Example 2-8 (Henze, p. 21)   Example 3-21 (Debussy, p. 54)
Example 2-13 (Debussy, p. 24)   Example 3-23 (Ives, p. 55)
Example 2-18 (Scriabin, p. 27)   Example 3-26 (Hindemith, p. 57)
Example 2-22 (Bartók, p. 30)   Example 3-31 (Persichetti, p. 59)

This "emancipation of the dissonance" has led some to suggest that the whole notion of dissonance should be reevaluated, since a dissonance by some definitions means a sound that requires resolution to a consonance. If sounds need not resolve, are there perhaps no longer any dissonances? This makes very good sense, but we still need a term to label the effect produced by certain combinations of sounds, and "dissonance" remains the most popular choice.

In spite of the repeal of the rules governing parallels and dissonance treatment, there are probably certain basic truths about voice leading that are independent of style. One of them is that counterpoint is threatened whenever voices move in parallel motion, and this is especially true when the intervals between the voices are exactly maintained. For example, parallel major 3rds would tend to destroy a two-voice contrapuntal texture faster than a mixture of major and minor 3rds. Another principle is that the smoothest effect when moving from one chord to another is gained if common tones are maintained where possible and all voices move by the smallest available interval. Finally, the effect of a dissonance can be softened by smooth motion—common tones or steps—into and out of the dissonance.

These truths are no longer conventions to be followed, but instead are merely tools or approaches that are among those available to the composer. So what conventions do remain to guide the composer, if the rules concerning parallels and dissonances no longer hold? None, really, which is what Stravinsky meant when he wrote of the "abyss of freedom" and of the "terror" he felt when faced with this multiplicity of choices. He went on to say that he defined a new set of compositional rules (Stravinsky referred to them as "limitations" and "obstacles") for each work.[5] The task of the composer is to create a work that is consistent, that is stylistically unified within its own self-defined universe. The task of the student is to try to understand what that universe is and how the different aspects of the composition fit into it.

ALIGNED INTERVAL CYCLES

We conclude our survey of voice leading with a rather insignificant but interesting detail: aligned interval cycles. Chapter 1 introduced the interval cycle, the transposition of an interval class two or more times by the same interval. Early in the twentieth century Alban Berg came up with the idea of aligning different interval cycles on top of each other, and he and others have made occasional use of this technique. In Example 4-11 Berg begins four lines on a middle C, but aligned C1, C2, C3, and C4 cycles lead the instruments to a sustained 4 × 5 chord. In performance the effect is difficult to hear because of a conflicting violin figure, not to mention Wozzeck's impassioned singing.

A more recent use of aligned interval cycles is found in Thomas Adès's Piano Quintet (2000), in which the composer makes use of various orderings of short aligned C2, C3, and C4 cycles.[6]

EXAMPLE 4-11 Alban Berg: *Wozzeck* (1921), Act II, m. 381

SUMMARY

Although many melodies composed since the tonal era make use of traditional approaches, what interests us here are those aspects of post-tonal melodies that set them apart from music of the past. Though the fragmentation of musical styles since 1900 makes any generalization difficult, a list of tendencies in post-tonal melodies would include the following:

More leaps
Wider range
Unconventional rhythm
More expression marks
More chromaticism
Less lyricism
Less emphasis on melody
Motivic use of pitch-class cells
Twelve-tone melody
Less regular phrase structure
Avoidance of traditional harmonic implications

Voice-leading procedures in post-tonal music are as varied as the multiplicity of musical styles would suggest. The traditional procedures are still available and have not been discarded entirely, but some important conventions of tonal harmony must now be considered as options rather than rules. As a result, parallel motion of all kinds is acceptable, including harmonic planing, while dissonances have been freed from conventional resolutions—and even from any requirement for resolution at all.

MUSIC FROM THE CHAPTER IN CHRONOLOGICAL CONTEXT

Year	Composer	Work	Reference
1894	Debussy	*Prelude to the Afternoon of a Faun*	Impressionism
1912	Schoenberg	*Pierrot Lunaire*	Expressionism
1913	Stravinsky	*Rite of Spring*	Primitivism
1918	**Stravinsky**	***The Soldier's Tale***	**p. 80**
1921	**Alban Berg**	***Wozzeck***	**p. 82**
1924	**Anton Webern**	**5 Canons, Op. 16**	**p. 73**
1930	Stravinsky	*Symphony of Psalms*	Neoclassicism
1931	**Bartók**	**Piano Concerto No. 2**	**p. 77**
1935	Berg	Violin Concerto	Serialism
1936	**Samuel Barber**	**String Quartet No. 1**	**p. 75**
1939	**William Walton**	**Violin Concerto**	**p. 72**
1946	**Roger Sessions**	**Symphony No. 2**	**p. 78**
1952	**Roy Harris**	**Symphony No. 7**	**p. 79**
1955	**Pierre Boulez**	***Le marteau sans maître***	**p. 70**

Works in **bold** are from the chapter; those not in bold are landmark pieces written around the same time.

NOTES

1. Throughout this chapter and much of the remainder of this book, "tonal" is used to refer to the system of functional harmonic tonality employed in Western art music from around 1600 to around 1900. This use of the term admittedly can be misleading, since it implies that all other music is atonal. The author's hope is that this disclaimer will head off any such misconceptions.

2. Parallel octaves were allowed when one part merely doubled another consistently at the interval of an octave. The same cannot be said of 5ths.

3. Some prefer to use the term "organum" for harmonic parallelism in post-tonal music, especially when it involves root-position triads.

4. Arnold Schoenberg, *Style and Idea*, pp. 216–217.

5. Igor Stravinsky, *Poetics of Music*, pp. 63–65.

6. Thanks to Philip Stoecker for this reference.

★

EXERCISES

Part A: Fundamentals

The Fundamentals exercises in this chapter provide a review of material from earlier chapters.

1. Find a doubly chromatic mediant relationship between two adjacent chords in some example in this chapter.

2. Notate the following scales:

    (a) Pentatonic on A♭

    (b) Whole-tone on G

    (c) Phrygian on F

    (d) Dorian on G♯

    (e) Hexatonic beginning B–C

    (f) Octatonic (diminished) beginning D–E

3. Review the summary at the end of Chapter 3. Of the nine chord types listed there, which term best describes:

    (a) the chords in mm. 3–4 of Example 4-8?

    (b) the chords in Example 4-9?

Part B: Analysis

1. Alban Berg: Violin Concerto (1935), I, mm. 84–93 (solo violin only)

    Discuss this melody, including the following points:

    (a) What elements are especially typical of post-tonal melody?

    (b) Is any part of this melody a twelve-tone melody?

    (c) Does this melody make use of pitch-class cells?

2. Edgard Varèse: *Density 21.5* (1936, 1946), mm. 1–17

Discuss this melody, including the following points:

(a) Which of its elements are especially typical of post-tonal melody?

(b) Is any part of this melody a twelve-tone melody?

(c) List those portions of the melody that could be analyzed as octatonic.

(d) How is the melody organized in terms of motives? Other aspects?

3. Karl Korte: *Aspects of Love* (1965), I, mm. 1–3

Write out the bass line of this excerpt, and under each bass note label the root and quality of the chord (except for the open 5ths, where the quality cannot be determined). Some of the chords are spelled enharmonically. Then answer the following questions:

(a) In what ways does the voice leading in this excerpt depart from conventional practice, especially in terms of "forbidden" parallels and dissonance treatment? List specific instances.

(b) Toward the end of the excerpt, the composer employs enharmonic spellings. Why not just use sharps or flats in all of the voices?

Used by permission of E. C. Schirmer Music Company. A division of ECS Publishing.

4. Study the voice leading in the following examples:

Example 2-5 (p. 19)	Example 3-10 (p. 47)	Example 3-23 (p. 55)
Example 2-11 (p. 23)	Example 3-20 (p. 54)	Example 3-29 (p. 59)
Example 2-13 (p. 24)	Example 3-21 (p. 54)	Example 3-B-8 (p. 66)

Then answer the questions below, using each example only once:

(a) Which one features two sets of parallel 5ths in imitation?

(b) Which one uses diatonic planing of triads?

(c) Which one uses real planing of triads?

(d) Which two use real planing of nontertian sonorities?

(e) Which one features clusters in parallel motion?

(f) Which one features unresolved dissonances?

(g) Which one adheres most closely to traditional voice leading?

Part C: Composition

1. Compose a melody exhibiting several of the characteristics of post-tonal melody discussed in the Summary section (but not including pitch-class cells or twelve-tone melody), and list those characteristics. Try not to let your melody sound too random, and see that every phrase includes a single high point.

2. Compose a melody following the preceding instructions, but using the cell E–G–G♯ and its mirror inversion E–C♯–C as a unifying factor. The cell and its inversion may be used in any transposition and in any octave, and the notes of the cell may be used in any order. Label each appearance of the cell with brackets.

3. Compose an adagio melody in the same style as the horn melody in Example 4-5, using the pitch classes from that melody, but in reverse order.

4. Compose a short example in which a Phrygian melody is accompanied by planed triads (diatonic planing).

5. Continue the following example, using real planing throughout:

6. Compose an excerpt similar in style to Example 4-B-3, following these guidelines:

    (a) Use triads, 7th chords, and open 5ths only. Label each chord.

    (b) Approach each 7th by step or common tone, and leave it by step up or leap down.

    (c) Include some parallel 5ths.

    (d) Be sure that each part is easy to sing.

FURTHER READING

Dallin, Leon. *Techniques of Twentieth Century Composition.* See Chapter 4, Twentieth Century Melodic Practices, and the section titled "Parallelism" in Chapter 7.

Hiller, Paul D. "Pärt, Arvo." *Grove Music Online*, Oxford Music Online.

Kliewer, Vernon L. "Melody: Linear Aspects of Twentieth–Century Music," Chapter 4 in Gary Wittlich, Ed., *Aspects of Twentieth-Century Music.*

Perle, George. "Berg's Master Array of the Interval Cycles." *The Musical Quarterly.*

Persichetti, Vincent. *Twentieth-Century Harmony.* Much of Chapters 3 through 7 is devoted to details of voice leading.

CHAPTER 5

Harmonic Progression and Tonality

INTRODUCTION

The late nineteenth and early twentieth centuries saw the decline of the tonal system, which had been an important organizing factor in music since the early Baroque period. In its place came not a new system but a splintering, a multiplicity of solutions to the problems of harmonic progression and tonality. At the most general level, music is either tonal or not tonal (usually termed "atonal"), but various approaches may be taken in both of those categories. As we shall see, even the "tonal" music of the twentieth century was of a new sort, one without a standardized vocabulary of harmonic progressions.

TRADITIONAL APPROACHES TO HARMONIC PROGRESSION

The beginnings of triadic tonality can be found in music composed many years before the beginning of the tonal era. Through evolutionary processes (influenced by voice-leading conventions and the nature of musical acoustics), certain chord successions became standard cadential formulas long before tonal harmony came into being and even longer before the development of the theory of chord roots. Chief among these was the progression that would later be analyzed as a V–I cadence, but other cadences, such as IV–I, vii°6–I, and iv6–V, were also used. As the language of tonality developed, the V–I progression became the prototype of the normative harmonic progression.

The tonal system turned out to be extremely flexible. It allowed a broad range of expression and made possible the composition of long works organized over a background harmonic structure. But late in the nineteenth century and in the early decades of the twentieth, compositional assaults on the system became so insistent that traditional tonality and its associated harmonic progressions all but disappeared from the works of "serious" composers. The procedures discussed in earlier chapters—the introduction of new scales and chord types and the redefinition of the fundamental principles of voice leading—had much to do with the decline of tonal harmony.

Conventional harmonic progressions still occur with some frequency, especially at cadences, in works from the early part of the twentieth century. Two such examples from earlier in this text are Example 3-3 (p. 44), by Debussy, and Example 3-B-5 (p. 64), by Ravel. Examples of conventional progressions from later in the century generally are found in works with a nationalistic or folk-music background, such as Copland's *Billy the Kid*; in the works by staunchly conservative composers such as Rachmaninoff; or in works of a lighter, more entertaining sort, such as Menotti's *The Telephone* (see Example 3-11, p. 48). Since the 1970s, conventional tonal music has found new life in an important style called "neoromanticism," to be discussed in Chapter 15.

Perhaps the healthiest and most vital continuation of traditional harmony has been in the "popular" music of the twentieth and twenty-first centuries, which includes everything from Broadway musicals to folk music to jazz to rock music. The harmonizations of most of this music can be analyzed using traditional approaches, but the analysis should concentrate on the composer's actual harmonization, not on the chord symbols that often appear in popular-music editions and that are frequently at odds with the original score. More recent rock music, especially since the introduction of electronic synthesizers, has shown an increasing tendency to leave behind its harmonic roots in the blues tradition and to concentrate on unconventional timbres and nonstandard progressions.

NEW APPROACHES TO HARMONIC PROGRESSION

We might expect that, as the older system declined, a new one would have developed to take its place, perhaps one built on root movements of a 3rd or on more involved cycles of root movements. In fact, this did not happen. There is no common harmonic language shared by all composers, although they are free to devise and follow their own stylistic "rules" (recall the Stravinsky quote on p. 81).

Even post-tonal modal music tends to avoid root movements by 5ths, as well as the voice-leading constraints of traditional major-minor music. But there are exceptions, as in Example 2-B-4 (p. 37), where a simple modal melody is accompanied by tertian chords. The harmonization of most of this excerpt is quite traditional, although the supertonic $^6_4$ chords in mm. 10 and 12 and the altered dominant in m. 18 are not. Nevertheless, this is a fairly close modal equivalent of a conventional tonal progression.

Composers who still make use of tertian sonorities generally do so in the context of unusual or unpredictable harmonic successions. In Example 3-9 (p. 47) Debussy ended a piece with the following progression:

Em–AM–Fm–CM^{add9}

This succession of chords is surely intended to be unpredictable to the listener, to delight and surprise rather than to perform the task of most tonal progressions, which is to satisfy expectations. It is of no help to the listener that a similar progression appeared earlier (mm. 4–5), because the similarity is one of gesture rather than of detail:

E♭M–A♭M–G♭M–Dm

Much of the element of surprise in these two passages is provided by doubly chromatic mediant relationships: A major–F minor and G♭ major–D minor.

EXAMPLE 5-1 Aram Khachaturian: Piano Concerto (1936), II, mm. 1–8

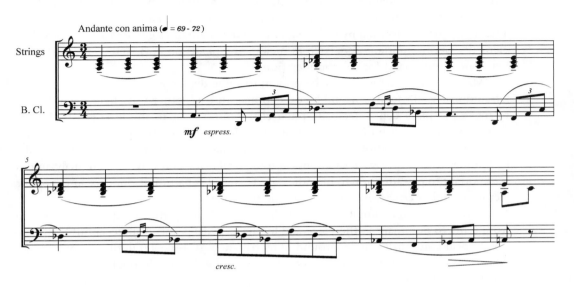

Examples of such successions—one hesitates to call them progressions—abound in post-tonal tertian music. Example 5-1 is simpler, the chords consisting of an A minor tonic triad and its B♭ minor neighbor. Notice the free use of nonchord tones in the bass clarinet melody.

The subject of harmonic progression becomes even murkier when nontertian chords are considered, because the roots of such chords are not defined by any generally accepted theory or by the common agreement of listeners. The most successful attempt to develop a universal theory of chord roots was carried out by Paul Hindemith in his *Craft of Musical Composition*,[1] first published in 1937. Although his theory does account for all possible chords (with the exception of microtonal chords) and had a certain amount of influence in the middle of the twentieth century, it has since fallen into disfavor, largely because, as Hindemith himself wrote, "A true musician believes only in what he hears,"[2] and his fellow musicians remained unconvinced.

ESTABLISHING A TONAL CENTER

Although the word "tonal" can be used to refer to any music that has a tonal center, we will restrict its use to music in which the tonal center is established through the traditional methods of common-practice music of the seventeenth through the nineteenth centuries, and we will use **pitch-centric** in reference to music that has a tonal center established through nontraditional means. Though not an ideal term (the cumbersome "pitch-class-centric" would be more accurate), it will help us to distinguish between traditional tonal music and the pitch-centric music of the twentieth and twenty-first centuries.

Before examining how tonality is established in pitch-centric works, let us review how this was accomplished in traditional tonal harmony. One important element was a descending perfect-5th root movement to tonic combined with a half-step leading-tone motion, also to tonic. The tonicizing effect was often made more convincing by a harmonic tritone formed by scale degrees 7 and 4 resolving stepwise to 1 and 3. Other elements were important also, such as melodic emphasis on 1, 3, and 5, melodic skips between 1 and 5, and formal considerations.

Many of these elements may be present to some degree in pitch-centric music, but a traditional V^7-I cadence would be exceptional. Instead, other ways have been devised to make the pitch center (actually pitch-class center) clear to the listener. Essentially, these methods establish **pitch center by assertion**—that is, through the use of reiteration, return, pedal point, ostinato, accent, formal placement, register, and similar techniques to draw a listener's attention to a particular pitch class. When analyzing, it is important to pay attention to melodic aspects as well as harmonic ones because melodic factors are often crucial in determining the pitch center.

For instance, in Example 5-2 the pitch center of D is clearly indicated by the motion from tonic to dominant in the voice and by the D pedal point. A three-chord harmonic progression continually circles around D by half-steps (C♯–E♭–D) until the Sonnet ends with the progression with which it began: D–C♯–E♭–C–D. Although there is no V–I harmonic progression here, Britten does outline a V^7 chord in the bass (by means of the notes A, C♯, and G) until the arrival of the penultimate chord.

EXAMPLE 5-2 Benjamin Britten: Serenade for Tenor, Horn, and Strings, Op. 31 (1943), "Sonnet," mm. 33–37.

Example 5-1 convinced us that A is the tonal center of the passage without the use of a pedal point. There is also no hint of dominant harmony or of any conventional scale on A, and the leading tone appears only once (in m. 7, as A♭); in addition, there are just as many measures of B♭ minor chords as there are of A minor chords. Yet we hear A as the pitch center because it was there first, before the melody began, and because A is important both melodically and harmonically at the beginning and end of the phrase. The B♭ minor triads, while interesting, do not distract our attention from the true pitch center.

TERTIAN AND NONTERTIAN PITCH-CENTRICITY

As we examine additional pitch-centric examples, we will attempt to categorize them into one of two types: tertian pitch-centricity and nontertian pitch-centricity. As the terms imply, the first type uses primarily chords built from 3rds, whereas the second type usually avoids such sonorities, except perhaps at cadences. Many examples will be of a mixed type, displaying features of both.

Examples 5-1 and 5-2 are both examples of tertian pitch-centricity. Another example of tertian pitch-centricity is seen in Example 2-B-4 (p. 37), whose harmonic progression was discussed earlier in this chapter. In that excerpt, the tonality of D is clearly established, both melodically and harmonically. Melodically, D is established by formal placement (beginnings and ends of phrases), by agogic accent, and by the frequent reiteration of D. The harmonic aspects that establish D as the tonal center include formal placement, pedal point, reiteration, and (in mm. 18–19) a V–I root movement (although not a traditional V⁷–I progression).

Much of the composition in which Example 5-3 appears is in a tertian pitch-centric style, but the excerpt shown here is nontertian. Even though there is an open 5th on D at the end of the excerpt, suggesting a tertian harmony, the excerpt is basically non-tertian, since there is little else about the harmony or melody that suggests tertian construction. The pitch center of D in Example 5-3 is established by both melodic and harmonic factors. Notice that the first phrase in the flute begins on A and ends on D,

EXAMPLE 5-3 Walter Piston: Flute Sonata (1930), I, last 6 measures

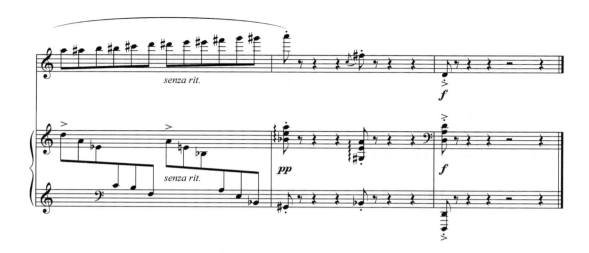

while the second begins on F (E♯) and ends on A, which is followed by F♯ and D. All of these notes are members of major or minor triads on D. In the piano part the emphasis on pitch classes D and A is obvious. Even though this music is basically nontertian, the traditional dominant-to-tonic relationship is employed to help establish the pitch center.

Example 5-4 has a mixture of tertian and nontertian elements. It begins with an F major triad, the third chord is an F minor triad, and the last sonority is an open 5th on F, but the other four chords in the excerpt sound more like quartal or mixed-interval chords. The pitch center in Example 5-4 is established by several factors. The melody obviously centers around F, and the harmony of the phrase begins and ends on F, while in the inner voices there is a double pedal point on F and C. Another interesting feature is the duet between alto and bass, moving in parallel major 10ths until the last two chords, where contrary motion takes over.

EXAMPLE 5-4 Hindemith: *Ludus Tonalis* (1943), "Interlude" (No. IX), mm. 8–10

POLYTONALITY

Polytonality is conceptually similar to the polychord, which was defined in Chapter 3 as a combination of two or more aurally distinguishable sonorities. Likewise, polytonality is the simultaneous use of two or more aurally distinguishable pitch centers, almost all examples consisting of two pitch centers rather than three or more. The term **bitonal** is sometimes used for polytonal music with two tonal centers. As a general rule, each tonal layer in a polytonal passage will be basically diatonic to its own scale.

The last section of Debussy's "Fireworks" (see Example 5-5) begins in Db, over which is superimposed a C major melody (a reference to "La Marseillaise") and its counterpoint. Only in the last three measures is the polytonal conflict resolved, with the Db tonality winning out.

EXAMPLE 5-5 Debussy: Preludes, Book II (1913), "Fireworks" ("Feux d'artifice"), mm. 91–99

In Example 5-6 bitonality occurs in a modal setting. Here the first violin is in E♭ Dorian, while the cello is in D Dorian (notice the planed triads). Meanwhile, the other instruments are playing only Ds and E♭s. In both Example 5-5 and Example 5-6, the pitch centers were a minor 2nd apart, but this is in no sense a "rule" of bitonality. Other relationships can and do occur.

EXAMPLE 5-6 Bartók: String Quartet No. 3 (1927), II, mm. 26–34

An interesting example of polytonality involving four tonal levels is found in the second movement of Henry Brant's *Angels and Devils* (1932, 1947), where a pair of piccolos and three pairs of flutes are notated in four different keys. It would take a sharp ear indeed to sort all of this out aurally, but most listeners are probably aware that some sort of polytonality is involved.

PANDIATONICISM

A great deal of music composed between the late nineteenth century and the present day is based on the chromatic scale. Presumably as a reaction against such pervasive chromaticism, some composers have employed a technique known as **pandiatonicism**. A pandiatonic passage uses only the tones of some diatonic scale but does not rely on traditional harmonic progressions and dissonance treatment. Pandiatonic passages may be pitch centric or not, tertian or nontertian.

An earlier excerpt by Ives, Example 3-23 (p. 55), illustrates nontertian pandiatonicism. Most of the sonorities in the excerpt are clusters derived from the C major scale. The three altered notes that appear do not seem to destroy the basically pandiatonic sound. The pitch center is not obvious, but it is probably G, which at the end is both the highest and lowest pitch class.

Tertian pandiatonicism can be seen in "O König aller Völker" from Arvo Pärt's *Magnificat Antiphons* (1988). In its first several measures, a D minor triad dominates, but there are no traditional harmonic progressions, and the dissonance treatment is anything but traditional.

The pandiatonic passage in Example 5-7 makes use of the C major scale. It is best classified as tertian, but the chords are sometimes difficult to identify with certainty. Later in the piece, the music "modulates" through several pandiatonic areas, including C♯, G♭, and F. We will see more instances of pandiatonicism in minimalist compositions, to be discussed in Chapter 15.

EXAMPLE 5–7 Stravinsky: Serenade in A (1925), I, mm. 52–58

ATONALITY

Atonality was a development even more radical than that of the various sorts of pitch-centricity used in post-tonal music. The ways in which atonality has been achieved and the analytical approaches that have been developed for atonal music are extensive and will be discussed in later chapters. For now it will suffice to define atonal music as music in which the listener perceives no pitch center. Because this is a subjective definition, listeners will not always agree as to whether a particular passage or piece is tonal or atonal, but the following examples from earlier in the text would probably be heard as atonal by most musicians:

Example 2-8 (Henze, p. 21)   Example 4-1 (Boulez, p. 70)
Example 2-18 (Scriabin, p. 27)   Example 4-5 (Schoenberg, p. 73).
Example 2-B-3 (Webern, p. 36)

NONHARMONIC MUSIC

In its broadest definition, harmony means the vertical aspect of music, and a harmony, or chord, is any collection of pitch classes sounded simultaneously. Such broad definitions are sometimes useful, but they may also distract us from the fact that a good deal of post-tonal music is not harmonic in conception. Sometimes the "simultaneities" in a piece are just that—the more or less uncontrolled coming-together of very independent lines. Although Schoenberg was certainly not completely indifferent to the vertical dimension, it would appear that the primary emphasis in Example 5-8, for instance, is on lines, rather than the chords that they produce. (Remember that the bass clarinet will sound a major 9th lower than written.) The term **linear counterpoint** is often used for music of this sort, where the compositional method is evidently overwhelmingly linear. This approach is typical of much atonal music, such as this excerpt, but it occurs in other styles as well.

EXAMPLE 5-8 Schoenberg: *Pierrot Lunaire*, Op. 21 (1912), "Madonna," mm. 1–4

Used by permission of Belmont Music Publishers.

SUMMARY

Traditional tonal harmony survived past the tonal era in various kinds of popular music and in a very small proportion of "classical" music. Otherwise, harmonic progression has to be regarded as a nonissue in an era without a common harmonic vocabulary and no generally accepted theory of chord roots. The declining interest in the vertical dimension is exemplified by linear counterpoint, in which the "chords" seem truly to be mere simultaneities created by the relatively uncontrolled relationships between independent lines.

For the most part, "serious" music since around 1900 has been either pitch-centric or atonal. Pitch-centric music, whether tertian or nontertian, relies on methods other than the V^7-I progression in order to establish a pitch center. These methods include such devices as pedal point and ostinato, accent (metric, agogic, or dynamic), and formal placement. Melodies play a larger role in determining the pitch center than was the case in tonal music.

Other developments in post-tonal music include polytonality, the employment of two or more pitch centers simultaneously; pandiatonicism, the use of a diatonic scale in a nontraditional context; and atonality, the avoidance of a pitch center.

MUSIC FROM THE CHAPTER IN CHRONOLOGICAL CONTEXT

Year	Composer	Work	Reference
1894	Debussy	*Prelude to the Afternoon of a Faun*	Impressionsim
1912	**Schoenberg**	***Pierrot Lunaire***	**Expressionism, p. 98**
1913	Stravinsky	*Rite of Spring*	Primitivism
1913	**Debussy**	**Preludes, Book II**	**p. 95**
1927	**Bartók**	**String Quartet No. 3**	**p. 96**
1930	Stravinsky	*Symphony of Psalms*	Neoclassicism
1930	**Walton Piston**	**Flute Sonata**	**p. 93**
1935	Berg	Violin Concerto	Serialism
1936	**Aram Khachaturian**	**Piano Concerto**	**p. 91**
1943	**Hindemith**	***Ludus Tonalis***	**p. 94**
1943	**Benjamin Britten**	**Serenade for Tenor, Horn, and Strings**	**p. 92**

Works in **bold** are from the chapter; those not in bold are landmark pieces written around the same time.

NOTES

1.   Paul Hindemith, *Craft of Musical Composition*, Vol. I.

2.   Hindemith, *Craft*, p. 156.

EXERCISES

Part A: Fundamentals

Define each of the following terms:

1.   Chromatic mediant relationship

2.   Cluster

3.   Mode of limited transposition

4.   Pitch-centricity

5.   Pandiatonicism

6.   Pitch-class cell

7.   Planing

8.   Polychord

9.   Real sequence

Part B: Analysis

Each of the following excerpts for analysis is to be approached in the same way:

(a)   Assuming the excerpt is pitch-centric (or even tonal), what is the pitch center, and what melodic and harmonic factors contribute to establishing it?

(b)   Is the pitch-centric style tertian, nontertian, or a mixture of the two?

(c)   Is the excerpt polytonal? If so, discuss.

(d)   Is the excerpt pandiatonic? If so, discuss.

(e)   Do you find any evidence of traditional harmonic progressions? Explain your answer.

1.   Example 2-5, p. 19 (Bartók: *Bluebeard's Castle*)

2.   Example 2-13, p. 24 (Debussy: "Footprints in the Snow")

3.   Example 3-5, p. 45 (Prokofiev: Sonata for Flute and Piano)

4.   Example 3-B-6, p. 65 (Ravel: Sonatina)

5. Example 3-B-8, p. 66 (Berg: "Warm Is the Air")

6. Copland: *El Salón México* (1936)

7. Darius Milhaud: *Saudades do Brasil* (1921), "Botafogo," mm. 1–10

Part C: Composition

As an alternative to any of the following exercises, disregard the music that is provided and compose your own example, illustrating the specified techniques.

1. Continue in B♭, illustrating tertian pitch-centricity.

2. Continue in a mostly nontertian pitch-centric style. Try to convince the listener of a tonal center on D.

3. Compose an excerpt using polychords with A as a tonal center. End your example with the following cadence.

4. Continue, illustrating C major pandiatonicism and the use of an ostinato.

5. Use bitonality (B and D) at the beginning of this example, resolving into a single tonality at the end.

FURTHER READING

Dallin, Leon. *Techniques of Twentieth Century Composition*. See Chapter 7, Harmonic Succession; Chapter 8, Tonality; and Chapter 9, Cadences.

Hindemith, Paul. *Craft of Musical Composition*, Vol. I. See especially the sections on interval roots (pp. 68–74, 79–89), chord roots (pp. 94–106), and harmonic tension (pp. 106–108, 158–164).

Persichetti, Vincent. *Twentieth-Century Harmony*. See the sections on "Progression" (pp. 182–188) and "Cadential Devices" (pp. 206–209), as well as pp. 248–261 in Chapter 12, Key Centers.

Reisberg, Horace. "The Vertical Dimension in Twentieth-Century Music," in Gary Wittlich, Ed., *Aspects of Twentieth-Century Music*. See the section titled "Negation of Harmony," pp. 372–385.

Steinke, Greg A., and Paul O. Harder. *Bridge to 20th-Century Music*. See Chapter 1, which deals with melodic tonality.

Zieliński, Tadeusz A. "Harmony and Counterpoint," in John Vinton, Ed., *Dictionary of Contemporary Music*.

CHAPTER 6

Developments in Rhythm

INTRODUCTION

One of the many features distinguishing post-tonal music from that of the tonal era is its preoccupation with rhythm. Though rhythm is an important element of tonal music, perhaps in ways that are still not completely understood, the surface rhythm of most tonal pieces is relatively straightforward and easy to comprehend, so much so that analyses of such pieces often make little or no mention of the rhythmic dimension. In contrast, in many post-tonal compositions the focus is on rhythm at least as much as on pitch, and the surface rhythms are frequently varied and complex. This chapter will explore some of the ways in which these varieties and complexities are achieved, but first it will be useful to review some terminology:

Rhythm—The organization of the time element in music
Beat—The basic pulse
Simple beat—Division of the beat into two equal parts
Compound beat—Division of the beat into three equal parts
Meter—The grouping of beats into larger units
Duple meter—The grouping of beats into twos
Triple meter—The grouping of beats into threes
Quadruple meter—The grouping of beats into fours
Measure—One full unit of the meter
Syncopation—An accent where one is not expected, or the lack of an accent where one would be expected.

The listener perceives the beat type (simple or compound) by listening to the way the beat divides (into twos or threes). The meter (duple, triple, or quadruple) is conveyed by the characteristic pattern of accents, although these are typically not explicitly notated in the music. The accents that express the meter are usually agogic ones, but subtle dynamic accents are also sometimes added by the performer.

WRITTEN RHYTHM AND PERCEIVED RHYTHM

Of course, it is perfectly possible to compose music in such a way that the listener will not be able to perceive the notated beat type or meter type or both. The first of Chopin's Preludes, Op. 28, is heard in compound time, but it is notated in $\frac{2}{8}$, with most of the beats being divided into sixteenth-note triplets. Contradictions between the way rhythm is heard and the way it is written are especially common in post-tonal music. An example similar to the Chopin prelude, but more complex, is the second movement of Webern's Variations for Piano, Op. 27. Although written in a very fast simple duple, it seems to most listeners to be in a slower compound meter, with occasional odd-length beats thrown in. The beginning of the piece is seen in Example 6-1, with the perceived rhythm notated below. (It could also be heard in $\frac{3}{8}$.) Notice the extra eighth-note rest in the second measure.

EXAMPLE 6-1   Webern: Variations for Piano, Op. 27 (1936), II, mm. 1–4

Often the conflict between written and perceived rhythms arises out of consideration for the performer. Example 6-2a shows an excerpt from the first edition of Kent Kennan's trumpet sonata, in which traditional $\frac{4}{4}$ and $\frac{3}{4}$ time signatures are used. By the time of the second edition, some 30 years later, performers had become so accustomed to untraditional time signatures that Kennan felt safe notating it as shown in Example 6-2b.

EXAMPLE 6-2A   Kennan: Sonata for Trumpet and Piano (1956), I, mm. 93–101

EXAMPLE 6-2b Kennan: Sonata for Trumpet and Piano (1986), I, mm. 90–99

In many of the examples discussed in this chapter, it will be very important to distinguish between rhythm as notated and rhythm as aurally perceived. In all cases we will take the perceived rhythm as the true rhythm.

CHANGING TIME SIGNATURES

Although changing from one time signature to another in the course of a movement certainly occurs in tonal works, it has seen much more use in the post-tonal era. Terms for this technique include **changing meter**, **mixed meter**, **variable meter**, and **multimeter**. Changing meters can be implied by shifted accents or syncopations, or they can be explicitly notated by the composer. Several examples have already illustrated changing time signatures, among them the following:

Example 2–21 (p. 29): $\frac{3}{4}$ $\frac{2}{4}$ $\frac{3}{4}$
Example 3–20 (p. 54): $\frac{3}{4}$ $\frac{5}{8}$ $\frac{4}{8}$
Example 4–5 (p. 73): $\frac{6}{4}$ $\frac{7}{4}$
Example 4–6 (p. 75): $\frac{4}{2}$ $\frac{5}{2}$ $\frac{4}{2}$
Example 6–2b: $\frac{9}{8}$ $\frac{7}{8}$ $\frac{2}{4}$ $\frac{8}{8}$ $\frac{5}{8}$ $\frac{8}{8}$ $\frac{5}{8}$ $\frac{6}{8}$ $\frac{5}{8}$ $\frac{7}{8}$

A more problematical example was Example 4–7 (p. 77), where the meter signatures fluctuate between $\frac{3}{8}$ and $\frac{2}{8}$, even though the perceived rhythm of the solo piano part remains steadfastly in $\frac{2}{8}$. A closer examination of the accompanying orchestral parts, however, reveals that the changing time signatures do reflect the rhythm of the accompaniment. This example will be discussed in more detail later.

NONTRADITIONAL TIME SIGNATURES

The top number of a traditional time signature is 2, 3, 4, 6, 9, or 12, but other top numbers have been used freely in post-tonal music. The numbers 5 and 7 have been especially favored (which is why some employ the term **asymmetric meter** for this device), but others, such as 1, 8, 10, and 11 have not been completely neglected.

The notated time signature in Example 4–9 (p. 79) is $\frac{4}{4}$, but it is obvious from the phrasing and accents that the perceived meter is $\frac{5}{4}$. Most examples of nontraditional meters can easily be heard as changing meters, and this is also true of Example 4–9, which sounds like $\frac{2}{4}$ alternating with $\frac{3}{4}$. However, Example 4–8 (p. 78), also in $\frac{5}{4}$, does not seem to divide clearly into 2 + 3 or 3 + 2. In Example 5–6 (p. 96), the divisions of the $\frac{5}{8}$ measures seem to imply 1 + 2 + 2, 2 + 2 + 1, and 2 + 3, with the first violin and the cello not always in agreement in any particular measure.

Example 6–2b illustrates several nontraditional time signatures: $\frac{5}{8}$, $\frac{7}{8}$, and $\frac{8}{8}$. Of course, $\frac{8}{8}$ contains the same number of 8th notes as $\frac{4}{4}$; Kennan presumably used $\frac{8}{8}$ to call the performer's attention to the irregular division of the measures into 3 + 3 + 2 eighth notes (instead of the customary 4 + 4).

The term **additive rhythm** is sometimes used for passages such as the one in Example 6–2, where some short note value (here the 8th note) remains constant but is used in groups of unpredictably varying lengths. Another instance of additive rhythm is seen in Example 5–B–6 (p. 101), which employs time signatures of $\frac{5}{8}$, $\frac{8}{8}$, $\frac{11}{8}$, and others.

When a traditional time signature is transformed into a nontraditional one by the use of a nonstandard metric accent, one approach is to indicate the new metric accent with dotted barlines, as in Example 5–B–6. Another way is to specify the new pattern of metric accents in the time signature itself, as Bartók did in the "Scherzo" of his String Quartet No. 5 (1934). There he transforms $\frac{9}{8}$ (traditionally 3 + 3 + 3) into a nontraditional 4 + 2 + 3 by use of a $\frac{4+2+3}{8}$ time signature, a type sometimes referred to as a **complex meter**. At a vivace tempo, the listener hears three beats of unequal length per measure, a variation on the traditional $\frac{3}{4}$ scherzo. The trio is in an unusual quadruple meter, predominantly $\frac{3+2+2+3}{8}$.

Another approach to transforming traditional time signatures is to use the traditional signature, but to use accents and phrase marks to indicate the metric accent. This is the case in Example 6–3, where the two hands play groups of 16th notes of varying length in notated $\frac{4}{4}$ and $\frac{3}{4}$ meters.

	m. 9	m. 10	m. 11	m. 12
R.H.:	rest	6 + 6	6 + 6	1 + 5 + 2 + 4
L.H.:	5 + 1 + 4 + 2	4 + 2 + 5 + 1	6 + 6	rest

EXAMPLE 6-3 Milton Babbitt: Three Compositions for Piano (1947), No. 1, mm. 9–12

In "*. . . quasi una fantasia . . .*" (1988) György Kurtág employs an unusual method of defining nontraditional time signatures, such as these:

The effect of the first two signatures is to create a measure of four or five beats with a short final beat. The last example creates a three-beat measure with a very long final beat.

The nontraditional time signature that is most difficult for performers is probably the **fractional time signature**. For example, in the fifth of his *Eleven Studies in Velocity* (1987), Colin Matthews uses a time signature of $\frac{2\frac{1}{2}}{4}$ for measures that generally have a ♩♪♪ rhythm and $\frac{3\frac{3}{4}}{4}$ for rhythms like this: ♩ ♪ ♩ ♪ ♩ ♪ .

In the third measure of Example 4-1 (p. 70) Boulez writes $\frac{4}{3}$ over 2, meaning four beats, each of them the length of one-third of a half note. Note also the use of $\frac{5}{8}$ and $\frac{7}{8}$ in the example, the latter apparently being divided into two $\frac{7}{16}$ segments. Although each note value maintains a nearly constant metronomic duration in this excerpt (the quarter note, for example, equals M.M. 104 or 105 throughout), the effect is of a fluid and constantly fluctuating tempo.

POLYMETER

The metrical equivalent of polytonality is **polymeter**, the simultaneous use of two or more aurally distinguishable meters. There are three possibilities: same time signature, but displaced (Example 6-4a); different signatures, with barlines coinciding (Example 6-4b); and different signatures, with barlines not coinciding (Example 6-4c). Though all three of these combinations occur, the third is perhaps the most striking aurally and the most frequently employed.[1] Remember that in each case we are referring to the aural effect, not necessarily to the actual notation.

EXAMPLE 6-4 Polymeter

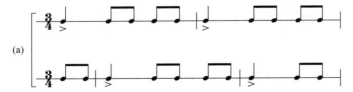

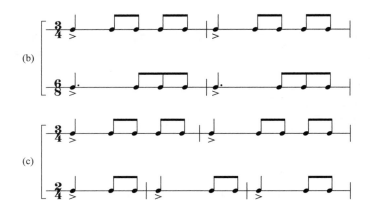

EXAMPLE 6-5 Bartók: String Quartet No. 3 (1927), II, mm. 15–21

Copyright © 1929 in the USA by Boosey & Hawkes, Inc. Copyright renewed. Reprinted by permission.

In Example 6-5 the polymeter (type c) is explicitly notated in the viola and cello parts. It comes about through the canon at the octave, with the viola leading the cello by one measure. The fourth and fifth measures of the viola part are in $\frac{3}{4}$ and $\frac{2}{4}$, while beneath those measures the cello plays the third and fourth measures of the canon with time signatures of $\frac{2}{4}$ and $\frac{3}{4}$.

Music with barlines that do not coincide, as in Example 6-5, may be troublesome for an ensemble or a conductor, so polymeter is often implied instead of explicitly notated. This is the case in Example 6-6, a few pages later in the same quartet—again a canonic example, this time between the two violins. Here the viola and cello are clearly in $\frac{3}{8}$, but the violins sound as if they are in a polymetric canon (type a) with each other, as well as being polymetric (type c) with the accompaniment. The rhythms might be rebarred as in Example 6-7.

EXAMPLE 6-6 Bartók: String Quartet No.3 (1927), II, mm. 95–103

Copyright © 1929 in the USA by Boosey & Hawkes, Inc. Copyright renewed. Reprinted by permission.

EXAMPLE 6-7 Explicit Polymetric Notation (compare with Example 6-6)

A less complicated example of implied polymeter was seen in Example 4-7 (p. 77), discussed above in connection with changing time signatures. In this instance the piano maintains a steady $\frac{2}{8}$ meter, although it is notated to conform with the changing meters of the brasses.

Polymeter with coinciding barlines (type b) is probably the least commonly used. Remember that the simultaneous use of $\frac{2}{4}$ and $\frac{6}{8}$, for instance, is not really polymeter but instead poly*division* of a single meter. One example of polymeter type b is seen in Example 6-8. Here the flutes and harps are continuing a $\frac{3}{4}$ waltz that was begun eight measures earlier. Meanwhile, beneath the waltz, the lower woodwinds and lower strings take up a $\frac{2}{4}$ melody that contrasts with the waltz in both meter and tonality.

EXAMPLE 6-8 Stravinsky: *Petrushka* (1911), third tableau

Excerpted from the Norton Critical Edition. Used by permission of W. W. Norton & Co., Inc., and Edwin F. Kalmus & Co., Inc.

AMETRIC MUSIC

We recognize the beat and meter type of a passage by listening to the way that the beat divides and the way that beats group into larger units. Once we have grown used to devices such as changing meters and nontraditional meters, we are able to identify them aurally as well. Yet some music seems to exhibit no perceivable metric organization, a style we will refer to as **ametric**. Gregorian chant is a good example of ametric music, as is much electronic music.

Some writers use the term "arhythmic" for music in which rhythmic patterns and metric organization are not perceivable. But if we accept a very general definition of rhythm as covering "all aspects of musical movement as ordered in time,"[2] then music cannot be arhythmic, but only ametric.

Not all music written without a time signature is ametric. For instance, four of the five movements of Hindemith's String Quartet No. 4 (1921) have no meter signature at all, but the music is barred, and the implied time signatures are clear both to the eye and to the ear. At the same time, some music notated *with* a time signature is written in such a way as to sound ametric. A good example of this is the Boulez excerpt discussed earlier in this chapter (Example 4-1, p. 70), which, although precisely notated, sounds free and improvisionary to the listener. The same is true of Example 4-B-2.

Music without barlines may be metric or not, depending on the composer's intention and the listener's interpretation. Although Ives used no time signature and no barlines in Example 3-B-7 (p. 65), a listener still might hear a steady $\frac{2}{4}$ organization. But Example 3-23 (p. 55), also by Ives, is almost certainly ametric, as is the rest of the movement from which it is excerpted.

Luciano Berio's *Sequenza I* (1958) uses a short barline (see Example 6-9), and the "measure" itself is assigned a specific tempo of "70 M.M." at the beginning. This composition is definitely ametric, however, because the actual durations are specified only by the placement of the notes within the measure. In the first measure, for example, the G5 is to be given the longest duration, because it occupies the greatest portion of the measure. Notation of this sort is sometimes called **proportional notation**. Accidentals in this excerpt affect only the notes they precede.

EXAMPLE 6-9 Berio: *Sequenza I* (1958), first staff

Many techniques developed after 1960 result in ametric effects, often involving some degree of improvisation, as in Example 6-9 and in Example 6-10. In Example 6-10 the temporal organization is determined by timed segments, with unmetered improvisation going on within them. These and other improvisatory techniques will be covered in more detail in Chapter 14.

EXAMPLE 6-10 Joseph Schwantner: *And the Mountains Rising Nowhere* (1977)

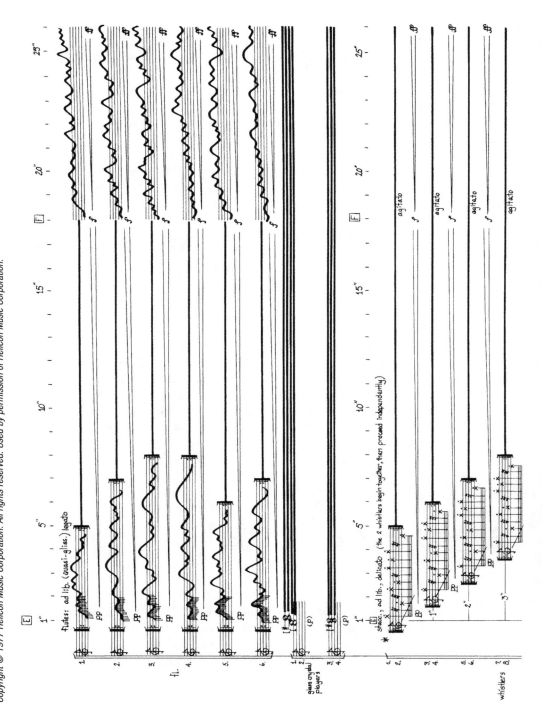

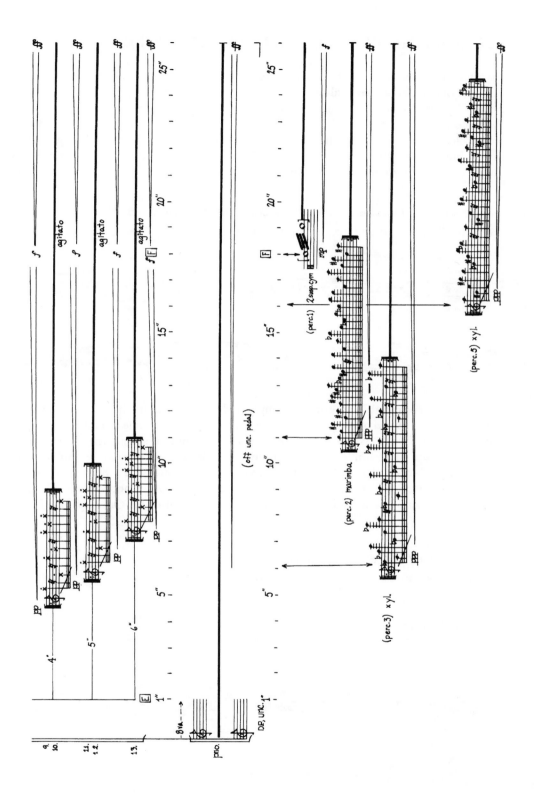

ADDED VALUES AND NONRETROGRADABLE RHYTHMS

Two techniques from the fertile imagination of Olivier Messiaen will be discussed here. The first one, called **added values**, involves complicating an otherwise simple rhythmic pattern by the addition of a short duration in the form of a dot, a note, or a rest. In Example 6–11 each added value is identified by a "+" sign. The first three measures would clearly be in $\frac{4}{4}$ without the added values; with them, the effect is still of quadruple meter, but with one or two longer beats in each measure. The rest of the example is more complicated rhythmically and would probably be perceived as ametric.

EXAMPLE 6-11 Messiaen: *The Technique of My Musical Language,* Example 13, mm. 1–6

Copyright © 1944 Editions Alphonse Leduc. Used by permission of the publisher.

A **nonretrogradable rhythm** is simply a rhythmic pattern that sounds the same whether played forward or backward (in retrograde). A trivial example would be a group of four 8th notes, but Messiaen is interested in more complicated patterns. The rhythm of each measure in Example 6-12 is nonretrogradable, and each measure also contains added values. Notice that the rhythmic activity builds gradually to a climax in the 7th measure, followed by an immediate relaxation through longer note values. Both of the Messiaen examples are drawn from the sixth movement of his *Quartet for the End of Time* (1941).

EXAMPLE 6-12 Messiaen: *The Technique of My Musical Language.*

Copyright © 1944 Editions Alphonse Leduc. Used by permission of the publisher.

Another way to look at nonretrogradable rhythms is that each one contains some rhythmic pattern followed by its retrograde, resulting inevitably in a rhythmic **palindrome**, a term used for any structure in language or music that reads the same forward as it does backward. Therefore, any piece that makes use of rhythmic retrogrades on a larger scale could also be considered an example of nonretrogradable rhythms. For instance, the second movement of Webern's Symphony, Op. 21 (1928), begins with an 11-measure theme that is a rhythmic palindrome, a technique that is found through much of the movement.

TEMPO MODULATION AND POLYTEMPO

Elliott Carter is generally credited with being the first to use a particular method of changing tempos precisely by making some note value in the first tempo equal to a different note value (or at least to a different proportion of the beat) in the second tempo. For example, to "modulate" from $\quarternote = 80$ to $\quarternote = 120$, one could begin using 8th-note triplets in the first tempo. These triplet 8ths have a duration of 240 per minute (three times the $\quarternote = 80$ rate). This rate of 240 turns out to be the rate of the simple division of the beat (the 8th note) at the new tempo of $\quarternote = 120$. (See Example 6-13). This device has been called "metric modulation" because it usually involves changing time signatures; however, a change of tempo is the real objective, so we will use the term **tempo modulation**. This technique does bear a resemblance to the common chord modulation of tonal music, in that one or more measures will contain elements of both tempos.

EXAMPLE 6-13 A Simple Tempo Modulation

Carter evidently employed tempo modulation for the first time in his Cello Sonata (1948). A relatively simple example is found in the second movement, which begins in cut time at $\quarternote = 84$. Later the meter changes to $\frac{6}{8}$ with the 8th note remaining constant. The most reliable way to calculate the new tempo is to first compute the tempo of the common note value in the first tempo:

If $\quarternote = 84$, then $\eighthnote = 4 \times 84 = 336$

and then to figure out what that means in terms of the beat in the second tempo:

If $\eighthnote = 336$, and the new beat is the dotted quarter,
then the new tempo is $336/3 = 112$.

A more complex example occurs in the third movement, which begins in $\frac{3}{4}$ with $\flat. = 70$. The tempo modulation then follows these steps:

1. Change to $\frac{6}{16}$, keeping the beat constant, so $\flat. = 70$.
2. Change to $\frac{21}{32}$, keeping the 32nd note constant. This unusual time signature is *not* compound septuple, as one might expect. Instead, it is a *triple* meter, with each beat equaling a doubly dotted 8th note. When $\flat. = 70$ (above), $\flat = 420$ (because there are six 32nds in one dotted 8th). Since the 32nd remains constant, and there are seven 32nds in the new beat value ($\flat..$), the new tempo is $420/7 = 60$.
3. Change to $\frac{2}{8}$, keeping the beat constant, so $\flat = 60$.

Similar in concept to polymeter but much less often encountered is **polytempo**, the simultaneous use of two or more aurally distinguishable tempos. One example of this is Ives's *The Unanswered Question* (1908), a work for four flutes, trumpet, and strings. The trumpet and strings maintain a steady tempo of $\quarternote = 50$, but the six statements by the flutes are heard at increasing tempos and dynamics, from *Adagio* and *p* to *Molto agitando* and *ffff*. A composer who devoted much of his life to the problem of polytempo and other rhythmic concerns is Conlon Nancarrow, who worked for decades in relative obscurity in Mexico, composing music with extremely complex ratios of tempos and rhythms that were realized on player piano rolls, the only practical way such music could be performed before the advent of the computer. (In Study No. 36, for example, the ratios between the tempos are 17: 18: 19: 20.) Recordings of his music finally became generally available in the 1980s, and these were followed by a number of nonmechanical works that explore the same issues.

In his String Quartet No. 1, Carter solves the problem of polytempo in a different way—by explicit notation. In Example 6–14 all of the parts are notated in the same tempo, $\quarternote = 120$, but only the cello *sounds* as if it is playing at that tempo. Because of the way the music is notated, the aurally perceived tempos, in terms of beats per minute are:

Violin I	36
Violin II	96
Viola	180
Cello	120.

Or, stated as ratios from top to bottom, 3: 8: 15: 10, meaning that the cello, for instance, will play ten notes in the span of three notes in violin I. All of this is part of a large-scale tempo modulation that will eventually settle into the tempo heard in the viola.

EXAMPLE 6-14 Carter: String Quartet No. 1 (1951), I, mm. 22–26

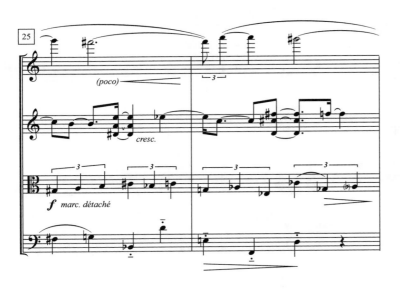

EXAMPLE 6-15 Alban Berg: *Wozzeck* (1921), Act III, Scene 3, mm. 187–198

SERIALIZED RHYTHM AND ISORHYTHM

The term **serialized rhythm** is generally used in connection with pieces in which the rhythmic aspects are governed by some preconceived series of durations. This will be discussed in more detail in Chapter 13.

The term **isorhythm** is applied to a technique that dates from the fourteenth century but that has been revived in the post-tonal era. Simply put, an isorhythm is a rhythmic pattern that repeats using different pitches. The pitches may or may not themselves form a repeating pattern, but if they do, it must be of a different length than the rhythmic pattern. (If the two are of the same length, what results is an *ostinato*, not an isorhythm.)

Much of Act III, Scene 3, of *Wozzeck* is isorhythmic, using the rhythmic pattern seen in the first three and a half measures of the bottom staff in Example 6-15—in fact, all of the music in the example is derived directly from that pattern. The effect here is polymetric, the three and a half-measure pattern in the low register rising inexorably over two whole-tone scales a major 7th apart, while Wozzeck tries desperately to explain to Margret how blood got onto his hand.

THE NEW COMPLEXITY

In the 1980s and 90s, Brian Ferneyhough, Michael Finnissy, James Dillon and others began writing music that combined extended techniques, microtonal intervals, and rhythms more complex than one could find in any previous composer's music, creating a style that is now commonly known as "the new complexity." The rhythms of this style are so complex that a live performer usually can only hope to approximate what is notated in the score during a performance, though the music is usually written for live performers (not intended for computer-generated realization). Example 6-16, the first four bars of Ferneyhough's *Intermedio alla ciaccona*, provides a clear illustration of how the complex rhythms are combined with microtones (see the discussion of microtonal scales on p. 29 for a guide to interpreting the microtonal accidentals), though it does not show any of the extended techniques that occur later in the piece.

Example 6-16 Brian Ferneyhough: *Intermedio alla ciaccona*, mm. 1–4

Peters Edition London, Copyright © 1986.

While the above definition of the style may accurately capture one's first impression when looking at a score, it doesn't speak to the driving force behind its composition, which is motivic development. In that way, it actually has much in common with the aesthetic behind the freely atonal music of Schoenberg, Webern, and Berg, though its incorporation of complex rhythms, microtonal intervals, and extended techniques gives it a very different sound.

SUMMARY

One aspect of rhythm in post-tonal music that must catch the attention of any performer is its difficulty. Certainly there was nothing in the rhythm of the tonal era to parallel the complexity of post-tonal rhythms, and one might have to go back to the late fourteenth century to find a comparable preoccupation with complicated rhythms. While most musicians could perform the rhythms of a tonal work at sight, it is doubtful that they would be as successful with the works from which Example 4-1 (p. 70) and Example 6-12 are drawn.

Some of the specific techniques discussed in this chapter included the following:

Syncopation
Changing time signatures
Nontraditional time signatures
    Using 5, 7, etc., for the top value
    Complex meters such as $\frac{3+2+3}{8}$
    Fractional top values
Polymeter
    Same signature, barlines not coinciding
    Different signatures, barlines coinciding
    Different signatures, barlines not coinciding
Ametric music
Proportional notation
Added values
Nonretrogradable rhythms
Tempo modulation
Polytempo
Serialized rhythm
Isorhythm

Certainly this chapter has not exhausted all of the details of rhythm in post-tonal music, but it has brought up some of the main points. One problem that you will discover if you do more reading in this area is that terminology relating to rhythm is not standardized. You will encounter terms such as "cross-rhythm" and "combined meters" that were not used in this chapter but refer to techniques discussed here using different terminology.

Finally, it is most important to remember that music is an aural experience, and you cannot always make an intelligent observation about the rhythm of a piece by a casual glance at the score. Such devices as polymeter and changing time signatures may be quite perceptible aurally, even though they are not explicitly notated. In all such cases, analyze the music by the way it sounds, not by the way it looks.

MUSIC FROM THE CHAPTER IN CHRONOLOGICAL CONTEXT

Year	Composer	Work	Reference
1912	Schoenberg	*Pierrot Lunaire*	Expressionism
1913	Stravinsky	*Rite of Spring*	Primitivism
1921	**Berg**	***Wozzeck***	**p. 120**
1927	**Bartók**	**String Quartet No. 3**	**p. 111**
1930	Stravinsky	*Symphony of Psalms*	Neoclassicism
1935	Berg	Violin Concerto	Serialism
1936	**Anton Webern**	**Variations for Piano, Op. 27**	**p. 106**
1947	**Milton Babbitt**	**Three Compositions for Piano**	**p. 108**
1951	**Elliott Carter**	**String Quartet No. 1**	**p. 119**
1952	John Cage	*4′33″*	Chance Music
1954	Edgard Varèse	*Poème Electronique*	Electronic Music
1956	**Kent Kennan**	**Sonata for Trumpet and Piano**	**pp. 106–107**
1958	**Berio**	***Sequenza I***	**p. 113**
1961	Krzysztof Penderecki	*Threnody: To the Victims of Hiroshima*	Aleatoric Music
1964	Terry Riley	*In C*	Minimalism
1977	**Joseph Schwantner**	***And the Mountains Rising Nowhere***	**pp. 114–115**
1986	**Brian Ferneyhough**	***Intermedio alla ciaccona***	**p. 124**

Works in **bold** are from the chapter; those not in bold are landmark pieces written around the same time.

NOTES

1. Some use "polyrhythm" to refer to the second type of polymeter.

2. Harold S. Powers, "Rhythm," in Don Randel, Ed., *The New Harvard Dictionary of Music.*

★

EXERCISES

Part A: Fundamentals

1. On what scale is Example 6-1 based?

2. Which example best illustrates planing?

3. The fourth movement of Corigliano's String Quartet (1995) is a fugue that features polytempo. Let's assume that the viola plays the fugue subject at a tempo of ♩ = 70. When the second violin enters, it has four notes to every five in the viola. The next entrance is by the first violin, which plays three notes to every two played by the second violin. The final statement of the subject is in the cello, which plays three notes to every four in the first violin. What would be the tempo for each of the instruments?

4. The following questions dealing with tempo modulation are based on techniques used by George Perle in his String Quartet No. 5 (1960, 1967).

    (a) In the first movement, Tempo I is ♩ = 96. To get to Tempo II, Perle specifies that the old triplet 8th note (one-third of a quarter note) be equal to the new 16th note. What is the tempo of the quarter note (not the half note) in Tempo II? Show your work.

    (b) In the third movement, Tempo II is ♩ = 96. To get back to Tempo I, Perle specifies that the old dotted half note be equal to the new half note tied to an 8th note. What is the tempo of the quarter note in Tempo I? Show your work.

    (c) Also in the third movement, Tempo III is ♩ = 120. To get back to another tempo, Perle specifies that the old 8th note be equal to one-fifth of the new half note. Is the new tempo Tempo I or Tempo II? Show your work.

5. Be able to perform the rhythms of the following examples:

    (a) Example 2-22 (p. 30 hand only, with the 8th note as the beat note.

    (b) Example 4-2 (p. 71).

    (c) Example 4-5 (p. 73) staff with the right hand, bottom with the left.

    (d) Example 4-B-2 (p. 85).

    (e) Example 5-6 (p. 96) staff with the right hand, bottom with the left.

    (f) Example 5-B-6 (p. 101) staff, vivace.

    (g) Example 6-2—both versions.

    (h) Example 6-5—bottom two staves.

    (i) Example 6-6-top two staves.

    (j) Example 6-11.

(k) Example 6-12.

(l) Example 6–13.

(m) Example 6-14—violin II and cello.

(n) Example 6-15—Wozzeck's line and the bottom staff.

Part B: Analysis

1. Example 2-22 (p. 30) has nine 8th notes to the measure, but the time signature is not $\frac{9}{8}$. What do you think would be an appropriate time signature for this example?

2. Discuss the rhythm and meter of Example 4-2 (p. 71), concentrating on those aspects that are characteristic of post-tonal music.

3. Analyze Example 6-3 in more detail. (*Note:* Each accidental affects only the note it precedes.) Do any measures share identical patterns of rhythms or accents? Are any the retrograde (reverse) of others? Are there any repeated or retrograded pitch patterns?

4. Analyze Example 6-12 in more detail. Can you find any relationship between the rhythms of successive or nonsuccessive measures? Is there any logic or pattern to the pitch choices?

5. Bartók: Forty-Four Violin Duets (1931), No. 33, "Song of the Harvest," mm. 6–15.

    Discuss rhythmic and tonal aspects of this excerpt. To what scale does the combined pitch material of both staves conform?

6. Francis Poulenc: *Promenades* (1921), V, "En avion," systems 3 and 4.

Discuss rhythmic and pitch aspects of this excerpt, including consideration of chord types and tonality.

Part C: Composition

1. Compose an example for clarinet or trumpet using several different nontraditional time signatures. All of the pitch material should be from a single diminished scale.

2. Compose a short polymetric passage for two violins in the Phrygian mode.

3. Compose a four-part clapping piece employing tempo modulation.

4. Compose and be able to perform a melody illustrating added values and non-retrogradable rhythms.

5. Compose an isorhythmic passage for three instruments in your class. Try to employ some of the techniques seen in Example 6-15.

6. Compose and perform an example that uses time signatures and strict tempos, yet sounds ametric to the listener.

FURTHER READING

Cope, David. *Techniques of the Contemporary Composer.* See Chapter 8, Rhythm and Meter.

Dallin, Leon. *Techniques of Twentieth Century Composition.* See Chapter 5, Rhythm and Meter.

Gann, Kyle. *The Music of Conlon Nancarrow.*

Kostka, Stefan, and Dorothy Payne. *Tonal Harmony with an Introduction to Twentieth-Century Music.* See the section titled "Rhythm and Meter" in Chapter 28.

Krebs, Harald. "Some Extensions of the Concept of Metrical Consonance and Dissonance."

Lester, Joel. *Analytic Approaches to Twentieth-Century Music.* See Chapter 2, Rhythm and Meter.

Simms, Bryan R. *Music of the Twentieth Century.* See pp. 92–108 of Chapter 5, Rhythm and Meter.

Smither, Howard E. "The Rhythmic Analysis of Twentieth-Century Music." See pp. 71–84.

Smither, Howard E., and Frederic Rzewski. "Rhythm," in John Vinton, Ed., *Dictionary of Contemporary Music.*

Winold, Allen. "Rhythm in Twentieth-Century Music," Chapter 3 of Gary Wittlich, Ed., *Aspects of Twentieth-Century Music.*

CHAPTER 7

Form in Post-Tonal Music

INTRODUCTION

All of the formal structures and procedures found in the tonal era survived in post-tonal music. That is, in post-tonal music we still encounter sonatas and rondos, canons and fugues, sectional and continuous variations, and binary and ternary forms. Not surprisingly, many works employing traditional formal structures date from the first few decades of the twentieth century or were composed by relatively conservative composers, but this is not always the case. For instance, Schoenberg, hardly considered by his contemporaries to be a conservative, often composed in classical forms.

Yet to many musicians some of the older forms seem uncomfortable in modern garb. The reason for this may well lie in the weakening of tonal centricity in almost all music since 1900, to the point of its total avoidance in atonal styles. The essence of sonata form, in particular, involved a dramatic conflict of tonalities—a large-scale tonal dissonance established in the exposition and resolved in the recapitulation. It can be argued that once that conflict of tonalities loses its impact, to the point that it seems to make little difference to the listener at what pitch level the piece ends, the drama of the sonata is lost.

Tonality is less of an issue in the traditional contrapuntal forms—canon and fugue, especially—which may explain in part their healthy survival in post-tonal music. The same could also be said of variations, whether sectional or continuous, and both have aged well. Ternary form, one of the most basic musical structures, has perhaps weathered the storm best of all, since its design—statement, contrast, return—can be applied to a wide variety of styles, from tonal to electronic.

In this chapter we will survey the survival of these and other forms from earlier periods, as well as the appearance of forms unique to post-tonal music. Because it is beyond the scope of this text to present long works or even extended excerpts, there are few musical examples in this chapter. However, all of the works referred to are readily available in both score and recording. In addition, a number of references will be made in the text and exercises to works found in the four widely available anthologies listed here. The abbreviations in parentheses will be used when referring to these anthologies.

Burkhart, Charles. *Anthology for Musical Analysis*, 6th ed. Belmont, Calif.: Schirmer, 2004 (BUR).

Kostka, Stefan, and Roger Graybill. *Anthology of Music for Analysis*. Upper Saddle River, N.J.: Prentice Hall, 2004 (K–G).

Turek, Ralph. *Analytical Anthology of Music*, 2nd ed. New York: McGraw-Hill, 1992 (TUR).

Wennerstrom, Mary H. *Anthology of Twentieth-Century Music*, 2nd ed. Englewood Cliffs, N.J.: Prentice Hall, 1988 (WEN).

The reader is assumed to have a general understanding of the terminology of musical form as it relates to tonal music. One departure from conventional terminology should be noted: no distinction is made in this chapter between "part forms" or "song forms" and the longer "compound forms." For instance, ABA will be labeled "ternary" and ABACA will be labeled "rondo" without regard to the length or complexity of the component parts.

BINARY FORM

Binary form (AA' or AB) is found as the structure of short pieces or movements or of sections within longer works. Examples are as varied as Hindemith's "A Swan" (1939) (BUR, p. 491), John Cage's Sonatas and Interludes (1948), Nos. 1 and 5 (TUR, p. 829), "Vocalise 2: Invocation," from George Crumb's *Apparition* (1980) (WEN, p. 91), and Ligeti's Sonata for Solo Viola (1994), fifth movement (K–G, p. 582). In its application, the binary principle is little changed in post-tonal music, except that the traditional tonal schemes are seldom used.

TERNARY FORM

The ternary principle is a flexible one that can be applied to small or large segments of music, and the contrast can be achieved in various ways. In Kenneth Gaburo's *Exit Music II: Fat Millie's Lament* (1965), an electronic piece, the A sections use voice and percussion sounds recorded at various tape speeds, while the B section is an excerpt from a jazz piece by Morgan Powell, providing a contrast in almost every aspect of the music.[1]

Many full-length movements are in ternary form, one example being the "Pastorale" from Britten's Serenade for Tenor, Horn, and Strings (1943) (K–G, p. 565), but it is also not uncommon to cast individual themes or sections in ternary form. An instance of this is the cornet solo in the third tableau of Stravinsky's *Petrushka* (1911) (WEN, p. 213).

One of the most obvious examples of ternary form in tonal music is the minuet or scherzo with trio, followed by a *da capo*, in multimovement sonatas (symphonies, string quartets, piano sonatas, and so forth). Although less common in post-tonal music, such forms do occur, as in the fifth movement of Schoenberg's Suite, Op. 25 (1923) (WEN, p. 175). A more complicated example is the third movement of Bartók's String Quartet No. 5 (1934). Here the trio is differentiated from the scherzo partly by its time signature ($\frac{4+2+3}{8}$ in the scherzo, $\frac{3+2+2+3}{8}$ in the trio) and partly by its faster tempo, as well as by more traditional thematic means. The *da capo* is written out and considerably varied, concluding with a coda (m. 58) that starts out with some very fast polymetric imitation.

Ternary form in tonal music generally exhibits something of a balance between the two A sections, and works with a shortened return of the A material are categorized by some writers as *rounded binary*. No such balance is expected in post-tonal ternary forms, and so the distinction between ternary and rounded binary may depend more on the presence or absence of a 2-reprise structure. An example of an unbalanced ternary structure from Debussy's Preludes appears in Example 7-1. Here the A section is found in mm. 1–10, the B in mm. 11–24, and the return of A in mm. 25–31. Actually, only two measures of the A material return (mm. 25–26), but this reference to the opening of the piece is enough to give the listener a feeling of return after contrast, the essence of ternary form.

EXAMPLE 7-1 Debussy: Preludes, Book 1 (1910), "Dancers of Delphi" (complete)

RONDO FORMS

The usual outlines of the rondo form in tonal music were the five-part rondo (ABACA) and the sonata-rondo (ABACABA). The key structure of the rondo required that the A theme always occur in the tonic key and that the B and C themes provide some kind of tonal contrast, except that the return of the B theme in the sonata-rondo was in the tonic key.

Both five-part rondos and sonata-rondos are found in post-tonal music, but the traditional tonal plans are not always used. Debussy's "Reflections in the Water" ("Reflets dans l'eau") (1905) follows fairly closely the conventional tonal scheme of a five-part rondo:

A	B	A	B	A
D♭	A♭	D♭	B	D♭

The second movement of Hindemith's String Quartet No. 4 (1921) (WEN, p. 125) is somewhat less conventional in its key relationships:

A	B	A	B	A
C♯	E♭	C♯	A	E♭, C♯

In addition, the B section is bitonal at its beginning, the E♭ harmonies supporting a melody that starts out in E Lydian. Bitonality is carried much further in "Song of the Harvest" from Bartók's Forty-Four Violin Duets (1931) (WEN, p. 9). In this miniature five-part rondo, the first four sections are bitonal, the two keys in each case being a tritone apart, and the A theme is in a different tonal setting in each appearance (the first B theme appears in Example 6-B-5, p. 125).

The third movement of Prokofiev's Piano Sonata No. 4 (1914) follows the traditional outline for a seven-part rondo:[2]

A	B	A	C	A	B	A
C	G	C	E♭	C	C	C

Because the rondo form is somewhat more dependent than some others (notably sonata form) on contrast of themes as opposed to contrast of key centers, it would seem better suited to the atonal style. The fourth movement of Schoenberg's Wind Quintet, Op. 26 (1924), is a seven-part rondo written using the twelve-tone technique, usually associated with atonality. The B theme is at a different pitch level when it returns, as one would expect, but the A theme also varies in pitch level (and in other ways) at each recurrence, a departure from the classical norm. Interestingly, the movement emphasizes E♭ at its beginning and end, and E♭ remains an important pitch class at the beginning and often at the end of each movement of this otherwise atonal work.

OTHER PART FORMS

Part forms other than binary, ternary, and rondo are frequently encountered, but many of them can be thought of as variants of more traditional structures. One that is very similar to the sonata-rondo is the seven-part rondo ABACADA. Examples of this form can be found in the last movement of Barber's *Capricorn Concerto* (1944) and in the "Interlude" from Debussy's Sonata for Flute, Viola, and Harp (1916). In the Debussy example the D section also contains elements of C. Another part form that resembles a seven-part rondo is ABACBA, one example of this occurring in the fourth movement of Bartók's Concerto for Orchestra (1943).

The interest that some post-tonal composers have in various kinds of symmetry is reflected in their use of *arch form*, a term for any formal structure that reads the same forwards and backwards. Some conventional forms, such as ternary and seven-part rondo, are examples of arch form, but we usually reserve the term for less-conventional formal structures.

Ternary:		A	B	A				
Seven-part rondo:		A	B	A	C	A	B	A
Arch:		A	B	C	B	A		
	or	A	B	C	D	C	B	A	etc.

Examples of arch forms in music range from single movements to entire multi-movement works. The third movement of Debussy's String Quartet (1893) can be analyzed as a ternary form or as a five-part arch form:

Ternary:	A	B^1	B^2	B^1	A
Arch:	A	B	C	B	A

The third movement of Bartók's Music for Strings, Percussion, and Celesta (1936) is a modified arch form, two of the parts being recapitulated simultaneously.

A	B	C	D	C+B	A

Bartók's String Quartet No. 5 (1934) is an arch form in terms of its overall plan:

I.   Allegro
II.   Adagio molto
III. Scherzo and Trio (vivace)
IV.   Andante
V.   Finale (allegro vivace).

The first movement of this work combines sonata form with the arch idea in various ways, the most obvious being a reverse recapitulation.[3] The second movement (K-G, p. 481) exhibits a more straightforward arch design:

A	B	C	B	A

Some part forms show the influence of the sonata by including a development. The second movement of Ravel's String Quartet (1903) combines the statement of new material with the development of previous material. The A and B parts each contain two themes:

A	A	B+Dev	A	Coda
a,c♯	a,C	unstable	a,c♯	a

Another movement containing a development is the fourth movement of Debussy's String Quartet, which contains elements of both rondo and sonata forms:[4]

A	B	A	C	Dev

Still other part forms are unique in that they do not seem to be similar to any more conventional form or to conform to the arch principle. One example is Debussy's prelude, "Canope" (K-G, p. 455), which has the following structure:

A	B	C	D	E	B	F	A /D /C

SONATA FORM

Sonata form was the most important musical form of the Classical and Romantic periods. Its essence involved a conflict between tonalities that would arise early in the exposition and continue until its resolution in the recapitulation.

Movements in sonata form are frequently encountered in post-tonal music. Some of them even make use of the traditional key relationships in the exposition of tonic–dominant as in Piston's Quintet for Flute and Strings (1942), I, or tonic–relative major as in Ravel's Sonatina (1905), I. But more often the tonal relationships in post-tonal sonata forms are not the traditional ones, as in Shostakovich's String Quartet No. 3 (1946), I (K-G, p. 540), in which the main tonal centers in the exposition are F and E. More problematic, however, are those movements in sonata form—and there are many—in which the tonality of one or both of the main themes is unclear. Obviously, a struggle between tonalities cannot occur if the tonalities are not firmly established. Some would say that other elements replace the tonal aspect in such pieces; others might argue that a movement based on a contrast of themes, for example, might be good music but is not a sonata.

The single movement of Berg's Piano Sonata, Op. 1 (1908), is an interesting mixture of traditional and experimental approaches to sonata form. The first theme, while tonally unstable, does cadence in B minor in the third measure of the exposition (although it does not do so in the recapitulation), and the exposition is even repeated. But Theme 2 (m. 29), which is tonally unstable, begins over an A9 chord in the exposition (implying D major) and a B9 in the recapitulation (implying E major), while the closing theme (m. 49) actually begins at the same pitch level in the exposition and the recapitulation.

Similar problems are encountered in the first movement of Bartók's String Quartet No. 6 (1939) (WEN, p. 11). In this work the first theme (m. 24) is in D, but the listener might be forgiven for not being certain about this until m. 60, where the first triad on D is heard. The second theme (m. 81) begins over a C pedal, which is apparently the dominant of the tonality of F, reached in m. 94. A third theme, tonally unstable and largely chromatic, begins at m. 99, climaxing at m. 110 on an E♭, but the exposition ends clearly on F at m. 157. In the recapitulation, the first theme returns in D, more or less, but the second theme returns over a C♯ pedal (m. 312), presumably the dominant of F♯, but certainly not in the tonality of D. The third theme climaxes on a B♭ chord at m. 343, but a D major triad is reached at m. 352, and the remainder of the movement is in D.

Tonal uncertainty is obviously a problem, in regard to sonata form, in the Berg and Bartók works discussed above, and the traditional objectives of sonata form are clearly achieved in neither instance. This is not a criticism, of course; both compositions are highly organized in their own ways, and each is a successful and well-known work. What is interesting here from a formal point of view is the effort required to make a tonal form function in an increasingly nontonal environment.

The whole notion of a tonal dissonance to be resolved in the recapitulation is essentially moot in any composition that is decidedly atonal, yet a good number of atonal pieces are cast in what appears to be sonata form. A good example is the first movement of Schoenberg's Wind Quintet, Op. 26 (1924), an early twelve-tone atonal composition. In this movement the first theme (m. 1) is recapitulated at the same pitch level (m. 128), whereas the second and closing themes (m. 42 and m. 55) are brought back a perfect 5th lower or a perfect 4th higher, a remarkable duplication of the traditional relationships found in a major-mode sonata form.

SECTIONAL VARIATIONS

The term *sectional variations* is used here to distinguish the theme with variations from the ground bass or continuous variations (passacaglia and chaconne). Many sets of sectional variations have been composed in the post-tonal era, works as diverse as Ravel's hyperemotional and tonal *Bolero* (1927) and Babbitt's cerebral and atonal *Semi-Simple Variations* (1957) (TUR, p. 526; BUR, p. 516). Although the compositions just cited use original themes, others such as Zoltán Kodály's *Variations on a Hungarian Folksong* (1939) and Frederic Rzewski's *The People United Will Never Be Defeated!* (1973) use borrowed material for the theme.

The theme of a traditional set of variations was relatively simple in order to allow for subsequent embellishment, and it was clearly set off from the music that followed so that the listener could easily identify and remember the theme. This is essentially the case with Copland's Piano Variations (1930), using a ten-measure theme that is set off from the first variation by a fermata. Carter's Variations for Orchestra (1955), on the other hand, begins with an introduction that is dovetailed into the beginning of the theme through sustained violin tones. The theme begins at the second of two tempo modulations that slow the tempo from allegro to andante, which does somewhat help the listener to identify the beginning of the theme. The theme itself is complex texturally and rhythmically; after 47 measures it runs into Variation I without pause but with another change of tempo. The nine variations are quite free, presenting a real challenge to the listener attempting to hear the relationship between them and the theme.

Some post-tonal works that are called variations are not variations in the customary sense. This tends to be especially true of serial, or twelve-tone, "variations" such as Webern's Piano Variations, Op. 27 (1936), and Luigi Dallapiccola's Variations for Orchestra (1954). In both of these works, the theme of the variations is not a short composition, as in traditional variations, but instead is the twelve-tone series itself; and though the series in both cases surely helps to unify the composition as a whole, the series is not presented initially as a tune or theme for the listener to remember. On the other hand, in some twelve-tone "variations" there is a true theme on which the subsequent variations are clearly based, an example being Schoenberg's Variations for Orchestra, Op. 31 (1928) (TUR, p. 443; WEN, p. 179).

CONTINUOUS VARIATIONS

The traditional forms of continuous variations are the *passacaglia*, based on a repeating bass line, or ground, and the *chaconne*, based on a repeating harmonic progression.[5] Though both forms have seen use since 1900, the decline of a common harmonic language has been paralleled by the relative decline of the chaconne as a compositional option.

As one would expect, passacaglia bass lines in post-tonal music tend to be complicated and nondiatonic. The fourth movement of Hindemith's String Quartet No. 5 (1923) consists of a passacaglia and a fugato based on the passacaglia theme, which is shown in Example 7-2. Notice that in the course of its seven measures this theme sounds every pitch class but one (E).

EXAMPLE 7-2 Hindemith: String Quartet No. 5, Op. 32 (1923), IV, mm. 1–8

Passacaglias using all 12 pitch classes have been used, a famous example being the passacaglia in Act I, Scene 4, of Berg's *Wozzeck* (1921). An intriguing passacaglia with a twelve-tone theme is "Little Blue Devil," from Gunther Schuller's *Seven Studies on Themes of Paul Klee* (1959) (WEN, p. 194). In this work a "jazzy" nine-bar bass line makes its way through three different (but related) twelve-tone "sets." This bass line, first heard in mm. 15–23, serves as the passacaglia theme for the movement. Another example is Crumb's "Voices from Corona Borealis" from his *Makrokosmos*, Vol. II (1973) (K-G, p. 585), which uses a 16-note passacaglia theme in the upper register.

The use of isorhythms (review Chapter 6, p. 121) can be thought of as an extension of the passacaglia principle. This is especially true when there is a pitch pattern associated with the rhythmic pattern, as in the "Crystal Liturgy" from Messiaen's *Quartet for the End of Time* (1941) (TUR, p. 511). Of course, the pitch pattern (the *color*) must not be the same length as the rhythmic pattern (the *talea*), or an ordinary ostinato would result. In the Messiaen work the rhythmic pattern contains 17 attacks and the pitch pattern contains 29 notes (ten different pitch classes), so the rhythmic pattern would have to be repeated 29 times before the beginnings of the two patterns would again coincide (because 493 is the lowest common multiple of 17 and 29). Messiaen stops the process long before that point.

CANON AND FUGUE

Canons and fugues are not "forms" in the sense that rondos and sonatas are. Instead, they are contrapuntal procedures that can be cast in any of a number of formal designs. Nevertheless, musicians customarily have referred to both "homophonic forms" and "contrapuntal forms," and it will be convenient in this chapter to follow that tradition.

The canon, a form that saw relatively little use in the century and a half after Bach, has enjoyed a new popularity among post-tonal composers. Whole sets of canons have been written, such as Webern's 5 Canons, Op. 16 (1924) (WEN, p. 271), and canons frequently appear as a major portion of a longer work, examples being the trio of the minuet from Schoenberg's Suite, Op. 25 (1923) (WEN, p. 177), and the second movement of Webern's Variations for Piano, Op. 27 (1936) (BUR, p. 485). In both of these works, the canonic imitation happens to be by contrary motion. The uninformed listener would almost certainly be unaware of the canon in the Webern work, and the same would be true of the sixth movement of Arvo Pärt's *Magnificat Antiphons* (1988) (K-G, p. 591), in which a canon by augmentation is hidden in the Soprano II and Tenor II parts (also see Example 4-11, p. 82). Canons also frequently appear as passages in otherwise noncanonic movements. For instance, although Schoenberg's "Summer Morning by a Lake," Op. 16, No. 3 (1909) (BUR, p. 424), is not a canon, it contains canonic passages, two of the clearest being mm. 3–9 and mm. 32–38.

Much of the challenge in writing a canon in the tonal idiom is to control the dissonance while at the same time creating harmonic interest. To a certain extent, these difficulties are alleviated in post-tonal music because of the "emancipation of the dissonance" and the lack of traditional harmonic progressions. Both can be seen and heard in the works cited in the preceding paragraph. In another example, the "Song of Harvest" from Bartók's Forty-Four Violin Duets (1931) (WEN, p. 9), the first canonic phrase (see Example 6-B-5 on p. 125) finds the violins a tritone apart, with no attempt at conventional preparation and resolution of the dissonances that result.

Terry Riley's *In C* (1964) (TUR, p. 540; BUR, p. 531) can be regarded as a canon in which the performers begin together but progress through the music at different rates. Each performer plays the same 53 musical segments for an indeterminate amount of time, usually for at least a minute, with each performer proceeding to the next segment on his or her own initiative, but not without regard for what the other players are doing. The resulting canon is a good example of phase music, or minimalism, to be discussed in more detail in Chapter 15.

The renewed interest in counterpoint since 1900 can also be seen in the collections of fugues composed after the model of *The Well-Tempered Clavier*. Hindemith's *Ludus Tonalis* (1942) is a famous collection of 12 fugues separated by 11 interludes, the entire work beginning with a prelude and ending with a postlude. Instead of arranging his fugues in chromatic order, as Bach did in *The Well-Tempered Clavier*, Hindemith follows Series 1 from his *Craft of Musical Composition*, an ordering that he first derives when discussing tuning. Hindemith felt that this ordering represented a "diminishing degree of relationship" with the beginning tonality of C:[6]

C   G   F   A   E   E♭   A♭   D   B♭   D♭   B   F♯

Fugue 5 from the *Ludus Tonalis* (TUR, p. 504) is a good representative of Hindemith's contrapuntal style.

Another collection of twentieth-century fugues is Shostakovich's *Twenty-Four Preludes and Fugues*, Op. 87 (1951). Here the order of keys is more traditional: C–a–G–e–D–b–A–f♯, etc. As in Bach's collection, each fugue is preceded by a prelude in the same key.

Fugues are also commonly encountered as individual movements within a longer work, as in the first movement of Bartók's Music for Strings, Percussion, and Celesta (1936) (BUR, p. 453) and the "Fantasy" from Elliott Carter's Eight Etudes and a Fantasy Woodwind Quartet (1950) (WEN, p. 57), or as a portion of a movement, as in Berg's *Wozzeck* (1921), Act III, Scene 1, consisting of a theme with seven variations followed by a fugue based on the theme.

The tonal conventions of the Baroque fugue need not restrict the post-tonal composer, and frequently they do not, but it is remarkable how often the traditional tonal relationships are found in the expositions of twentieth-century fugues. Three examples:

Bartók: Sonata for Solo Violin (1944), II
Shostakovich: String Quartet No. 8 (1962), V
Rochberg: String Quartet No. 4 (1977), II.

Each of the movements cited above begins with a fugue exposition in which the first and third statements of the subject are in the tonic and all of the others are in the dominant. Coincidentally, each also happens to be in the key of C.

PROPORTION: THE GOLDEN MEAN

Some post-tonal composers and writers have been interested in the "golden mean" or "golden section," a proportion used for centuries in art and architecture to obtain aesthetically pleasing designs. To understand this ratio, consider a line <u>ac</u> with line segments <u>ab</u> and <u>bc</u>:

a   b   c

If the proportion of ab to bc is the same as the proportion of bc to the whole line, then ac is segmented according to the golden mean. This relationship can be expressed as:

$$\frac{ab}{bc} = \frac{bc}{ac}$$

The resulting fraction is about 0.618.

Integers (whole numbers) that approximate the golden mean can be generated by means of a **Fibonacci sequence**, an endless series of numbers in which each number is the sum of the previous two. The farther you go in the sequence, the closer you get to the true value of the golden mean:

Integers	1	2	3	5	8	13	21	34 etc.
Ratios:	0.5	0.67	0.6	0.625	0.615	0.619	0.618	

The most obvious way that this ratio can be used musically is in the proportions of a musical form. For example, the beginning of "Minor Seconds, Major Sevenths," from Bartók's *Mikrokosmos* (BUR, p. 483), could be subdivided in this way:

m. 8   =   strong cadence; first whole–note chord
m. 21   =   strong cadence; first appearance of "glissando"
m. 34   =   end of long accelerando and of first main section.

There is some evidence that Bartók used the golden mean not only in formal proportions but in other aspects of his music as well,[7] and this is also true, if to a lesser extent, of some other post-tonal composers.[8] In Example 7-3 Karel Husa employs a series of durations that expresses the Fibonacci series in terms of multiples of 16th notes: 1, 2, 3, 5, 8, 13, and 21. On the surface, at least, this appears to be the only use of the series in this work. Notice also the strict mirroring between the two hands.[9]

EXAMPLE 7-3 Karel Husa: *Sonata a Tre* (1982), II, extract from piano part

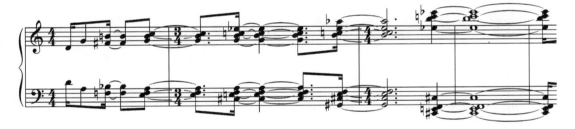

NONTHEMATIC DELINEATORS OF MUSICAL FORM

The primary determinants of musical form in tonal music were tonality and theme, with contrast of tonalities being a generally stronger force than contrast of themes. The decline in tonality as an organizing force has often led to a greater reliance on thematic contrast; but in many pieces, themes, in the sense of melodies, play a small or nonexistent part. The most obvious example is electronic music, where texture, register, dynamics, and especially timbre are usually more important as shaping elements than themes are. Tempo and rhythmic activities are also organizing factors, as in Bartók's "Increasing— Diminishing" from the *Mikrokosmos* (1937), where rhythmic activity creates an arch form. Another work in which nonthematic elements are important in delineating the form is the second movement of Webern's Concerto, Op. 24 (1934) (K-G, p. 502).

The ABCB form of the first movement of Arvo Pärt's *Collage on B-A-C-H* (1964) is delineated by nonthematic means. The A section (see Example 7-4a) begins with a repeated B♮4 that unfolds in m. 2 to a B♭ major triad. The triad arpeggiates slowly outward until it spans four octaves by m. 7. The B section (Example 7-4b) also consists of repeated notes, but here the sonorities are dissonant and include 16th-notes. The repeated notes in part C (Example 7-4c) also create dissonances, but here they are staccato and pit downbeats against upbeats. The dissonant climax of the movement in mm. 47–48 is followed by eight measures of retransition and the return of the B material. The movement ends with an unexpected *p* B minor triad in mm. 81–84. Although the form is clear to the listener, nothing resembling a melody is heard.

EXAMPLE 7-4 Pärt: *Collage on B-A-C-H* (1964), 1, mm. 2, 11, 30

Copyright © 1964, Musikverlag Hans Sikorski, Hamburg.

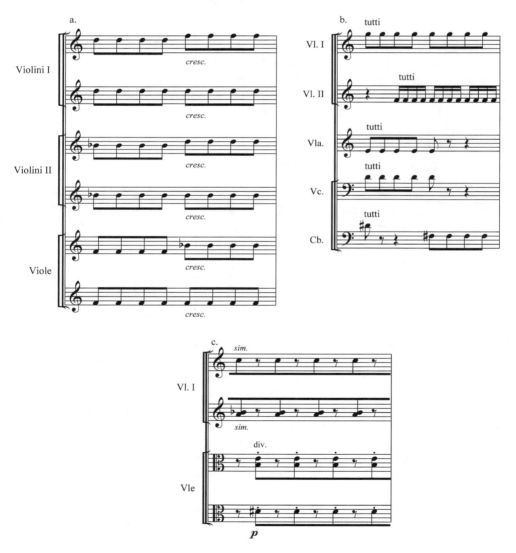

The primary form-determining element in Krzysztof Penderecki's *Threnody: To the Victims of Hiroshima* (1961) is texture, with a good deal of assistance from dynamics, timbre, and register. To this listener the piece is in four sections, with a number of subsections:

Section	Begins at	Material
Part 1	0'0"	High entrances, *ff*, *dim*, with texture thinning; "busy" sounds, random effects
Part 2	1'50"	Clusters *pp*, expanding, contracting, sliding, ending with stationary cluster; *ff* climax, followed by simultaneous ascent and descent
Part 3	4'30"	Individual entrances build up to *ff* cluster; clusters center on one pitch, slow vibrato, *dim.*; silence
Part 4	5'45"	Busy, random sounds (different from Part 1); high cluster superimposed, then crescendo to climax; sub. *pp*; silence; huge *ff* cluster ends the piece at 8'30".

Certainly there are different ways to hear this piece—more or fewer sections, and so forth—but probably every listener would agree that its shape is determined largely by texture and other elements that traditionally have had a secondary role in musical form. Incidentally, the final cluster covers the two octaves from C3 to C5 in quarter-tone intervals distributed among the 52 performers, obviously a prime example of sound–mass. The "busy" music from Part 1 appears later in this book in Example 11-4 (p. 222).

NONORGANIC APPROACHES TO MUSICAL FORM

A traditional painting depicts something, and if the painting is a good one, every part of the canvas contributes to the effectiveness of the visual message that the artist is trying to convey. In traditional literature every passage has its purpose—fleshing out a character, setting the mood, developing the plot, and so on. The same is generally true of music in the European tradition: the composition is considered to be greater than the sum of its parts, a work of art in which each passage has a function that is vital to the overall plan of a work. Think of any tonal work that you know well, and imagine what it would be like if its parts—themes, transitions, and so forth—were randomly rearranged. It might be interesting to see how it would turn out, but the piece would almost certainly not be as effective as a whole.

Some composers have reacted against this traditional "organic" (or "teleological") approach to musical composition. One such reaction led to what Karlheinz Stockhausen called "moment form," an approach that treats every portion of a piece as an end in itself, without any intentional relationship to what precedes or follows it. The listener is not supposed to try to identify traditional shaping forces such as motivic development, dynamics, and rhythmic activity in an attempt to understand where the music is going, because it is not going *anywhere*, in the traditional sense. Even the beginning and ending of the work lose their traditional functions, because "a proper moment form will give the impression of starting in the midst of previously unheard music, and it will break off without reaching any structural cadence, as if the music goes on, inaudibly, in some other space or time after the close of the performance."[10]

Stockhausen first used the term "moment form" in discussing *Contact* (1960), a work for prerecorded tape, piano, and percussion, but other works by various composers, both before and since, show the same avoidance of linear growth. Some of these works employ a high degree of chance, an early example being Cage's *Williams Mix* (1952), a tape piece composed by juxtaposing at random hundreds of prerecorded sounds. Tape music and the use of chance in music are both discussed in more detail in later chapters.

SUMMARY

All of the forms of the tonal era survived into the post-tonal era, in spite of problems relating to the function of tonality in those forms. Not only was there a decline in the influence of tonality on form, but in many post-tonal compositions the "theme" also ceased to be an important element of form. Formal proportions are often less balanced than in the Classical period, but interest in the golden mean by some composers, notably Bartók, shows a desire for a systematic aesthetic. Coexisting with the traditional forms are a large number of works that do not conform to earlier models. Some of these can be thought of as variants of traditional part forms or as related to the sonata; others are arch forms; and still others would seem to be unique in the sense that they do not have traditional analogues. Even more radical is the nonorganic approach to musical form seen in the "moment form" works of Stockhausen and others and in some works composed using chance procedures.

MUSIC FROM THE CHAPTER IN CHRONOLOGICAL CONTEXT

Year	Composer	Work	Reference
1903	**Ravel**	**String Quartet**	**p. 136**
1910	**Debussy**	**Preludes, Book I**	**p. 131**
1912	Schoenberg	*Pierrot Lunaire*	Expressionism
1913	Stravinsky	*Rite of Spring*	Primitivism
1914	**Prokofiev**	**Piano Sonata No. 4**	**p. 134**
1923	**Hindemith**	**String Quartet No. 5**	**p. 138**
1930	Stravinsky	*Symphony of Psalms*	Neoclassicism
1934	**Bartók**	**String Quartet No. 5**	**p. 135**
1935	Berg	Violin Concerto	Serialism

1936	**Bartók**	**Music for Strings Percussion and Celesta No. 5**	**p. 135**
1952	John Cage	*4′33″*	Chance Music
1954	Edgard Varèse	*Poème Electronique*	Electronic Music
1961	**Penderecki**	***Threnody: To the Victims of Hiroshima***	**Aleatoric Music p. 143**
1964	Terry Riley	*In C*	Minimalism
1964	**Arvo Pärt**	***Collage on B–A–C–H***	**p. 142**
1982	**Karel Husa**	***Sonata a Tre***	**p. 141**

Works in **bold** are from the chapter; those not in bold are landmark pieces written around the same time.

NOTES

1. Barry Schrader, *Introduction to Electro-Acoustic Music*, p. 33.

2. For a detailed analysis of the form of this work, see Wallace Berry, *Form in Music*, pp. 216–224.

3. For a detailed analysis of this movement, see Mary Wennerstrom, "Form in Twentieth-Century Music," in Gary Wittlich, Ed., *Aspects of Twentieth-Century Music*, pp. 19–33.

4. For an analysis of this movement, see Gail De Stwolinski, *Form and Content in Instrumental Music*, pp. 546–548.

5. These definitions are used for convenience, but the difference between the two was not so clearly defined in the Baroque period, during which both the passacaglia and the chaconne first flourished.

6. Paul Hindemith, *The Craft of Musical Composition*, Vol. I, p. 56. The derivation of this series of tones is found on pp. 32–43.

7. Ernö Lendvai, *Béla Bartók: An Analysis of His Music*.

8. See Howat and Kramer in the "Further Reading" section.

9. Thanks to Craig Cummings for this example.

10. Jonathan D. Kramer, "Moment Form in Twentieth Century Music," p. 180.

★

EXERCISES

Part A: Score Analysis

Each of the pieces below can be found in one of the four anthologies listed at the beginning of this chapter. Analyze the form of whatever piece you are assigned, including a diagram down to the phrase level, if possible. Be sure to include measure numbers.

1. Bartók: *Mikrokosmos* (1931), No. 94, "Tale" (K-G, p. 477).

2. Berg: *Wozzeck* (1921), "Marie's Lullaby" (WEN, p. 28).

3. Debussy: Preludes, Book I (1910), "The Engulfed Cathedral" ("La Cathédrale engloutie") (BUR, p. 421).

4. Debussy: Preludes, Book I (1910), "The Hills of Anacapri" ("Les Collines d'Anacapri") (K-G, p. 449).

5. Hindemith: *Ludus Tonalis* (1942), Fugue in C (BUR, p. 490) and Fugue in A (WEN, p. 140). Before beginning work on these fugues, review the terms "double fugue" and "triple fugue."

6. Ives: Sonata No. 2 for Violin and Piano (1910), III (WEN, p. 147). Though this movement is not a canon, it contains some canonic passages. Locate and comment on each one.

7. Schoenberg: Six Short Pieces for Piano, Op. 19 (1911), No. 6 (K-G, p. 463; WEN, p.173).

8. Schoenberg: *Pierrot Lunaire*, Op. 21 (1912), No. 8 (TUR, p. 438).

9. Schoenberg: Variations for Orchestra, Op. 31 (1928), Var. 2 (TUR, p. 443). Concentrate on the issue of imitation in this variation.

10. Shostakovich: String Quartet No. 3, Op. 73 (1946), I (K-G, p. 540).

11. Webern: Five Movements for String Quartet, Op. 5 (1909), IV (BUR, p. 484).

Part B: Aural Analysis

Listen several times to any of the works listed below. Name the form, and provide a diagram of the main parts. For each section, provide the approximate time at which it begins and try to sketch or describe the salient features (rhythms, contours, etc.) of each section.

1. Barber: Piano Concerto, Op. 38 (1962), III.

2. Bartók: String Quartet No. 6 (1939), II.

3. Dallapiccola: *Quaderno Musicale* (1952), No. 3.

4. Hindemith: String Quartet No. 4 (1921), V.

5. Prokofiev: Symphony No. 5 (1944), IV.

6. Shostakovich: String Quartet No. 1 (1935), II.

7. Stravinsky: Septet (1953), I.

8. Stravinsky: *Symphony of Psalms* (1930), II.

9. Stravinsky: Septet (1953), II.

10. Arnold Walter, Myron Schaeffer, and Harvey Olnick: *Summer Idyll* (1959).

FURTHER READING

Berry, Wallace. *Form in Music*. This text—like De Stwolinski's, cited next—does not deal exclusively with post-tonal music.

De Stwolinski, Gail. *Form and Content in Instrumental Music*.

Howat, Roy. "Bartók, Lendvai, and the Principle of Proportional Analysis."

———. *Debussy in Proportion*.

Kramer, Jonathan D. "The Fibonacci Series in Twentieth Century Music."

———. "Moment Form in Twentieth Century Music."

Lendvai, Ernö. *Béla Bartók: An Analysis of His Music*. See the sections titled "Golden Section," pp. 17–26, and "Chromatic System," pp. 35–66.

Wennerstrom, Mary. "Form in Twentieth-Century Music," in Gary Wittlich, Ed., *Aspects of Twentieth-Century Music*, pp. 1–65.

CHAPTER 8

Imports and Allusions

INTRODUCTION

This chapter is concerned with some of the external influences that have had an effect on post-tonal music. These influences came chiefly from three sources:

The Past

> Neoclassicism
> Quotation, paraphrase, and collage

The Present

> Folk music
> Jazz
> Rock

The Unfamiliar

> Music from other cultures

There is little new technical information in this chapter, and few exercises follow it. In many ways it deals more with music history than with music theory. But the currents outlined here are important ones, and they had a significant role in shaping the sound of post-tonal music.

INFLUENCES FROM THE PAST

Post-tonal composers have shown a greater awareness of and concern for the music of past centuries than did any of their predecessors. In earlier chapters we have seen the revival of modal scales and isorhythm and renewed interest in older forms such as the *passacaglia*. This historical consciousness has also led to the developments discussed in the next two sections: neoclassicism and quotation. *Neoclassicism* was a reactionary movement in the sense that it rejected the chromatic saturation and other characteristics of both the late Romantic style and atonality. Although it was not truly an attempt to revive the Classical style, as the term might suggest, it did reflect a desire for clarity, balance, and greater detachment, and the music of the Baroque and Classical periods provided a starting place for the style.

Quotation of already existing music was not unknown before the twentieth century. The use of plainsong melodies in Renaissance polyphonic compositions and the borrowed themes for sets of variations are but two examples. But quotation in post-tonal music is of a different sort, at times a dramatic juxtaposition of contrasting styles, at others an almost poetic allusion to another composer. Thus "quotation music" has become another catchword of post-tonal music.

Neoclassicism

"Let's say that I was a kind of bird, and that the eighteenth century was a kind of bird's nest in which I felt cozy laying my eggs."[1] In this picturesque way Stravinsky characterized his own involvement in neoclassicism, an approach to composition that was especially widespread from around 1920 to around 1950. Many composers wrote works in the neoclassical style—Hindemith and Poulenc, for example—but the central figure in the movement was Stravinsky. Important neoclassical works by Stravinsky include the Octet for Wind Instruments (1923), the *Symphony of Psalms* (1930), the Symphony in C (1940), and the Symphony in Three Movements (1945).

Donald Jay Grout defines neoclassicism as "adherence to the Classical principles of balance, coolness, objectivity, and absolute (as against Romantic program) music, with the corollary characteristics of economy, predominantly contrapuntal texture, and diatonic as well as chromatic harmonies."[2] William Austin, referring to Stravinsky's neoclassical works in particular, writes:

> They presumed sophistication. They alluded not simply to Bach and Beethoven, but to separate traits of the classical styles. They treated those traits with such dry irony, such jerky stiffness, and such evident distortion that even a sympathetic listener needed several hearings to penetrate beneath the wit and skill to the glowing warmth of the melodies and the subtle continuity of the forms.[3]

From these definitions it is clear that neoclassicism was not an attempt to compose new works in the style of Haydn and Mozart. For one thing, it made use of Baroque techniques as well as Classical ones. But more important, neoclassicism was a reaction against the style of late Romanticism in favor of a sparser texture and less chromaticism, using clear rhythms and definite cadences, all combined with twentieth-century developments in melody, meter, and the treatment of dissonance.

The techniques of neoclassicism are not new, and all of them have been discussed in earlier chapters of this text. The best way to get acquainted with the style is through listening and score study, but Example 8-1 is included here as a representative of several aspects of neoclassicism. First of all, notice the metric subtleties between the bass-clef instruments and the treble-clef instruments. The changing time signatures accurately reflect the rhythm of trumpet I and the clarinet; however, the bass-clef instruments move along with a steady pattern of 8th notes followed by 8th rests, sometimes agreeing with the time signature and sometimes not, ironically creating through their steady pulse a

EXAMPLE 8-1 Stravinsky: Octet for Wind Instruments (1923), "Sinfonia," last 9 mm

destabilizing polymeter. Meanwhile, in the flute and trumpet II, which imitate trumpet I, the $\frac{3}{4}$ measure four bars from the end is notated in $\frac{2}{4}$, creating a third polymetric element.

Another aspect to be noted in Example 8-1 is the prevailing pandiatonicism (see p. 97). Because trumpet II sounds in unison with the flute (but two octaves lower), the only pitches in the excerpt that are not diatonic to E♭ major are the D♭s in bassoon I and trombone II. But there is no harmonic progression in the traditional sense, even though the bass-clef accompaniment is triadic, and no attempt is made to control the dissonances that occur among the treble-clef instruments or between them and the bass-clef accompaniment.

The ballet *Pulcinella* (1920) is one of Stravinsky's earliest neoclassical works. An excerpt from the Suite Italienne (1932), derived from the ballet, appeared earlier as Example 3-10 (p. 47), and it will serve as our second example of neoclassicism. Here the rhythm is quite straightforward, as is the harmonic progression, but the nontraditional treatment of dissonance in this excerpt is a fine example of the dry irony to which Austin referred in the passage quoted earlier.

Though the neoclassical style has nearly died out, music of the past still attracts the interest of many composers. A more recent movement, dubbed *neoromanticism*, will be discussed in the final chapter of this book.

Quotation, Paraphrase, and Collage

Neoclassicism rarely involved the actual quotation of already existing music, exceptions including Stravinsky's *Pulcinella* (1920) and *The Fairy's Kiss* (*Le baiser de la fée*) (1928), which used the music of Pergolesi and Tchaikovsky, respectively. But many other post-tonal composers not connected with the neoclassical style have quoted, arranged, and paraphrased earlier music extensively. Though this practice has become especially common since the mid 1960s, earlier examples include Debussy, who quoted Wagner in "Golliwog's Cakewalk" from *The Children's Corner* (1908) and Bach in *In Black and White* (*En blanc et noir*) (1915), and Berg, who quoted Wagner in the last movement of the *Lyric Suite* (1926) and Bach in the concluding "Adagio" movement of the Violin Concerto (1935). The style of another composer from the early part of the century, Charles Ives, depended to a great extent on the quotation of music—hymn tunes, popular songs, and the like—familiar to most Americans in the early part of the century. Patriotic songs were grist for his mill as well, as seen in Example 8-2, where the "Marseillaise" (voice, mm. 30–33), "Columbia, the Gem of the Ocean" (voice, mm. 34–35), and "America" (piano, mm. 30–33) can all be heard. Notice as well the polymeter in the first few measures, where the piano sounds as if it is in $\frac{3}{4}$.

Other works that quote national anthems include Debussy's "Fireworks" (Example 5-5, p. 95) and Stockhausen's *Hymns* (*Hymnen*) (1966), an electronic work in which the "program" is not nationalistic, as Ives's presumably was, but instead is concerned with world unity.

A composer does not always quote existing music for programmatic reasons. The second act of George Rochberg's *Music for the Magic Theater* (1965) begins with a "transcription" (actually a rather free arrangement) of the fourth movement from Mozart's Divertimento in B-flat, K. 287 (1777). In the preface to the score Rochberg discusses the reaction of the audience:

EXAMPLE 8-2 Ives: "In Flanders Fields" (1917), mm. 30–35

> It seems to test the perceptual courage of listeners (musicians and laymen alike) by
> putting in question the whole concept of what is "contemporary," how far that
> concept may be stretched today and what it can include. The presence of the
> transcription abrogates the 19th to early 20th century notion of "originality."[4]

Rochberg goes on to provide more insight into the compositional aesthetic that justifies
quotation in his music:

> The world of this music is surreal more than it is abstract. In its combinations of the
> past and the present, seemingly accidental, unrelated aural images whose
> placement in time obeys no conventional logic, it attempts to create a musical
> soundscape which is strangely and oddly familiar.[5]

This idea of juxtaposing seemingly unrelated ideas was encountered in Chapter 7
in the discussion of nonorganic approaches to musical form. Crumb takes up the same

topic in discussing his *Ancient Voices of Children* (1970), which contains a quotation from Bach: "I was conscious of an urge to fuse various unrelated stylistic elements. I was intrigued by the idea of juxtaposing the seemingly incongruous . . ."[6]

Juxtaposition of the incongruous is certainly a feature of Example 8-3. The work from which the example is taken is a chillingly dramatic representation of the anguished madness of King George III. Various composers are quoted, or suggested, in the course of the piece, the most recognizable being from Handel's *Messiah* (1742), which was composed when George III was a child. In Example 8-3 a "Country Dance" is interrupted by the famous "Comfort ye" quotation from the *Messiah*, which is then continued and grossly distorted by the mad king. Both lines are sung by the same performer, who must play both a female vocalist and the king in this excerpt. It is said that Roy Hart, the singer for whom the work was written, could sing chords, as you see at the end of the excerpt. This use of multiphonics for the voice is very unusual, although they are more frequently called for in instrumental writing. Multiphonics will be discussed in more detail in Chapter 11.

EXAMPLE 8-3 Peter Maxwell Davies: *Eight Songs for a Mad King* (1969), VII

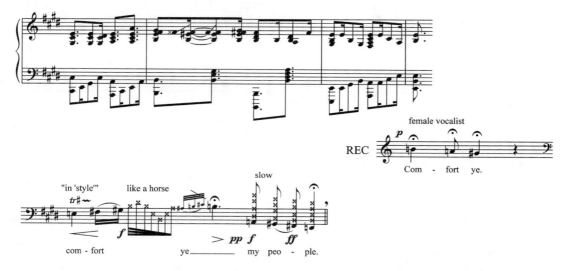

The material borrowed by a composer is often transformed, or paraphrased. This was true to some extent of the Ives excerpt in Example 8-2. Electronic compositions might use recorded excerpts, with or without alteration, as in Kenneth Gaburo's *Exit Music II* (see p. 130) and Stockhausen's *Opus 1970* (1969). Example 8-4 shows the beginning of the composition that inspired *Ô Bach!* by Betsy Jolas. In Example 8-5 you can find the first ten notes of the toccata (C–E–G–B–F–A–B–D–G–E), sometimes displaced by several octaves, and with some other notes added. (The opening G3 is not struck; the key is held down silently.) The eight-note descending C major scale that follows in the Bach is represented in mm. 6–7 of the Jolas by a nine-note descent from C4 to C♯3, followed by a B diminished triad, which also occurs in the Bach. In the rest of the composition (204 measures in all) references to the Bach are much more indirect.

EXAMPLE 8-4 Bach: Toccata in C, BWV 564 (1712?), mm. 1–2

EXAMPLE 8-5 Jolas: *Ô Bach!* (2007), mm. 1–7

Copyright © 2007 by permission of Editions Durand Allan Kozinn, "Eclectice Mix Through a Contemporary Prism" New York Times.

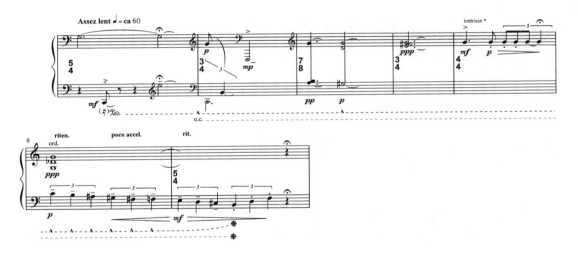

Quotation in Bernd Alois Zimmermann's music is an important stylistic element rather than the exceptional event, a good example being *Photoptosis* (1968), an orchestral work with quotations from various sources. In *Petroushkates* (1980), Joan Tower has composed a sort of paraphrase variation on Stravinsky's original. Direct quotations in *Petroushkates* are most apparent at the beginning, but chords, rhythms, and melodic figures drawn from Stravinsky can be heard throughout the work, most of which maintains the exhilarating spirit of the opening of *Petrushka*.

Bach's Partita in E Major for solo violin serves as the basis for the third movement of Lukas Foss's *Baroque Variations* (1967). Far removed from the traditional theme and variations, this dramatic and effective work often views the Bach work through a wildly distorted lens. Chapter 14 includes additional discussion of this movement.

A very famous example of quotation is the third movement of Berio's *Sinfonia* (1968), a work for eight voices and orchestra. The entire movement is based on the third movement of Mahler's Symphony No. 2 (1894), sometimes obviously but often more subtly, with additional quotations from Bach, Berg, Brahms, Debussy, Ravel, Schoenberg, Strauss, Stravinsky, and others, these quotations being alluded to on occasion by the chorus.[7] Most of the text, however, is drawn from Samuel Beckett's novel *The Unnamable*. The connections between Mahler, Joyce, Beckett, and Berio have been convincingly shown, including the suggestion that Joyce's stream-of-consciousness style of writing has its parallel in Mahler's music, and presumably in Berio's as well.[8] The result is a musical collage but also a complex and fascinating work, much more than a haphazard pastiche.

Alfred Schnittke is a Russian composer who used quotations and stylistic allusions in his music beginning in the late 1960s, one example among many being his *Moz-Art*, a blend of Mozartean gestures and post-tonal dissonances, multiphonics, and other effects. His use of earlier materials is sometimes humorous and sometimes serious.

> Sometimes I'm tweaking the listener. And sometimes I'm thinking about earlier music as a beautiful way of writing that has disappeared and will never come back; and in that sense, it has a tragic feeling for me.[9]

David Fanning finds something similar in Shostakovich's Symphony No. 15 (1971). This symphony, the composer's last, has quotes and references to his own music as well as to that of Rossini, Wagner, Mahler, and others.

> The Fifteenth Symphony is haunted by a legion of ghosts—subtle allusions to Shostakovich's own past works and to musical styles that had influenced him. Paradoxically, these allusions make the overall tone of the work all the more difficult to define. The last pages gaze back over the past with unfathomable sadness, and the coda is probably the most desolate music ever to have been written in A major.[10]

References to earlier music can be literal and specific, as in parts of Berio's *Sinfonia*, or more oblique. Speaking of his *Lontano* (1967), György Ligeti put it this way: "I do not actually quote composers, only allude to nineteenth-century music, evoking late Romantic orchestral effects."[11]

This fascination with artifacts of the past is found to some extent in the visual arts, as well. George Deem (1932–2008) was an American artist who carefully reproduced masterworks from the past, but with subtle variations and containing additional images imported from still other paintings, creating what he called "paintings of paintings, new works from existing works."[12]

INFLUENCES FROM FOLK MUSIC, JAZZ, AND ROCK

Composers of the nineteenth century were certainly not unaware of folk music, as witnessed by the influence of Polish folk music on Chopin and the arrangements of German folk songs by Brahms. The rise of nationalism in the late nineteenth century spawned an increased interest on the part of composers of all countries in the music that was indigenous to their own cultures, and this interest continued into the twentieth century, especially in the first several decades.

Probably the composer whose name first comes to mind in connection with folk music in the twentieth century is Béla Bartók. Shortly after the beginning of the century, he and his compatriot Zoltán Kodály began a serious study of folk music, at first only Hungarian, but soon including that of neighboring countries as well. Bartók's interest in this area is seen explicitly in the titles of many of his works; for example, the following titles appear in Volumes 4–6 of the *Mikrokosmos*:

100.	"In the Style of a Folk Song"
112.	"Variations on a Folk Tune"
113 and 115.	"Bulgarian Rhythm"
127.	"New Hungarian Folk Song"
128.	"Peasant Dance"
138.	"Bagpipe"
148–153.	"Six Dances in Bulgarian Rhythm."

An excerpt from No. 148 appeared as Example 2-22 (p. 30), and the beginning of No. 112 is given in Example 8-6. The folk song melody appears in octaves in mm. 1–8. The first variation follows without pause, parallel 6ths in the right hand being imitated canonically in the left hand at the 12th below.

EXAMPLE 8-6 Bartók: *Mikrokosmos* (1926–37), No. 112, "Variations on a Folk Tune," mm. 1–17

The music of composers such as Bartók, Kodály, and the Czech composer Leoš Janáček often shows the influence of folk music even when folk materials are not being explicitly quoted—hence, the frequent references to their "folk-like" melodies and rhythms. But it would be a serious mistake to think of the music of these composers only in terms of folk songs. Though folk music is an important element in their work, it merges with the currents of change in twentieth-century music, to which these composers made significant contributions.

Interest in folk music was of some importance in all European countries. Spain had a particularly strong nationalist movement in the music of Isaac Albéniz, Enrique Granados, and Manuel de Falla. Representative figures in the New World included Heitor Villa-Lobos in Brazil and Carlos Chávez and Silvestre Revueltas in Mexico.

In the United States the influence of folk song is seen in the music of Ives, Copland, and Roy Harris, among others. One of the first to make use of the folk songs of black Americans was the English composer Samuel Coleridge-Taylor, whose father was African. His *Twenty-Four Negro Melodies* (1905) may have inspired the black American composers William Grant Still and William Dawson. Another English work that uses black folk music is Michael Tippett's *A Child of Our Time* (1941), an oratorio dealing with racial persecution.

Jazz music first caught the attention of "serious" composers around the end of World War I (1918). A large number of works were composed during the next few decades that borrowed certain obvious features from jazz. Some of the better known of these compositions include:

Igor Stravinsky: "Ragtime" (1918)

Paul Hindemith: Chamber Music No. 1 (Kammermusik No. 1) (1922)

Darius Milhaud: *The Creation of the World* (*La création du monde*) (1923)

George Gershwin: *Rhapsody in Blue* (1924)

Aaron Copland: *Music for the Theater* (1925)

Aaron Copland: Piano Concerto (1927)

Ernst Krenek: *Johnny Plays On* (*Jonny spielt auf*) (1927)

Kurt Weill: *The Threepenny Opera* (*Die Dreigroschenoper*) (1928)

Maurice Ravel: Concerto for the Left Hand (1930)

George Gershwin: *Porgy and Bess* (1935)

Igor Stravinsky: *Ebony Concerto* (1945).

One of the first such pieces was the "Ragtime" from Stravinsky's *The Soldier's Tale* (*L'histoire du soldat*) (1918), the beginning of which is seen in Example 8-7. The syncopations and dotted rhythms are evident here, as is an imitation of the functions of bass and percussion in an early jazz band, while later in the piece "jazzy" trombone glissandos are used. Of course, this music does not really sound like jazz, any more than neoclassical music sounds Classical; in fact, Stravinsky's comment concerning his neoclassical style (see p. 150) is equally appropriate here.

EXAMPLE 8-7 Stravinsky: *The Soldier's Tale* (*L'histoire du soldat*) (1918), "Ragtime," mm. 1–8

EXAMPLE 8-8 Schuller: Suite for Woodwind Quintet (1957), II, mm. 16–23

With some important exceptions, jazz does not seem to have exerted much influence on concert music after World War II (i.e., since 1945). The main exception to this has been the so-called Third Stream movement, chiefly associated with Gunther Schuller, which attempted to blend jazz and concert music without condescending to either. In Example 8-8 Schuller evokes the sound of a blues through the "walking" bass in the bassoon, the prevailing compound meter (Schuller instructs the performers to accent the 8th note in any figure), the bends and glissandos in the horn, and other means as well. Another of Schuller's Third Stream pieces, "Little Blue Devil" (1959) is discussed on p. 138.

Third Stream music never seemed to "catch on" to the extent that might have been expected, but there are still quite a few postwar jazz-influenced works. Examples include David Amram's Triple Concerto (1970); Mark-Anthony Turnage's *Blood on the Floor* (1996), which also includes rock elements; and the Anthony Davis operas *X (The Life and Times of Malcolm X)* (1986) and *Amistad* (1997), both of which share with Gershwin's *Porgy and Bess* the combination of jazz idioms with serious subject matter. The use of jazz styles even found its way into Schnittke's first quotation piece, his First Symphony (1972). Nevertheless, Reginald Smith Brindle is no doubt correct when he points out that most jazz has three characteristics that avant-garde composers since 1945 generally have wanted to avoid: clear melodic lines, conventional harmonic progressions, and a strong beat.[13] Ironically, "progressive jazz" itself seems to have done away with those characteristics one at a time—first by means of the disjunct, complex melodies of bebop in the 1940s, then through the harmonic stasis of the "time-no changes" style associated with Miles Davis in the 1960s,[14] and finally, in the performances of musicians such as Keith Jarrett, by the development of an ametric approach to rhythm. In fact, some of the experimental jazz ensembles that exist today play compositions that resemble in significant ways some postwar avant-garde music.

All jazz by definition contains some improvisation, usually a significant amount, and this is the primary difference between jazz and most but not all of its concert-hall derivatives. Improvisation has been an important aspect of certain "serious" music in recent decades (see Chapter 14), and the improvisatory styles of Charlie Parker and his heirs may well have had an influence on the performers of this kind of music. In addition, some of the instrumental timbres introduced into concert music in the twentieth century—notably the vibraphone and the cup mute for brass instruments—probably got there by way of jazz.

Rock music, now often referred to generically as "pop," has a shorter history than jazz does, but its influence on "classical" concert music is on the rise, at least in places such as New York City, where the avant-garde can find a venue and an audience more easily. Much of this involves music for small ensembles that typically play in clubs rather than on concert stages, and study scores are difficult for students of this music to come by. A few composer/performers, such as John Zorn, and experimental ensembles, such as Bang on a Can, have become well known outside of the great artistic centers, and that trend will probably continue.

Rock has certainly weighed in to some extent as well in more traditional genres, such as opera. For example, the rental score of Jake Heggie's opera *Dead Man Walking* (2000) comes with prerecorded rock songs that are to be played at points specified in the score.

MUSIC FROM OTHER CULTURES

Composers have shown occasional interest since the late eighteenth century in the music of "exotic" lands, which in this context means anything from the islands of the Western Pacific to the Middle East to Africa. A broader definition could easily include Hungary and Spain, since each had absorbed a certain amount of Eastern culture through long periods of occupation. Under such a definition, Debussy's "La Puerta del Vino" (1910) and Ravel's *Bolero* (1927) would be examples of musical exoticism.

Until the twentieth century, most examples of musical exoticism, such as the "Alla Turca" movement from Mozart's Sonata in A Major, K. 331 (1783) and Rimsky-Korsakov's *Scheherazade* (1888), made use of only the most superficial elements of the musical style being imitated. Two obvious ways of evoking the sound of the Far East are through timbre—the use of gongs, wood blocks, and pitched percussion instruments in imitation of the gamelan orchestra—and through certain compositional techniques such as parallelism and pentatonic scales.

Debussy makes use of some of these in Example 8-9. The upper two voices move in parallel motion up and down a four-note scale: (C♯–D♯–F♯–G♯), while the entrance of the bass in m. 29 provides a B, which when added to these four produces a pentatonic scale.

The middle voice in the texture moves more quickly than the bass but more slowly than the upper pair, and it seems to emphasize the important notes of the topmost voice. The total effect—pentatonicism, slow-moving bass, heterophony between topmost and middle voices—resembles some of the characteristics of the Javanese gamelan orchestra, indicating that Debussy had perhaps absorbed more of the authentic technique of exoticism than had his predecessors.

EXAMPLE 8-9 Debussy: *Estampes* (1903), "Pagodes," mm. 27–30

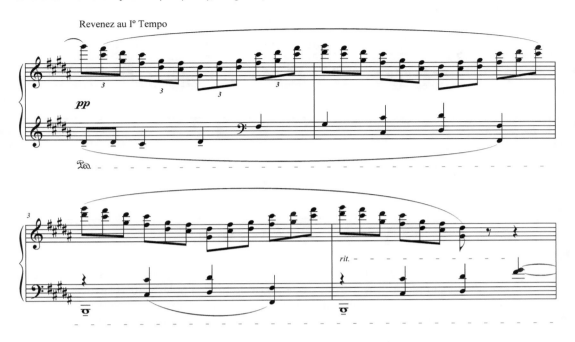

Composers became still more sophisticated about the music of other cultures as the century progressed: Messiaen, who studied the music of India and adapted its rhythms and scales to his own purposes, and Lou Harrison, who studied in Japan, Taiwan, and Korea, are but two examples. Some representative works:

Gustav Holst: *Choral Hymns from the Rig Veda* (1910)

Albert Roussel: *Padmâvatî* (1914)

Henry Cowell: *Persian Set* (1957)

Messiaen: *Sept haïkaï* (1953)

Alan Hovhaness: *Fantasy on Japanese Woodprints* (1965)

Karlheinz Stockhausen: *Telemusik* (1966)

David Fanshawe: *African Sanctus* (1972).

This blending of Western and Eastern musical styles has been furthered by various non-Western composers, including the Japanese composers Toru Takemitsu and Toshiro Mayuzumi, the Chinese Chou Wen-chung and Tan Dun, and Jacob Avshalomov, a Chinese-born American.

Harrison's *Concerto in Slendro* (1961) is a work for violin, celesta, two tack pianos (pianos in which a thumbtack is pressed into each hammer), and percussion, including gongs, triangles, washtubs, garbage pails, pipes, and wooden sticks. The term "Slendro" refers to certain Indonesian tunings of the pentatonic scale, and Harrison states in the score that the piece may be performed with or without these tunings. The third

EXAMPLE 8-10 Harrison: *Concerto in Slendro* (1961), III, mm. 19–23

Copyright © 1978 by C. F. Peters Corporation. Used by permission.

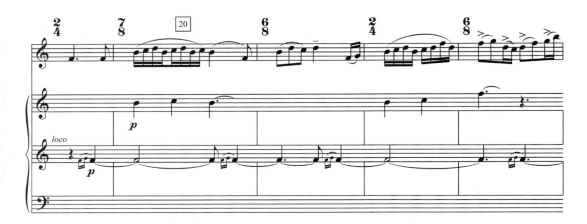

movement is a blend of Indonesian timbres and compositional practices with Western ones (for example, the recurring strict canons). In Example 8-10 (Harrison does not provide here the key signature of four sharps given at the beginning of the movement), one of the tack pianos provides a pedal point on F♯ while the violin and celesta play in heterophony, a texture in which simple and ornamented versions of a melody are played simultaneously.

The past decade has seen the inception and flourishing of The Silk Road Project, directed by Yo-Yo Ma, and The Silk Road Ensemble, a group of performers dedicated to playing concert music from around the world, much of it recently composed.

Eastern philosophy (or at least the Western understanding of it) has also been important for some post-tonal composers, especially for John Cage. Questioning the whole notion that art can "communicate" anything, Cage turned to Indian aesthetic theory, where he found the idea that "the purpose of music is to sober and quiet the mind, thus making it susceptible to divine influences."[15] His study of Zen, which "leads to a mistrust of the rational mind and a searching out of ways to nullify its powers of decision,"[16] led Cage to compose music by chance, the compositional decisions being made by the use of chance procedures from the *I-Ching*, a Chinese treatise on probabilities (discussed in more detail in Chapter 14). For Cage the influence of Zen was central to his development as a composer; he has said that "without my engagement with Zen I doubt whether I would have done what I have done."[17]

We have not discussed in this chapter what is broadly referred to as "world music," which has come to mean any music not part of the tradition of Western art music, because the focus here is on the *influence* such music has had on the Western tradition, not on world music itself. As cross-cultural influences continue, both from the "other" on the West and from the West on the other, distinctions between cultural styles may become less and less distinct. Although it is highly unlikely that this will ever lead to a single global musical style, it does open doors to creative and aesthetic experiences that can only enrich our musical lives.

SUMMARY

In many ways post-tonal music has broken with the past as completely as has any period in history. Neoclassicism and quotation, while providing important connections to the music of earlier times, are in no sense equivalent to the veneration of the past represented by the *stile antico* of the Baroque. Some composers have reached out in other directions—to folk music, to jazz, and rock, to the music of other cultures—and have adapted these new materials and techniques to their own needs. These trends are an important part of the amazing diversity of styles found in post-tonal music.

MUSIC FROM THE CHAPTER IN CHRONOLOGICAL CONTEXT

Year	Composer	Work	Reference
1912	Schoenberg	*Pierrot Lunaire*	Expressionism
1913	Stravinsky	*Rite of Spring*	Primitivism
1917	**Ives**	**"In Flanders Fields"**	**p. 153**
1918	**Stravinsky**	**The Soldier's Tale**	**p. 159**
1923	**Stravinsky**	**Octet for Wind Instruments**	**p. 151**
1926–37	**Bartók**	***Mikrokosmos***	**p. 157**
1930	Stravinsky	*Symphony of Psalms*	Neoclassicism
1935	Berg	Violin Concerto	Serialism
1952	John Cage	*4'33"*	Chance Music
1954	Edgard Varèse	*Poème Electronique*	Electronic Music
1957	**Gunther Schuller**	**Suite for Woodwind Quintet**	**p. 160**
1961	Krzysztof Penderecki	*Threnody: To the Victims of Hiroshima*	Aleatoric Music
1961	**Lou Harrison**	***Concerto in Slendro***	**p. 164**
1964	Terry Riley	*In C*	Minimalism
1969	**Peter Maxwell Davies**	***Eight Songs for a Mad King***	**p. 154**
2007	**Betsy Jolas**	***Ô Bach!***	**p. 155**

Works in **bold** are from the chapter; those not in bold are landmark pieces written around the same time.

NOTES

1. Robert Craft, *Stravinsky: Chronicle of a Friendship, 1948–71*, p. 103.

2. Donald Jay Grout, *A History of Western Music*, pp. 714–715.

3. William Austin, *Music in the 20th Century*, p. 330.

4. George Rochberg, *Music for the Magic Theater*, p. 6. "Notion" appears as "notation" in the original.

5. Ibid., p. 6.

6. George Crumb, *Ancient Voices of Childen*.

7. A thorough list is given in Chapter 4 of David Osmond-Smith's *Playing on Words*.

8. Michael Hicks, "Text, Music, and Meaning in the Third Movement of Luciano Berio's *Sinfonia*."

9. Bernard Holland, "Alfred Schnittke, Eclectic Composer, Dies at 63."

10. David Fanning and Laurel Fay, "Shostakovich, Dmitry."

11. Ligeti, György. *György Ligeti in Conversation*, p. 56.

12. Deem, George. *How to Paint a Vermeer*, p. 14.

13. Reginald Smith Brindle, *The New Music*, pp. 137–138.

14. Ian Carr, *Miles Davis*, p. 145.

15. Ev Grimes, "Ev Grimes Interviews John Cage," p. 48.

16. Brindle, *The New Music*, p. 123.

17. Michael Nyman, *Experimental Music*, p. 43.

★

EXERCISES

Part A: Analysis

1. *Bartók: Fourteen Bagatelles*, Op. 6 (1908), No. 4, mm. 1–8.

    This excerpt contains the beginning of a folk song harmonization by Bartók (the remainder of the piece simply repeats mm. 5–8). Bartók uses different compositional techniques in the harmonization of each phrase. Analyze both the song and the accompaniment in detail, summarizing your findings in prose with musical examples. Do not neglect such issues as voice leading and scale formations.

2. Look back at Example 8-1. The "Clarinet in Si♭" (B♭) sounds a M2 lower than written, and "Trumpet II in La" (A) sounds a m3 lower than written.

    (a) List the chords used in the accompaniment (bassoons and trombones) using lead-sheet symbols such as C7 and FM7.

    (b) How much of this harmonic accompaniment conforms to traditional harmonic progressions in E♭? Be specific.

    (c) Point out some dissonances between the accompaniment and the upper parts that would be difficult to explain in traditional terms.

    (d) Comment on imitation in this excerpt.

3. A very basic harmonic pattern for a twelve-bar blues in B♭ is:

    | B♭7 | ✗ | ✗ | ✗ | E♭7 | ✗ | B♭7 | ✗ | F7 | E♭7 | B♭7 | ✗ ||

    Discuss how Example 8-8 compares to the first eight measures of that pattern. Remember to transpose the clarinet and horn parts.

4. One B♭ "blues scale" can be derived by combining the three 7th chords listed in the previous exercise, producing a nine-tone scale: B♭–C–D♭–D–E♭–F–G–A♭–A. Part of the flavor that we associate with the blues results from the use, either melodically or harmonically, of the altered and unaltered "blues notes" (D♭/D and A♭/A) in close proximity. Point out any examples that you can find of this technique in Example 8-8.

Part B: Listening

Listen to as many of the following examples as you can. For each one, explain how the example is relevant to the present chapter, and try to describe how the music *sounds*—how the use of folk materials or quotation, for example, helps to give the music its own particular sound.

1.   Amram: Triple Concerto for Woodwind, Brass, and Jazz Quintets, and Orchestra (1970), I.

2.   Bartók: Fifteen Hungarian Peasant Songs (1917).

3.   Berio: *Sinfonia* (1968), III.

4.   Copland: *Appalachian Spring* (1944).

5.   Falla: Nights in the Gardens of Spain (1916).

6.   Harrison: Double Concerto for Violin and Cello with Javanese Gamelan (1982).

7.   Still: Afro-American Symphony (1933).

8.   Stravinsky: Octet for Wind Instruments (1923).

FURTHER READING

Brindle, Reginald Smith. *The New Music*. See Chapter 13, The Search Outwards—The Orient, Jazz, Archaisms.

Chou, Wen-Chung. "Asian Concepts and Twentieth-Century Western Composers."

Cope, David H. *New Directions in Music*. See the sections titled "Non-Western Influences," pp. 109–113, and "Quotation," pp. 355–357.

Gann, Kyle. *American Music in the Twentieth Century*. See Chapter 11, Interfaces with Rock and Jazz.

Griffiths, Paul. *Modern Music and After*. See the section titled "Of Elsewhen and Elsewhere," pp. 151–170.

Grout, Donald Jay. *A History of Western Music*. See the section titled "Musical Styles Related to Folk Idioms," pp. 685–700, and "Neo-Classicism and Related Movements," pp. 700–722.

Losada, C. Catherine. "Between Modernism and Postmodernism: Strands of Continuity in Collage Compositions by Rochberg, Berio, and Zimmermann."

Metzer, David. *Quotation and Cultural Meaning in Twentieth-Century Music*.

Ringo, James. "The Lure of the Orient."

Simms, Bryan R. *Music of the Twentieth Century*. See Chapter 10, Neoclassicism in France, Germany, and England, and Chapter 15, Eclecticism.

Taylor, Timothy D. *Beyond Exoticism: Western Music and the World*.

CHAPTER 9

Nonserial Atonality

INTRODUCTION

In the first decade of the twentieth century, a few composers developed an approach to composition that, in retrospect, was perhaps inevitable and that Liszt anticipated toward the end of his life with his "Bagatelle without Tonality" (1885). The chromaticism of the nineteenth century had chipped away at the tonal system so successfully that it was only a natural outcome for the system eventually to be abandoned altogether. This new music without a tonal center eventually became known as "atonal" music, although not without objection by some of the composers who originated the style.

Atonality is one of the more important aspects of post-tonal music, and it is a major factor that distinguishes much of the music since 1900 from any other music in the Western tradition. Nonserial, or "free," atonality led in the 1920s to a more organized atonal method called serialism or twelve-tone music, but nonserial atonal music continued to be composed and is still being composed today. We will discuss serialism in later chapters. For now we are concerned only with nonserial atonal music, which, for the present, we will refer to simply as atonal music.

It is not surprising that the analysis of atonal music has required the development of new theoretical terms and approaches. Although analytical methods are still being developed and experimented with, most of the current literature owes a debt to the work of Allen Forte, whose book *The Structure of Atonal Music* is a standard reference on the subject.[1] Most of the information in this chapter derives from Forte's work or from that of his followers. Although the basics of this theory may be totally unfamiliar to you, the concepts are not very difficult, and you will find them applicable to a wide range of post-tonal styles.

CHARACTERISTICS OF ATONAL MUSIC

Atonal music has several characteristics that set it apart from other styles. The first of course, is that it is not pitch-centric. This aspect is a subjective one, for any two listeners might differ concerning the degree to which a tonal center is audible in a particular work; nevertheless, a great many pieces are widely accepted as being atonal. This atonality is achieved by avoiding the conventional melodic, harmonic, and rhythmic patterns that help to establish a tonality in traditional tonal music. In their place we find unresolved dissonances, a preponderance of mixed–interval chords, and pitch material derived from the chromatic scale. Textures often are contrapuntal, with themes or melodies in the traditional sense occurring less often, and the metric organization is frequently difficult for the listener to follow.

Example 9-1 is from the beginning of one of the earliest atonal works. Although it is not the most representative example that could have been chosen, it does have the advantage of being easy to play, and you will get more out of the following discussion if you play the example several times before going on. The piece opens with a slow tremolo between D and F over a sustained F, perhaps suggesting D minor. (Octave doublings such as the octave here on F were soon discarded by some atonal composers on the theory that they put too much emphasis on a single pitch class.) The melody that enters in m. 2 does little to confirm D as a tonality. Two short melodic phrases, one beginning in m. 2 and the other in m. 3, use the pitch classes C, D♭, D, E♭, A♭, and A, with many of these pitches being freely dissonant against the accompaniment. Following the rest under the fermata, a third phrase interrupts the tremolo figure in the low register and closes the excerpt. Melodically this third phrase begins with an expressive motion up to D5 (notice that the accompanying chords here do not suggest a D tonal center), followed by the same pitch classes that ended the second phrase: C–E♭–D♭. The tremolo figure returns as the melody settles in on its last two notes. In this excerpt the D/F *dyad* (pair of notes) in the accompaniment is clearly in opposition to the D♭ in the melody, but neither D nor D♭ is strongly established as a tonal center, and this, along with the prevailing chromaticism, leads us to classify this music as atonal rather than polytonal (review Chapter 5).

EXAMPLE 9-1 Schoenberg: Three Piano Pieces (1909), Op. 11, No. 2, mm. 1–5

Used by permission of Belmont Music Publishers.

PITCH-CLASS SETS

It soon became clear to musicians that the pitch aspect of atonal music required a new vocabulary if the analysis of this music was ever to be more than descriptive. It was recognized that atonal music often achieved a certain degree of unity through recurrent use of a new kind of motive. This new kind of motive was given various names, including **cell**, **basic cell**, **set**, **pitch set**, **pitch-class set**, and **referential sonority**. It could appear melodically, harmonically, or as a combination of the two. The set also could be transposed and/or inverted (that is, in mirror inversion; for example, G–B–C inverts to G–E♭–D), and its pitches could appear in any order and in any register. Most pieces were found to employ a large number of different kinds of pitch sets, only a few of which might be important in unifying the piece. The analysis of atonal music usually includes the process of identifying and labeling these important pitch sets, a process that involves **segmentation**.

Segmentation is in some ways much more difficult than the analysis of chords in traditional tonal music. The first problem is that, when beginning the analysis, one usually does not know which sets will turn out to be significant in the piece and which ones will not, meaning that various musically convincing segmentations may have to be tried and discarded before the significant ones appear. We will demonstrate the process of segmentation throughout this chapter.

A second problem is labeling the sets for ease of comparison, and it is in this area that Allen Forte's work has proved so helpful. Because an atonal chord or melodic fragment can consist of any combination of pitches, thousands of different sets are possible. As we shall see, Forte's system of pitch-class sets reduces this number considerably.

PITCH-CLASS INTERVALS

In Chapter 1 we introduced the idea of representing pitch classes with the integers 0 through 11 (C = 0, C♯/D♭ = 1, etc.; remember that pitch class 0 represents every C, every B♯, every D♭♭, etc., regardless of octave). We will often find it convenient to use integers to represent the intervals between pitch classes as well. A **pitch-class interval** (more properly, an "ordered pitch-class interval") is an integer between 0 and 11 that indicates the distance in half steps from the first pitch class *up* to the second pitch class. (We will use the abbreviations **PC** for pitch class and **PCI** for pitch-class interval.) To calculate this, *subtract the first PC from the second PC.* Here are some examples:

First PC	Second PC	PCI
0 (C)	2 (D)	2
3 (E♭)	10 (B♭)	7
5 (F)	11 (B)	6

If the integer representing the first PC is larger than the second (as in 9 up to 2), we have to use **mod 12 arithmetic**, which brings every number within the range 0 to 11 by adding or subtracting 12 until that range is reached. Three ways to accomplish this are shown here; use the one that works best for you:

1. Visualize a clock face with the 12 replaced by a 0. You can easily see that there are five hours from 9:00 to 2:00, and 5 is the correct answer.
2. Add 12 to the second number before you subtract the first number from it: $(2 + 12) - 9 = 5$.
3. Convert 9 up to 2 into A up to D, which is a P4; if you know how many half steps are in a P4, you know the answer is 5.

Here are some more examples:

First PC	Second PC	PCI
11 (B)	0 (C)	1
7 (G)	4 (E)	9
5 (F)	4 (E)	11

The following table lists all of the pitch-class intervals along with the traditional labels for those intervals. **Enharmonic equivalence** always applies when dealing with pitch classes; for example, an A2 and a m3 are both PCI 3. You will want to learn the information in this table, either through use or by memorization.

PCI	Traditional Label	PCI	Traditional Label
0	P1 (unison)	6	A4, d5 (tritone)
1	m2	7	P5
2	M2	8	m6
3	m3	9	M6
4	M3	10	m7
5	P4	11	M7

OCTAVE EQUIVALENCE, TRANSPOSITIONAL EQUIVALENCE, AND NORMAL ORDER

In the analysis of tonal music, we routinely reduce sonorities to basic forms. For instance, through the theories of **octave equivalence** and chord roots, we analyze all of the chords in Example 9-2a as C major triads and all of those in Example 9-2b as F major triads. In addition, we consider C major triads and F major triads to be **transpositionally equivalent**, to be members of a class of sonorities referred to collectively as major triads. These concepts are so obvious to us that it seems trivial to mention them, but in fact the theory that classifies the sonorities in Example 9-2 into one chord type is only a few centuries old.

EXAMPLE 9-2 Major Triads

To analyze and compare the pitch-class sets in atonal music, we need a process that will reduce any set to some basic form in the same way that we reduce the chords in Example 9-2 to the three notes of the major triad in root position. This basic form in pitch-set analysis is called the **normal order**. The procedure to follow in determining the normal order will be illustrated by means of the segmentations shown in Example 9-3. All of the segmentations are circled except for Sets 3 and 4; these sets are the three-note chords that accompany the melody.

EXAMPLE 9–3 Schoenberg: Three Piano Pieces (1909), Op. 11, No. 2, mm. 1–5

Used by permission of Belmont Music Publishers.

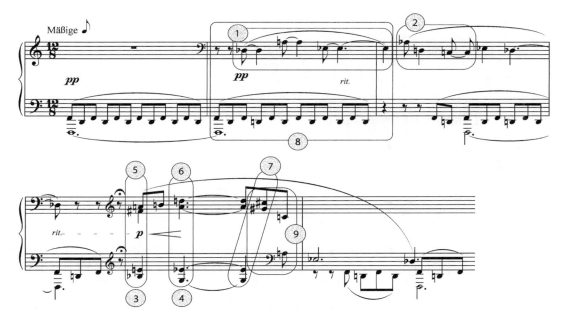

The normal order of a pitch-class set is that ordering of the PCs that spans the smallest possible interval. In that sense, it is similar to putting a triad into root position. To find the normal order of a set, notate or list the PCs as an ascending "scale" within an octave, as in Example 9-4a. You can begin the scale on any of the PCs, and they may be spelled enharmonically if you wish. Leave out any duplicated PCs, but continue up to the octave (the second D♭ in Example 9-4a). Now find the largest interval between any two adjacent PCs (PCI 6 in Example 9-4a); the *top* note of this largest interval (the A in Example 9-4a) is the *bottom* note of the normal order. The normal order of Set 1 is shown in Example 9-4b. To write out a normal order without using musical notation, list the PCs or the note names, separate them with commas, and enclose the normal order with brackets, as in [9,1,3] or [A,D♭,E♭].[2]

EXAMPLE 9-4 Normal Order of Set 1

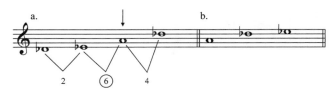

When we put Set 2 into normal order in Example 9–5b, we discover that it is [8,0,2] or [A♭,C,D], the same as Example 9–4b, but a half step lower; in other words, Set 2 is transpositionally equivalent to Set 1.

EXAMPLE 9-5 Normal Order of Set 2

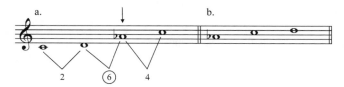

Sets 3 and 4 are the three-note chords that accompany the melody in m. 4. The normal orders of these two sets are shown in Example 9–6. Notice that Set 4 [3,7,9] or [E♭,G,A], is transpositionally equivalent to Sets 1 and 2, but Set 3 is not.

EXAMPLE 9-6 Normal Orders of Sets 3 and 4

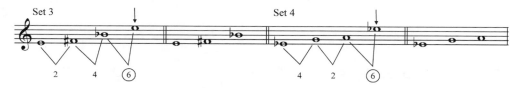

Sets 5, 6, and 7 result from a different segmentation of m. 4. Each one contains four pitch classes. The first column of Example 9-7 shows these sets in scalar form. Notice that in Set 7 the G♯ and C♯ have been spelled enharmonically for convenience. The normal orders of these sets are shown in the second column of Example 9-7. None of these sets is transpositionally equivalent to any of the others.

EXAMPLE 9-7 Normal Orders of Sets 5, 6, and 7

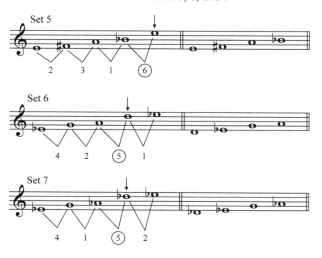

We are making good progress here in learning how to put pitch sets into normal order, which, you will recall, refers to the order that spans the smallest interval. A complication that occasionally arises is seen in a set that has no single largest interval, but instead has two or more intervals that are tied for largest. Set 8 is an example of such a set. Notice in Example 9-8a that there are two occurrences of PCI 4 and that all of the other intervals are smaller. This means that we have two candidates for the normal order, Examples 9-8b and 9-8c. The tie is broken by comparing the intervals between the first and next-to-last notes in both versions (A–E♭ in Example 9-8b versus C♯–F in Example 9-8c). The normal order is the version with the *smaller* interval—Example 9-8c—because that version is the one that is packed most tightly to the left.

EXAMPLE 9-8 Normal Order of Set 8

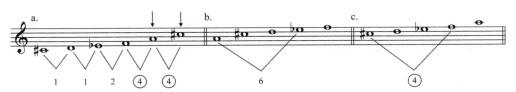

If the intervals between the first and next-to-last notes in Examples 9-8b and 9-8c had been the same, we would have proceeded to the intervals between the first and third-to-last notes, and so on, until the tie was broken. In some sets, however, the tie cannot be broken, and in such cases we choose the ordering that begins with the smallest pitch-class integer. Consider the set in Example 9-9a (not taken from the Schoenberg excerpt). It contains two instances of its largest interval, PCI 3, so there are two candidates for the normal order. These are shown in Example 9-9b and 9-9c. The interval successions in the two versions are identical (because they are transposition-ally equivalent), so it is impossible to break the tie, and so we compare the pitch classes that begin each ordering, 10 (A♯) and 4 (E), and choose Example 9-9c, because 4 is a smaller number than 10. A set such as this is called a **transpositionally symmetrical set**, because it reproduces its own pitch-class content under one or more intervals of transposition. In the case of the set in Example 9-9, transposition by PCI 6 reproduces the set. A few traditional tertian sonorities are transpositionally symmetrical, includ-ing the augmented triad, the diminished 7th chord, and the French augmented sixth chord.

EXAMPLE 9-9 A Transpositionally Symmetrical Set

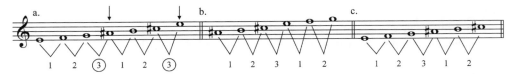

INVERSIONAL EQUIVALENCE AND BEST NORMAL ORDER

We have seen that tonal and atonal analyses share the concepts of octave equivalence and transpositional equivalence. Atonal analysis goes a step further, however, and considers pitch–class sets that are related by inversion to be equivalent. This is called **inversional equivalence**. (To "invert" a set in atonal music means to reverse the order of the intervals.)

This would not be a useful approach in tonal music, because the major and minor triads, for example, are related by inversion, as are the dominant 7th chord and the half–diminished–7th chord, and we need to be able to distinguish between them in tonal analysis. But in atonal music a set and its inversion (and all transpositions of the set and of its inversion) are considered to be different representations of the same "set class" (discussed in more detail below).

If we are going to have a single classification for any set and its inversion, then we will have to carry the concept of the normal order a step further, to something called the **best normal order**. This concept is important because the best normal order is the generic representation of all possible transpositions and inversions of a set. To find the best normal order of any set, first find its normal order and then notate its inversion. In most cases the inversion will already be in normal order; however, it may or may not be in normal order if there are two or more occurrences of the largest PCI (discussed later). Finally, compare the two normal orders: the "better" of the two is considered to be the best normal order.

Let us see how this works with Set 1 from Example 9-3. Its normal order was given in Example 9-4. An easy way to invert the normal order of a set is to use the same top and bottom notes, and then fill in the remaining notes by reversing the order of the intervals. In Example 9-10a the intervals of the normal order are analyzed. Then, keeping the outer notes the same, these intervals are reversed in Example 9-10b to form the inversion. Finally, we choose between the two orders by comparing the intervals between the first and next-to-last notes in both versions, just as we did with Example 9-8. We select as the best normal order the version with the smaller interval—in this case, Example 9-10b.

EXAMPLE 9-10 Set 1 and Its Inversion

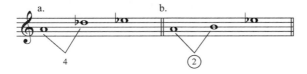

Looking back over Examples 9-4, 9-5, and 9-6, you can see that Sets 1, 2, and 4 were transpositionally equivalent to one another, and that all three were inversionally equivalent to Set 3. In other words, all four sets have the same normal order and therefore are all representatives of the same set class.

Set 5 is analyzed in Example 9-11. The normal order of the original set is in Example 9-11a, and its inversion is in Example 9-11b. When the two normal orders, Examples 9-11a and 9-11b, are compared, we see that the PCI 4 in Example 9-11b is smaller than the PCI 5 in Example 9–11a, so Example 9–11b is selected as the best normal order. If the intervals between the first and next-to-last notes in Examples 9–11a and 9–11b had been the same, we would have proceeded to the intervals between the first and third-to-last notes, and so on, until the tie was broken.

EXAMPLE 9-11 Best Normal Order of Set 5

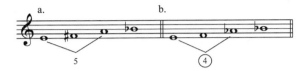

In Example 9–12, Set 6 is analyzed. The normal order of the original set, Example 9–12a, turns out to be the best normal order.

EXAMPLE 9-12 Best Normal Order of Set 6

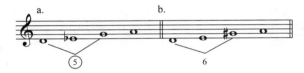

Set 7 is analyzed in Example 9–13. The best normal order is Example 9–13b. Because the best normal orders of Sets 6 and 7 (Example 9–12a and Example 9–13b) are transpositionally equivalent, Sets 6 and 7 are representatives of the same set class.

EXAMPLE 9-13 Best Normal Order of Set 7

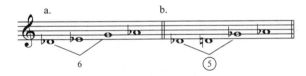

It is not uncommon to find a set in which the normal order of the set and the normal order of its inversion are identical or transpositionally equivalent. An example is Set 9, shown in normal order in Example 9–14a. In Example 9–14b the normal order is inverted, and we see that the normal order of the inversion is the same as the original. A set such as this is called an **inversionally symmetrical set** because it reproduces its pitch-class content at one or more levels of inversion. Several traditional tertian sonorities are inversionally symmetrical, including the augmented triad, the minor 7th chord, and others.

EXAMPLE 9-14 Best Normal Order of Set 9

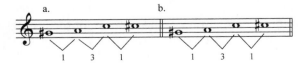

The method that we have been using so far to find the best normal order will not always work with pitch-class sets that have more than one occurrence of the largest interval (such as the one in Example 9–8). Consider the set in Example 9–15a. There are two occurrences of the largest interval, PCI 4, so we have to consider the two candidates for the normal order in Examples 9–15b and 9–15c. The interval between the first and next-to-last notes in Example 9–15b is smaller than that in Example 9–15c, so the normal order is [4,7,8,0], or [E,G,A♭,C].

EXAMPLE 9-15 A Pitch-Class Set

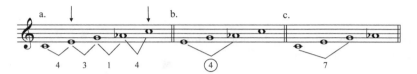

The normal order of this set is given again in Example 9–16a along with its inversion in 9–16b. However, because we know that there are two occurrences of the largest interval (PCI 4), we have to consider another ordering of the inversion, shown in Example 9–16c. Comparing our three candidates for best normal order, we see that two of them span PCI 4 between the first and next-to-last notes, which eliminates Example 9–16b from the competition. We now back up one interval and compare the intervals between the first and third-to-last notes in Examples 9–16a (PCI 3) and 9–16c (PCI 1), looking for the smaller interval. As it turns out, the last version of our set wins out over the other two and is in fact the best normal order. The lesson here is that you must try out as many orderings of the inversion as there are occurrences of the largest interval or you may not discover the best normal order.

EXAMPLE 9-16 The Normal Order Inverted

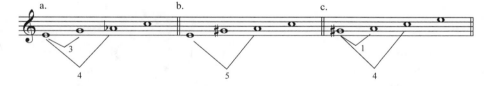

PRIME FORMS AND SET CLASSES

Once we know the best normal order of a set, we need to be able to give it a name, which is done by applying numbers to the best normal order. The resulting series of numbers is called the **prime form**, and it represents all of the pitch-class sets in that **set class**, just as "major triad" represents all possible major triads in all possible arrangements. The first number of a prime form is always 0, and it stands for the lowest note of the best normal order. The other numbers give the distance in half steps (the PCI) each successive note is above that lowest note. For instance, in Example 9–10b we notated the best normal order of Set 1 as [A,B,E♭]. Because B is two half steps above A (PCI 2) and E♭ is six half steps above A (PCI 6), the name of this set class is [026], and [026] represents all transpositions and/or inversions of Set 1. Sets 1, 2, 3, and 4 are all [026] trichords. Notice that the set class is enclosed in brackets and that the numbers are not separated by commas or spaces. In the event that you need a 10 or 11 in a set name, use T or E; hence, a whole-tone scale would be [02468T].

Let's look at a few more illustrations: The best normal order of Set 5 (Example 9-11b) is [E,F,A♭,B♭], yielding [0146] as a prime form. The best normal order of Set 6 (Example 9-12a) is [D,E♭,G,A], so its prime form is [0157], and Set 7 (Example 9-13b) is also a [0157] tetrachord. Set 9 (Example 9-14a) is a [0145] tetrachord.

By adopting the concepts of transpositional and inversional equivalence, the thousands of possible pitch combinations have been reduced to a manageable number of prime forms or set classes. The following table shows how many set classes there are for combinations of from two to ten pitch classes:

6	Dyads (two pitch classes)
12	Trichords (three pitch classes)
29	Tetrachords (four pitch classes)
38	Pentachords (five pitch classes)
50	Hexachords (six pitch classes)
38	Septachords (seven pitch classes)
29	Octachords (eight pitch classes)
12	Nonachords (nine pitch classes)
6	Decachords (ten pitch classes)
220	TOTAL

THE INTERVAL-CLASS VECTOR

Most of pitch-set analysis is concerned with identifying sets that recur in a piece in compositionally significant ways. This includes, of course, transpositions and inversions of the original set, since we recognize transpositional and inversional equivalence. But analytical theory is much less advanced when it comes to comparing nonequivalent sets. Consider, for example, Sets 5 and 6 from the Schoenberg excerpt, reproduced here in best normal order beginning on G.

EXAMPLE 9-17 Sets 5 and 6

[0146]   [0157]

It would appear that [0146] and [0157] are very similar, the only difference being the interval between the second and third notes; thus, [0157] is a kind of expansion of [0146]. But there are other differences, one of them being that [0157] contains two perfect intervals (G–C and G–D), but [0146] contains only one (A♭–C♯). This may mean that [0157] is potentially a more consonant sound than [0146]. One way of comparing sets that contain the same number of pitch classes, as these do, is to tabulate their interval contents. Because inversional equivalence is still in effect, we consider PCI 1 and PCI 11 (the m2 and M7) to be equivalent, also PCI 2 and PCI 10 (the M2 and m7), and so forth. We then have six **interval classes** ("interval class" is sometimes abbreviated as **IC**):

Interval Class	Pitch-Class Interval	Traditional Interval
1	1, 2	m2, M7
2	2, 10	M2, m7
3	3, 9	m3, M6
4	4, 8	M3, m6
5	5, 7	P4, P5
6	6	A4, d5

To analyze a set according to its interval content, tabulate all of the ICs between each note in the set and all of the notes *above* it. This way, the interval between each pair of notes in the set will be counted only once. The following tables demonstrate this procedure for Sets 5 and 6 (refer again to Example 9-17):

Set 5				Set 6		
From	Up to	IC		From	Up to	IC
G	A♭	1		G	A♭	1
G	B	4		G	C	5
G	C♯	6		G	D	5
A♭	B	3		A♭	C	4
A♭	C♯	5		A♭	D	6
B	C♯	2		C	D	2

You can see from this that Set 5 contains exactly one occurrence of each IC. Set 6, on the other hand, contains two occurrences of IC5 but none of IC3. This information is usually presented in the form of an **interval-class vector** (or **ICV**), which lists the number of occurrences of each IC, beginning with IC1 and continuing through IC6. In this text we will enclose the list with angled brackets, as in <001110>. Set 5, because it contains one of each IC, has an ICV of <111111>, whereas the ICV for Set 6 is <110121>. The ICVs of Sets 5 and 6 illustrate their similarity and give us a general picture of their potential consonance or dissonance.

The interval-class vector provides one tool for comparing pitch-class sets of the same size, but it is not without its problems. At the beginning of Example 3-B-8 (p. 66) Berg employs two set classes in alternation (the chords marked a, b, c, d, and e). The first two chords are shown in Example 9-18, both in their original versions (but compressed spacing) and in their best normal orders, transposed to begin on G. The first chord is set class [0137], and the second is [0146], the same as Set 5 from the Schoenberg excerpt. The surprising thing here is that both sets have an ICV of <111111>. Because they are different set classes, we know they are not related by transposition or inversion, yet their ICVs are identical. Pairs of sets that share the same vector (they come only in pairs) are known as **Z-related sets**. This is the only pair of Z-related tetrachords, but there are three pairs of Z-related pentachords and 15 pairs of Z-related hexachords. It is obvious from this that the ICV alone cannot be used to compare set classes, although it does provide some useful information.

EXAMPLE 9-18 Two Chords from Berg's "Warm Is the Air"

[0137]   [0146]

INVARIANCE

One thing an interval-class vector can do is predict how many pitch classes will be retained under any level of transposition. For example, the ICV of a major triad (or a minor one, for that matter) is <001110>. This means that if we transpose a triad up *or* down by a minor 3rd, a major 3rd, or a perfect 4th, exactly one pitch class will be held **invariant**— that is, it will be retained. Conversely, transposing a triad by any other interval will produce a fresh crop of three new pitch classes. (Prove this to yourself by starting with a C major triad.) An important point, however, has to do with IC6: transposition by a tritone will keep *twice* the number of pitch classes invariant as are found in the last digit of an ICV. For instance, Set 6 from the Schoenberg example was a [0157] set with an ICV of <110121>. If it is transposed by a tritone, two—not one—pitch classes will be retained:

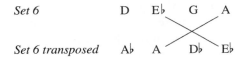

Set 6   D   Eb   G   A

Set 6 transposed   Ab   A   Db   Eb

An **inversion matrix** will allow us to predict how many PCs will be held invariant under inversion. To make such a matrix, we convert our (D, Eb, G, A) set to (2, 3, 7, 9) and add each PC to itself and to every other PC in the set (using mod 12 arithmetic, of course):

	2	3	7	9
2	4	5	9	11
3	5	6	10	0
7	9	10	2	4
9	11	0	4	6

Next, invert the set, not by using notation, but by subtracting each note from 0 and reversing the order:

(−2,−3,−7,−9) mod 12 = (10,9,5,3) reversed = (**3**,5,**9**, 10)

This is considered the 0th transposition. If you look in the matrix, you will find two occurrences of the number 0, which means that two PCs will be held invariant— in this case PCs 3 and 9. There are no occurrences of the number 1 in the matrix, which means that transposing the inversion by PCI 1 will yield no invariant PCs: (4,6,10,11). There is one occurrence of the number 2, so transposing by PCI 2 will keep one PC invariant: (5,7,11,0), and so on.

FORTE LABELS

Music theorists often use the labels for prime forms that are found in Allen Forte's *Structure of Atonal Music*. Once you know the prime form of a set, you can look up its Forte label as well as its ICV in the Appendix at the back of this book. A Forte label has three parts: a number that indicates how many pitch classes the set contains, a hyphen, and a number that is sometimes preceded by the letter Z. For example, the chromatic trichord, [012], has 3–1 as its Forte label, while the augmented triad, [048], is 3–12. The letter Z is used for pairs of sets that have identical interval-class vectors. You may recall that [0137] and [0146], discussed earlier, both have an ICV of <111111>, so their Forte labels include a letter Z, as in 4–Z29 and 4–Z15, respectively. Forte labels are frequently used in the theoretical literature, so it is useful to know where you can look them up and find their associated prime forms.

SUBSETS

Sometimes pitch-class sets that do not belong to the same set class may be related to each other by sharing common **subsets**, just as C7 and Cadd6 are closely related because they have the C major triad in common. For example, the pitch-class sets below all have forms of the set class [026] as a subset:

[E, F♯, A, B♭], set class [0146], includes subset [E, F♯, B♭], a form of set class [026]
[D, E♭, G, A], set class [0157], includes [E♭, G, A], another form of [026]
[D♭, D, E♭, F, A], set class [01248], includes [D♭, E♭, A], another form of [026]

These are the pitch-class sets labeled chords 5, 6, and 8 in Example 9-3 (p. 173), and their [026] subsets make them not only related to each other but also to the chords labeled 1 and 2 in that example, both of which are forms of [026] as well. Chord 1 is a **literal subset** of chord 8 because it shares not just the same intervals but literally the same pitch classes: D♭, E♭, and A. The other subset relationships above are all **nonliteral subsets**, because those forms of [026] are all related by transposition or inversion, but do not literally share the same three pitch classes.

A special kind of subset is the **scalar subset**, which is a subset that is derived from a particular scale type, usually diatonic (as in the white keys of the piano), octatonic, or whole tone. For example, even if a passage is not based on a single whole-tone scale, it would be of interest to discover that most or all of its sets are whole-tone subsets. In Example 9-19a, the violin states a figure that, while not octatonic, is constructed from octatonic subsets. The piano a few measures later answers with some octatonic subsets of its own with another non-octatonic figure (Example 9-19b).

EXAMPLE 9-19 Zwilich: Sonata in Three Movements (1974), III

Reprinted by permission of Carl Fischer, LLC.

AGGREGATES

Nonserial atonality does not offer a systematic method of achieving atonality, as serialism does, but atonal composers have at times shown a concern that all 12 pitch classes be heard within a fairly short period, which is one of the fundamental notions of twelve-tone serialism. The term **aggregate** is used to refer to any such statement of all 12 pitch classes, *without regard to order or duplication*. In atonal analysis, it is sometimes helpful to look for aggregates, especially at the beginning of a piece or major section, or even within certain parts of the texture.

Concerning his Bagatelles, Op. 9, a nonserial atonal work, Anton Webern wrote, "While working on them I had the feeling that once the twelve tones had run out, the piece was finished."[3] This does not mean that each Bagatelle is only 12 notes long, although they are quite short, but it might mean that Webern has used aggregates in significant ways in these pieces. The first half of the fifth Bagatelle (Example 9-20) contains an extreme example of what Webern was talking about.

In the first measure of this piece, Webern introduces a nearly chromatic set, C–C♯–D♯–E, which is filled in by the D in m. 2, giving us:

C   C♯   D   D♯   E
├─────── mm. 1–2 ───────┤

Measure 3 begins with a chord that extends the chromatic set by two more PCs:

B   C   C♯   D   D♯   E   F
├────── mm. 1–2 ──────┤

The chord in m. 4 expands the chromatic set to nine PCs:

B♭   B   C   C♯   D   D♯   E   F   G♭
├────── mm. 1–2 ──────┤

Measure 6 continues the set upwards by two PCs:

B♭   B   C   C♯   D   D♯   E   F   G♭   G   A♭
├──────mm. 1–2 ──────┤

And the chromatic set is completed by the A in m. 7:

A   B♭   B   C   C♯   D   D♯   E   F   G♭   G   A♭
├────── mm. 1–2 ──────┤

What we have in mm. 1–7 is an aggregate, but it is a highly unusual one in that the pitch classes are introduced according to a preconceived pattern and within a single octave (A3 to A♭4). Even the pitch classes that are repeated, like the E and E♭ in m. 3, recur in the same octave, with the single exception of the C5 in m. 5.

EXAMPLE 9-20 Webern: Six Bagatelles for String Quartet, Op. 9 (1913), V, mm. 1–7

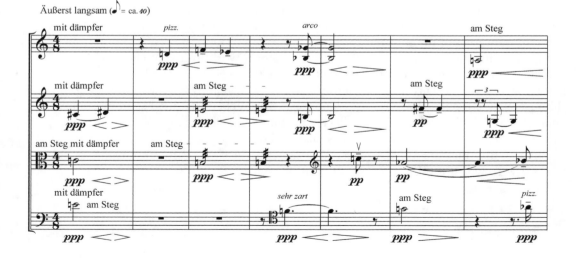

Aggregate completion is also important in the first movement of Ligeti's Ten Pieces for Wind Quintet (1968). In this twenty-five-measure work, the composer employs 11 pitch classes, omitting only C♯, until the middle of m. 16, where C♯s are introduced to produce the climax of the movement.

MORE ABOUT SEGMENTATION

Earlier in this chapter we said that atonal analysis is largely a matter of segmentation, or identifying and labeling significant pitch-class sets. The Schoenberg excerpt provided some experience with this process. Segmentation is largely a hit-or-miss analytical procedure, because a set that occurs only once and is not significantly related to any more important set is not really of much interest. In the Webern excerpt (Example 9-20), for instance, you might isolate these three sets in m. 1:

C–C♯–E	[014]
C–D♯–E	[014]
C–C♯–D♯–E	[0134]

The fact that the first two sets are representatives of the same pitch–class set is encouraging to the analyst, but they may or may not recur later in the piece. Another segmentation that could be tried would be to join the "melodies" in the violins:

C♯–D♯–D–F–E♭	[0124]

Other musically defensible segmentations could be made on the basis of timbre (for instance, *am steg* versus *pizzicato*) or register. The most important thing is that the segmentations should reflect the way the music sounds and should not divide musical units such as chords or melodic figures in unmusical ways. Good atonal analysis requires a high degree of musical sensitivity and a very keen ear.

SET THEORY IN OTHER CONTEXTS

While set theory is often applied to atonal music, it can be just as effective in any context where non-tertian harmonies are common, even in pandiatonic and octatonic music. Consider the strongly centric music given as Example 5–4 (p. 94), which contains a double pedal on C and F throughout. Of the seven chords in the example, only the first, third, and last harmonies could easily be called tertian; the second, fourth, and fifth chords are better described as quartal, while the sixth is a chord of mixed intervals. Example 9-21 below provides the set class labels for each of the seven chords in Example 5-4.

EXAMPLE 9-21 Set Class Analysis of Chords in Example 5-4

A set class analysis of the passage reveals that the harmonies are more unified than one might initially think by labeling them only as tertian, quartal, and mixed interval harmonies. Example 9-22 shows the trichordal subsets of the second, fourth, and sixth chords.

EXAMPLE 9-22 Trichordal Subsets of Chords 2, 4, and 6

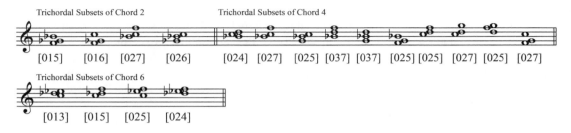

Trichordal Subsets of Chord 2

[015]   [016]   [027]   [026]

Trichordal Subsets of Chord 4

[024]   [027]   [025] [037] [037]   [025] [025]   [027] [025] [027]

Trichordal Subsets of Chord 6

[013]   [015]   [025]   [024]

Notice how the [027] subset of the second chord is embedded three times in the fourth chord while [037], the set class representing both major and minor triads, and thus both the first and the third chords, is embedded twice in the fourth chord. The fourth chord thus serves to bind together the disparate harmonies of the first three chords by including elements of both. Comparing Examples 9-21 and 9-22, we can now understand more fully why the fifth and sixth chords seem to flow naturally from those that came before: the fifth chord is literally the second chord again, just with an added G-natural (i.e. the second is a literal subset of the fifth), and the sixth chord is related to the second by the trichordal subset [015], and to the fourth by the trichordal subsets [024] and [025].

SUMMARY

The most essential characteristic of nonserial atonal music is its atonality, which is achieved by avoiding the melodic, harmonic, and rhythmic patterns used to establish tonality in tonal music. Some of the other characteristics of nonserial atonal music include unresolved dissonances, a preponderance of mixed-interval chords, contrapuntal textures, ambiguous metric organization, and use of the chromatic scale.

An important aspect of atonal analysis is the segmentation of the texture into smaller sets, or cells, which are then identified according to set class. This process involves arranging each set in normal order and then in best normal order for the identification of its set class, represented by its prime form. This classification process depends on both transpositional and inversional equivalence in order to reduce to 220 the number of possible sets that contain between two and ten pitch classes. Forte labels provide reasonably short names for each of these set classes. Some set classes are transpositionally or inversionally symmetrical, or both.

Nonequivalent sets may be compared by means of their interval-class vectors, by subset relationships (including scalar subsets), and by other means not introduced here. Aggregate completion is another element to look for in the analysis of atonal music, especially at the beginning of a piece.

Probably the best way to analyze atonal music, as well as tonal music, is at the piano keyboard. Finding the best normal order and prime form becomes considerably faster at the piano. More important, as you work at the analysis, you hear the sound of the set and gradually learn to associate the sounds with the set classes.

MUSIC FROM THE CHAPTER IN CHRONOLOGICAL CONTEXT

Year	Composer	Work	Reference
1909	**Schoenberg**	**Three Piano Pieces, Op. 11**	**pp. 170, 173**
1912	Schoenberg	*Pierrot Lunaire*	Expressionism
1913	Stravinsky	*Rite of Spring*	Primitivism
1913	**Anton Webern**	**Six Bagatelles for String Quartet**	**p. 184**
1930	Stravinsky	*Symphony of Psalms*	Neoclassicism
1935	Berg	Violin Concerto	Serialism
1952	John Cage	*4'33"*	Chance Music
1954	Edgard Varèse	*Poème Electronique*	Electronic Music
1961	Krzysztof Penderecki	*Threnody: To the Victims of Hiroshima*	Aleatoric Music
1964	Terry Riley	*In C*	Minimalism
1974	**Ellen Taaffe Zwilich**	**Sonata in Three Movements**	**p. 183**

Works in **bold** are from the chapter; those not in bold are landmark pieces written around the same time.

NOTES

1. Allen Forte, *The Structure of Atonal Music.*

2. The conventions for notating normal orders and other constructs introduced in this chapter are still in flux. Your instructor may wish to employ other conventions that are equally useful.

3. Webern, *The Path to the New Music*, p. 51.

★

EXERCISES

Part A: Fundamentals

1. Transpose each unordered PC set by the PCI indicated by adding the PCI to each PC. Remember to use mod 12 arithmetic in order to keep your answers in the range of 0 to 11. You do not need to put the sets into normal order.

    Example: (7,9,6,1,2) by PCI 9 = (4,6,3,10,11)

    (a) (6,1,4,2) by PCI 6

    (b) (3,9,6,4) by PCI 3

    (c) (10,11,3,6) by PCI 2

    (d) (8,2,1,5) by PCI 7

    (e) (4,5,7,1,6) by PCI 8

    (f) (5,4,0,9,7) by PCI 11.

2. Analyze the pitches in each exercise below as a single PC set. Notate the set in its normal order and in its best normal order (which may or may not be different). Above the best normal order provide the prime form (as in [0157]) and below it provide the Forte label (as in 4-16) from the Appendix.

3. Provide the interval-class vector for each set in Exercise A-2.

4. Classify each set from Exercise A-2 as (a) transpositionally symmetrical, (b) inversionally symmetrical, (c) both transpositionally and inversionally symmetrical, or (d) neither transpositionally nor inversionally symmetrical.

5. Which two sets in Exercise A-2 are Z related?

6. Notate the four trichordal subsets that can be derived from Exercise A–2f. Notate them in normal order, not in best normal order. Which two belong to the same set class?

7. There are 12 trichord set classes. See if you can list their prime forms without referring to the Appendix. Be sure that none are related by inversion.

8. Construct an inversion matrix for this PC set: (G,A♭,C,E). Is this set inversionally symmetrical? How can you tell from looking at the matrix? At what transposition level(s) will the inversion have no invariant PCs?

Part B: Analysis

1. See Example 3-15 (p. 50). What tetrachord type (prime form) is featured in the piano?

2. See Example 3-21 (p. 54). What trichord type (prime form) is featured in this passage from a tonal composition by Debussy?

3. See Example 3-27 (p. 57). What is the prime form of this hexachord? Is this set class transpositionally symmetrical, inversionally symmetrical, or both?

4. See Example 3-29 (p. 59). The same two tetrachord types appear in each measure on beats 1 and 2. What are the prime forms of these tetrachords? Are either or both of them transpositionally and/or inversionally symmetrical?

5. See Example 3-B-8 (p. 66). We saw in connection with Example 9-18 that the music alternates between [0137] and [0146] in the first two measures. What trichord type is found in the right hand in those measures? What set class ends the piece?

6. See Example 4-1 (p. 70). What tetrachord begins the flute part? The voice part? Where is the first aggregate completed? Is this a structurally significant location, such as a climactic pitch or the end of a phrase?

7. See Example 4-4 (p. 73). What trichord type appears under each of the three phrase marks?

8. See Example 4-5 (p. 73). Using reasonable segmentations of the bassoon part, find two recurrent tetrachords.

9. See Example 4-B-1 (p. 84). One way to segment this would be into three tetrachords and a final trichord. Analyze each one.

10. See Example 4-B-2 (p. 85). Analyze this melody in terms of set classes and large scale (mostly chromatic) motion.

11. See Example 5-3 (p. 93). What trichord type is most prominent in this excerpt?

12. See Example 9-1 (p. 170). Where in this excerpt is the first aggregate completed? Is this a structurally significant location?

13. Takemitsu: *And then I knew 'twas Wind* (1992), mm. 1–10 (harp).

Takemitsu presents some of the important pitch material in this piece in m. 1, where six pitch classes are heard. Determine the set class of this hexachord, and then analyze the set classes of the circled trichords in the following measures. All of the pitch material in mm. 3–10 comes from m. 1 except for the mysterious B♮ in m. 8.

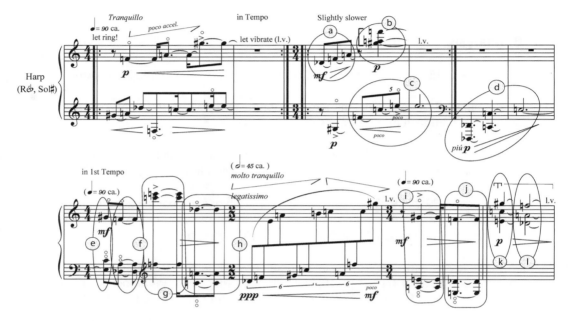

14. Crumb: Madrigals, Book I (1965), No. 1, "To see you naked is to remember the earth," mm. 1–6 (see p. 227).

This excerpt is based primarily on one set class. Decide what that set class is and mark its occurrences in the music. Try to make your segmentations musically justifiable.

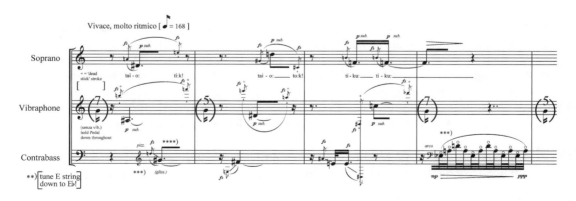

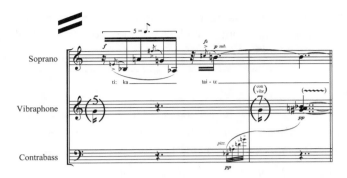

Part C: Composition

1. Compose an instrumental melody based on the [0157] tetrachord in various transpositions and in inversion. Every fourth note should be the end of one statement of the tetrachord and the beginning of another:

Because the [0157] tetrachord has an interval-class vector of <110121>, your melody can have a good deal of intervallic variety. Include an analysis of your melody.

2. Continue the example below or compose one of your own, basing the passage on a single trichord type, used both melodically and harmonically. Circle all occurrences of the set. The trichord used in the example is [016].

3. Compose a fanfare for three trumpets, based on one melodic trichord type and a different harmonic trichord type. Label all of the trichords.

4. Compose a harmonic "progression" in four parts using a single tetrachord type. The pitch content of each chord should be a transposition of the preceding one, and you are to use all six ICs as intervals of transposition. Label the transpositions.

Keep any invariant pitch classes in the same voices, and move the remaining voices as smoothly as possible. What is the interval-class vector of your tetrachord? How does that ICV relate to the invariants?

FURTHER READING

Cope, David. *Techniques of the Contemporary Composer*. See Chapter 7, Pitch–Class Sets.

Forte, Allen. *The Structure of Atonal Music*. See Part I, Pitch–Class Sets and Relations.

Kostka, Stefan, and Dorothy Payne. *Tonal Harmony with an Introduction to Twentieth-Century Music*. See pp. 541–552.

Lansky, Paul, and George Perle. "Atonality," in Stanley Sadie, Ed., *The New Grove Dictionary of Music and Musicians*.

Lester, Joel. *Analytic Approaches to Twentieth-Century Music*. See Unit 2, Pitch Structures.

Perle, George. *Serial Composition and Atonality*. See Chapter 2, "Free" Atonality.

Rahn, John. *Basic Atonal Theory*.

Schmalfeldt, Janet. *Berg's Wozzeck*. See pp. 14–24.

Simms, Bryan R. *Music of the Twentieth Century*. See Chapter 2, Harmonic and Motivic Associations and the "Emancipation of Dissonance" section.

Straus, Joseph N. *Introduction to Post-Tonal Theory*. See Chapter 2, Pitch–Class Sets.

Winold, Allen. *Harmony: Patterns and Principles*. See Chapter 28, Integer Notation and Analysis.

Wittlich, Gary. "Sets and Ordering Procedures in Twentieth-Century Music," in Gary Wittlich, Ed., *Aspects of Twentieth-Century Music*. See pp. 455–470.

CHAPTER 10

Classical Serialism

INTRODUCTION

When Schoenberg composed the first twelve-tone piece in the summer of 1921,[1] the "Prelude" to what would eventually become his Suite, Op. 25 (1923), he carried to a conclusion the developments in chromaticism that had begun many decades earlier. The assault of chromaticism on the tonal system had led to the nonsystem of free atonality, and now Schoenberg had developed a "method [he insisted it was not a 'system'] of composing with twelve tones which are related only with one another."[2]

Free atonality achieved some of its effect through the use of aggregates, as we have seen, and many atonal composers seemed to have been convinced that atonality could best be achieved through some sort of regular recycling of the 12 pitch classes. But it was Schoenberg who came up with the idea of arranging the 12 pitch classes into a particular series, or row, that would remain essentially constant throughout a composition.

Various twelve-tone melodies that predate 1921 are often cited as precursors of Schoenberg's tone row, a famous example being the fugue theme from Richard Strauss's *Thus Spake Zarathustra* (1895). A less famous example, but one closer than Strauss's theme to Schoenberg's method, is seen in Example 10-1. Notice that Ives holds off the last pitch class, C, for three and a half measures until its dramatic entrance in m. 68.

In the music of Strauss and Ives the 12-note theme is a curiosity, but in the music of Schoenberg and his followers the 12-note row is a basic shape that can be presented in four well-defined ways, thereby assuring a certain unity in the pitch domain of a composition.

This chapter presents the basics of "classical" serialism, the serial technique developed by Schoenberg and adopted by Webern and Berg (somewhat more freely by the latter), as well as many other composers. Chapter 13 will deal with more advanced serial topics, concentrating on integral serialism.

EXAMPLE 10-1 Ives: *Three-Page Sonata* (1905), mm. 62–68

Copyright © 1949 Mercury Music Corporation. Used by permission of the publisher.

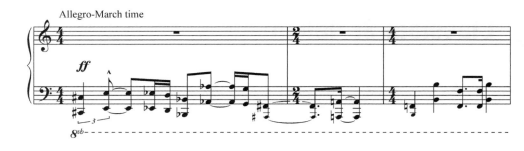

BASIC TERMINOLOGY

The core of the twelve-tone system is the **tone row** (**basic set**, **series**), an ordered arrangement of the 12 pitch classes (not 12 pitches), with each one occurring once and only once. The row itself has four basic forms:

1. **Prime:** the original set (not to be confused with the prime form of an unordered set, discussed in Chapter 9)
2. **Retrograde:** the original set in reverse order
3. **Inversion:** the mirror inversion of the original set
4. **Retrograde Inversion:** the inversion in reverse order.

The row that Schoenberg used for his first serial work is shown in its four basic forms in Example 10-2. The notes could have been written here in any octave and with enharmonic spellings—it would still be the same row. We follow the convention in this and in similar examples of omitting natural signs; any note without an accidental is natural. The numbers under the notes are called **order numbers** and simply indicate each note's position in the row form. We use the integers 0 through 11 (rather than 1 through 12) for order numbers in order to be consistent with PC numbers and to lay the groundwork for some more advanced serial operations that are beyond the scope of this book.

In addition, each of the four basic forms has 12 transpositions—that is, each one may be transposed to begin with any of the 12 pitch classes—so a single row has 4 × 12, or 48, versions that are available to the composer. In simple terms, a twelve-tone work consists of the presentation of various row forms at various transpositions, though the details of how this is done vary from composer to composer and from piece to piece.

EXAMPLE 10-2 Schoenberg: Suite, Op. 25 (1923), row forms

Used by permission of Belmont Music Publishers.

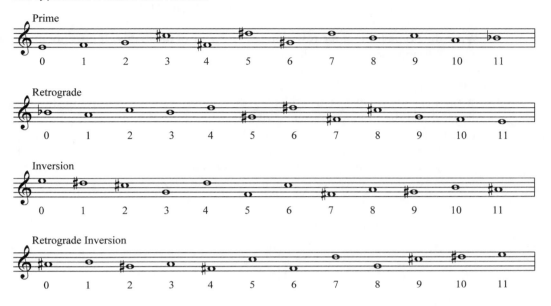

When analyzing a serial composition we label the row forms using abbreviations:

P = prime
R = retrograde
I = inversion
RI = retrograde inversion.

After the abbreviation comes a number, from 0 to 11, which specifies the transposition level of the row. A prime form or an inversion that begins on C would have a transposition level of 0 (P-0 or I-0), one beginning on C♯/D♭ would have a transposition level of 1 (P-1 or I-1), and so on, to the pitch class B, which is represented by an 11. However, the transpositional level of an R or RI form is indicated by the pitch class that *ends* the row: R-0 and RI-0 would both *end* with a C because they are the retrogrades of P-0 and I-0.[3] Therefore, the row forms in Example 10-2 are P-4, R-4, I-4, and RI-4.

THE TWELVE-TONE MATRIX

It is sometimes helpful when composing or analyzing serial music to be able to see all 48 versions of the row. The **matrix**, or "magic square," allows you to see all 48 versions after writing out only 12 of them. Example 10–3 is the matrix for the row for Schoenberg's Suite. The prime forms can be read from left to right along the rows of the matrix, while the retrogrades are read from right to left. The inversions are read along the columns from top to bottom, and the retrograde inversions from bottom to top. The transposition number is next to the first note of each row form. Looking down the left-hand side of the matrix, you can see that P-4 begins on E, P-3 on D♯, P-1 on C♯, and so on. There are several ways to fill in a twelve-tone matrix. Here is one of them:

1. Write the prime form of the row along the top row of the matrix. It does not matter what transposition level you choose.
2. Fill in the main diagonal (the one that runs from upper left to lower right) with the first PC in the top row of the matrix.
3. In the next row of the matrix, identify the interval between the PC in the main diagonal and the PC immediately above it.
4. Transpose the other 11 PCs of that row by the same interval. Use simple spellings (not B♯ or F♭, for example), and make sure that there are exactly five PCs with accidentals when you finish the row. (In Example 10-3, we have used all sharps, but you could use all flats or a combination of the two.)

EXAMPLE 10-3 Matrix for Schoenberg's Suite, Op. 25

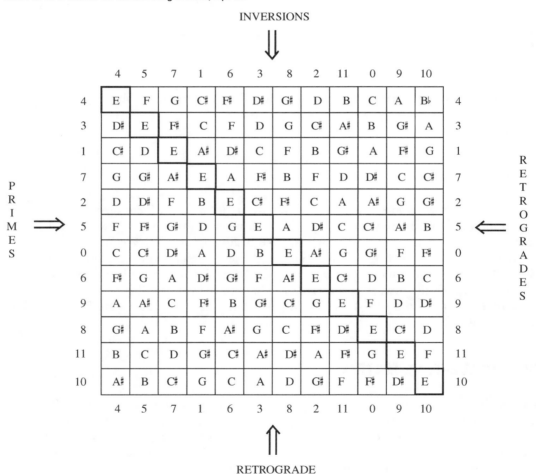

5. Repeat Steps 3 and 4 until all 12 rows have been filled.
6. Fill in the transposition levels along the top and left borders (only), with C = 0, C♯/D♭ = 1, and so on.
7. Copy the numbers from the left border onto the right border, and from the top border to the bottom one.

You may prefer to use PC numbers instead of letter names when you make a matrix. In that case, Step 4 will involve mod 12 addition and subtraction; otherwise, the method would be the same.

A FIRST EXAMPLE

Before going on to some more technical information, it would probably be of interest at this point to see how Schoenberg used the row we have been discussing. The beginning of the work is given in Example 10-4. Because this is the first serial piece that Schoenberg composed, you might expect it to be fairly simple in terms of row usage, but this is really not the case. While reading the discussion of the example, it would be good practice for you to add the order numbers 0 through 11 to the example for each row, using Example 10-3 as a reference.

The "Prelude" is the first movement of the Suite, and the first row form to be used is P-4. Here the first row occurs in the treble clef, beginning on E5 and ending on B♭3. P-4 is accompanied at the beginning by P-10, and the careful listener will hear the imitation between the two voices at this point:

P-4:   E   F   G   D♭

P-10   B♭   C♭   D♭   G

P-10 continues toward the end of m. 2 with notes 4–7 in the tenor voice: C–A–D–G♯, in imitation of G♭–E♭–A♭–D in the soprano, while beneath the tenor the bass sounds notes 8–11: F–F♯–E♭–E. Notice that notes 8–11 here do not follow notes 4–7, but occur simultaneously with them.

The B♭ that ends P-4 becomes the bass for a time, and it also serves as the first note of I-10, the next row form. Trace notes 0–3 of this row form, B♭–A–G–D♭, as they move from the bottom staff to the top staff and finally, in m. 5, to the melody. Some listeners would be able to recognize that the 16th-note line, B♭3–A3–G4, is the inversion of the opening motive, E5–F5–G4, and that G–D♭ occurs here in the same octave as in m. 1. The highest voice from the end of m. 3 through m. 4 is made up from notes 4–7 of I-10, A♭–C♭–G♭–C, while the alto has notes 8–11, E♭–D–F–E.

To recapitulate: We have seen that P-4 and P-10 were used in counterpoint at the beginning, whereas in the next measures a single row form, I-10, accompanied itself. We have also seen that the row does not always have to proceed strictly from the first note to the last, but instead that segments of the row may appear simultaneously.

EXAMPLE 10-4 Schoenberg: Suite, Op. 25 (1923), Prelude, mm. 1–5

Used by Permission of Belmont Music Publishers.

ANALYZING A ROW

Because the tone row serves as the source of the pitch material of a composition, we really should analyze the row itself before beginning the analysis of the piece. The first step should be to play (or sing) it several times. Listen for sequences or familiar patterns. In general, composers avoid using in a row any combination of pitches that would recall tonal music, such as triads, scale segments, and traditional bass or melodic formulas. If the composer chooses to include such patterns, as occasionally happens, you should make note of this and its effect on the music. For example, play through the series Berg used for his *Lyric Suite* (1926):

F	E	C	A	G	D	G#	C#	D#	F#	A#	B
0	1	2	3	4	5	6	7	8	9	10	11

This row contains triads on A minor and D# minor, and the row ends with a figure that suggests a B tonality, F#–A#–B. (The end of the retrograde, C–E–F, would suggest an F tonality.) The first hexachord (the first six notes) is diatonic to C major or F major, and the second hexachord is diatonic to F# major or B major. Schoenberg's row (Example 10-2) contains fewer tonal references, but it ends with the retrograde of the famous B–A–C–H motive (in German B♭ is written as B, and B♮ as H), and we might expect Schoenberg to do something with this in the piece.

The next step in the analysis might be to label the ICs (interval classes; review Chapter 9) found between adjacent notes of the row. For instance, for Schoenberg's Op. 25 we find:

IC:	1	2	6	5	3	5	6	3	1	3	1
Note: E	F	G	C#	F#	D#	G#	D	B	C	A	Bb

Totals:	ICI	IC2	IC3	IC4	IC5	IC6
	3	1	3	0	2	2

We see from the totals (do not confuse this interval tabulation with the interval vector, discussed in Chapter 9) that there are no appearances of IC4 (major 3rd or minor 6th) and that IC1 (minor 2nd, major 7th) and IC3 (minor 3rd, major 6th) predominate. Some rows are composed so as to emphasize particular intervals, as is the case here, while others are not. The **all-interval row** contains one occurrence of each of the 11 pitch–class intervals. For example, consider the row from Berg's *Lyric Suite*:

PCI:	11	8	9	10	7	6	5	2	3	4	1
	F	E	C	A	G	D	G#	C#	D#	F#	A#	B

If the row that you are analyzing has two of each IC except for IC6, which appears once, check to see if it is an all-interval row.[4]

Some rows use the first three, four, or six notes as a pattern from which the rest of the row is derived; such a row is called a **derived row**. In such a set the pattern is transposed, inverted, retrograded, or inverted and retrograded to "generate" the remainder of the set. For example, the first hexachord of Berg's row from the *Lyric Suite* in the previous paragraph in retrograde and transposed by a tritone would produce the second hexachord, so the row is a derived set. The row of Webern's Concerto, Op. 24 (1934), is generated by applying the RI, R, and I operations to the first trichord:

B	Bb	D	Eb	G	F#	G#	E	F	C	C#	A
0	1	2	3	4	5	6	7	8	9	10	11
pattern			RI of 0–2			R of 0–2			I of 0–2		

Even if the row is not a derived set, it may well contain patterns that are transposed, inverted, or retrograded. Patterns of ICs or PCIs that are repeated or reversed may help us to find these pitch–class patterns. In Schoenberg's Suite the repeated 9–1 at the end of the row is caused by two overlapping statements of a trichordal pattern:

PCI:	1	2	6	5	9	5	6	9	1	9	1
Note: E	F	G	C#	F#	D#	G#	D	B	C	A	Bb
							[D	B	C]		
								[C	A	Bb]	

The pattern 6–5 within the row is reversed later as 5–6, and it is also part of a larger palindromic pattern: 6–5–9–5–6. Such patterns may indicate that a segment of the row is its own retrograde or retrograde inversion. Here the patterns 6–5–9–5–6–9–1–9 and 1–9–1 reproduce themselves under retrograde inversion. As it turns out, two of these segments are duplicated in RI-5, whereas the third is duplicated in RI-7, as shown in Example 10-5.

EXAMPLE 10-5 Recurring Row Segments

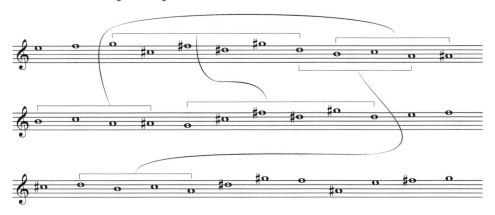

These patterns that we have found may have implications in the piece motivically, and in this case they certainly have implications in the area of **invariance**. An invariant pitch class is one that is shared by any two collections of pitches (two chords, for example). Similarly, an **invariant subset** is one that appears intact in two forms of the row. The order of the notes was not important when dealing with unordered sets in Chapter 9, but it is important when talking about rows. Looking again at Example 10-5, you can see that RI-5 is a reorganized version of P-4, beginning with notes 8–11 from P-4, then notes 2–7 and ending with notes 0–1. Each prime row transposition in the matrix has a similar RI "cousin," and there also are 12 similar I/R pairs. The matrix of a derived set may exhibit even more invariance. The row from Berg's *Lyric Suite*, for instance, has only 24 different row forms instead of the usual 48, because each R form is the same as some P form, and each RI form is the same as some I form.

The next step in a thorough analysis is to analyze the subsets in terms of the pitch-class set types we learned in Chapter 9. This is not the same thing as the row segment analysis we were doing above, because there we were looking for exact transpositions (or inversions, etc.) of row segments. Here we are looking for set types, and we know that the notes of a pitch-class set may appear in any order and may be inverted to find the best normal order and the prime form. For example, there are ten trichords in any row, the first one made up of notes 0–2, the second of notes 1–3, and so on, with the last one made up of notes 10–12. There are also nine tetrachords, eight pentachords, and seven hexachords. The set types contained in Schoenberg's row are as follows:

First note	Trichords	Tetrachords	Pentachords	Hexachords
E	[0,1,3]	[0,2,3,6]	[0,1,2,3,6]	[0,1,2,3,4,6]
F	[0,2,6]	[0,1,2,6]	[0,1,2,4,6]	[0,1,2,3,5,7]
G	[0,1,6]	[0,1,4,6]	[0,1,2,5,7]	[0,1,2,5,6,7]
C♯	[0,2,5]	[0,2,5,7]	[0,1,2,5,7]	[0,1,2,4,7,9]
F♯	[0,2,5]	[0,1,4,6]	[0,1,4,6,9]	[0,1,3,4,7,9]
D♯	[0,1,6]	[0,1,4,7]	[0,1,3,4,7]	[0,1,3,4,6,7]
G♯	[0,3,6]	[0,2,3,6]	[0,1,3,4,6]	[0,1,2,3,4,6]
D	[0,1,3]	[0,2,3,5]	[0,1,2,3,5]	
B	[0,1,3]	[0,1,2,3]		
C	[0,1,3]			
A				
B♭				

In practice, it is usually enough to analyze only the trichords and tetrachords; the first and last hexachords will always be either of the same type or Z related,[5] and most of the pentachords and hexachords overlap too much to be of interest. The trichord analysis shows us that [0,1,3] and [0,1,6] are unifying elements in the set; the composer might possibly make use of them as melodic motives or as chords to help unify the piece. The set [0,2,5], although it occurs twice, is less useful because its two appearances overlap. The tetrachords [0,2,3,6] and [0,1,4,6] also might fulfill a unifying function, although the two appearances of [0,1,4,6] overlap by two notes.

COMPOSITIONAL USES OF THE ROW

Rows are used in a number of ways in compositions. Generally, a twelve-tone work consists of the presentation of various row forms at a number of transpositions, the forms being used sometimes in succession and sometimes simultaneously. The notes may appear in any octave, and the order of the notes of each row form is usually preserved, but there are exceptions. Notes can be sounded simultaneously, as in a chord, and there is no "rule" as to how the notes in this case must be arranged. Repeated notes are not considered to alter the order of the row, and neither are tremolo figures—using two of the notes repeatedly in alternation. You may also occasionally encounter overlapped segments of a row (as in Example 10-4) and arbitrary reordering of the row for compositional purposes.

Because most music involves more than a single line, the composer must either present two or more row forms simultaneously or distribute a single row form among the various voices. Both of these approaches are widely used, which complicates the task of determining the original row at the beginning of an analysis. Turn back to Example 10-4 for a minute, and imagine that you had no prior knowledge of the row. You might notice that the melody in the right hand comes to a stop after 8 PCs (on the D) and that the left hand in the same passage contains 4 PCs, making 12 in all, so you would check out the possibility that the row has been distributed between the two lines. This could have been done in various ways, such as:

R.H. 0(E) 1(F) 2(G)   5(Db) 7(Gb) 8(Eb)   10(Ab) 11(D)

L.H.   3(Bb) 4(Cb)   6(Db)   9(G)

or

R.H. 0(E) 1(F) 2(G)   3(Db) 4(Gb) 5(Eb)   6(Ab) 7(D)

L.H.   8(Bb) 9(Cb)   10(Db)   11(G)

The first of these diagrams is the more commonly used method of distributing a row, but we could not rule out the second possibility. Even if we want to go ahead on the assumption that the first diagram is basically correct, we still would not be sure of the entire order, because some of the notes are played simultaneously (2–3 and 6–7), and notes in a simultaneity do not have to be arranged in any particular vertical order with respect to the row. In any case, we would have to analyze more of the piece to find the answers to these questions.

As it turns out, we can see that Schoenberg has not distributed the row between the two hands, because the eight notes in the treble and the four in the bass include only ten of the pitch classes: C and A are missing, and Db and G occur twice. Instead, P-4 continues through the Bb in m. 3, while P-10 is used in the bottom staff. In mm. 3–6 Schoenberg uses the other basic approach, which is to distribute a single row form among the voices. In this and in some of his other works, Schoenberg breaks his row into three tetrachords, which he then uses somewhat independently. That is, he might begin with the third tetrachord in some voice and introduce the first and second tetrachords later. Sometimes the order of pitches within each tetrachord is maintained, and at other times it is not. A more frequently used method is the one shown in the first diagram above, where the notes of the row are presented in order.

Turn back to Example 4-5 (p. 73) for an especially interesting example of row technique. (Remember that in this example the horn is written at concert pitch.) The excerpt, from Schoenberg's Wind Quintet, Op. 26, consists of three statements of P-3 (plus a final Eb) of the following row:

Eb	G	A	B	Db	C	Bb	D	E	F♯	G♯	F
0	1	2	3	4	5	6	7	8	9	10	11

Schoenberg distributes the notes so that the horn melody (the **H⁻** symbol designates the primary line) uses each member of the row only once (disregarding immediate repetitions):

Horn:	0		5 6		11 1	4	7	10

Horn: 0   5 6   11 1   4   7   10
Bassoon: 1 2 3 4   7 8 9 10   0   2 3   5 6   8 9   11
(Horn, cont.):   2 3   8 9
(Bassoon, cont.):   0 1   4 5 6 7   10 11 0

The resulting succession of 12 pitch classes in the horn forms a new twelve-tone row, drawn from but distinct from the original row.

Ernst Krenek demonstrates another approach in Example 10-6. The row on which this work is based is:

C	Eb	Db	Gb	D	Bb	A	Ab	B	G	F	E
0	1	2	3	4	5	6	7	8	9	10	11

Here Krenek keeps the initial pitch of P–0 as a pedal point, doubled at the octave, while the other instruments unfold the remainder of the row in a harmonic progression until the cadence on F. The next two measures (not shown) are similar, ending with a strong Bb–F cadence. Although this is a serial work, it is clear that the Cs here are acting as a dominant of the F, and both pitch classes are prominent at the end of the opera as well.

EXAMPLE 10-6 Krenek: *Karl V* (1933), I, mm. 1–4

ROW SUCCESSION

Although a composer has 48 row forms available, few twelve-tone compositions make use of all of them—in fact, some works use only the prime form and at a single transposition. One of these is another of Schoenberg's early serial works, the fourth movement from his Serenade, Op. 24 (1923), for voice and seven instruments. The text features 11-syllable lines, which Schoenberg sets to permutations of his row:

Line 1: notes 0–10
Line 2: notes 11–9
Line 3: notes 10–8
etc.

Not many twelve-tone works are so restricted, however. Most employ all four basic forms and several transpositions. One of the more difficult tasks of the analyst is attempting to determine why a particular row form and transposition have been chosen. It is not enough to put the label "R–3" on the score without considering why a retrograde form was chosen and why R–3 instead of some other transposition, even though we may not be able to find an explanation in every case.

Invariance is frequently a factor in the choice of transpositions. In the Schoenberg excerpt, Example 10-4, B♭ is the invariant pitch class in m. 3 between P-4, where it is the last note, and I-10, where it is the first. It is not uncommon for one or more pitch classes to serve as common tones between two row forms in this manner. Schoenberg's reasons for choosing P-10 as the first row in the left hand are not hard to guess. Presumably he chose imitation at the tritone as an effect analogous to the imitation at the dominant that is so much a part of Baroque style, and it offered the advantage of keeping intact the pitch classes that form the two tritones in the top voice:

G/D♭ answered by D♭/G

A♭/D answered by D/G♯

Also, Schoenberg's choice of I-10 and P-10 conforms to his overall plan for the work, which is to use only P-4, P-10, I-4, I-10, and their retrogrades. Each of these row forms begins on E and ends on B♭ (or the reverse), and each contains the tritone G/D♭ (or D♭/G).

Luigi Dallapiccola's overall plan for "Fregi," the sixth movement of his *Musical Notebook for Annalibera* (*Quaderno Musicale di Annalibera*) (1952), goes as follows:

1. Compose a melody for mm. 1–6 to be played by the right hand.
2. In mm. 7–12, invert that melody and give it to the left hand.
3. To carry the idea of inversion a step further, accompany mm. 1–6 with an I form, and mm. 7–12 with a P form.

The prime form of the row is:

A♯	B	D♯	F♯	G♯	D	D♭	F	G	C	A	E
0	1	2	3	4	5	6	7	8	9	10	11

Notice that this row has tonal implications (for example, the triads on B and A) that we might expect Dallapiccola to make use of. The melody in mm. 1–6 of Example 10-7 actually consists of two row forms, P-10 (mm. 1–4) and R-5 (mm. 4–7). Here the link between the rows is the E, which is the *second* note of R-5:

B	(E)	G	D	C	G♯	A	E♭	D♭	B♭	G♭	F
0	1	2	3	4	5	6	7	8	9	10	11

This allows a diatonic "progression" from the A minor triad at the end of P-10 to the E minor triad at the beginning of R-5. It also allows for a quintal chord (A–E–B) that is beautiful in context. All of this happens in the fourth measure of Example 10–7. The accompaniment in mm. 3–6 is provided by I-8:

A♭	G	E♭	C	B♭	(E)	F	D♭	B	F♯	A	D
0	1	2	3	4	5	6	7	8	9	10	11

EXAMPLE 10-7 Dallapiccola: *Musical Notebook for Annalibera* (1952), "Fregi," mm. 1–8

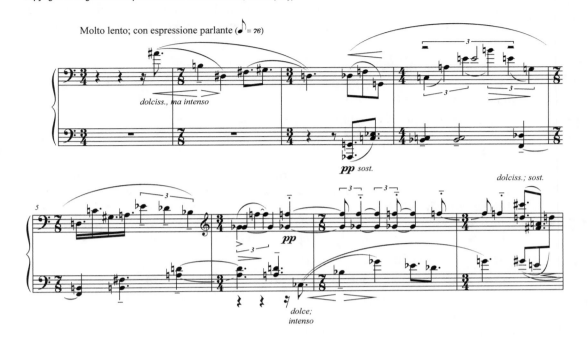

Just as P-10 is ending and R-5 is beginning in m. 4, I-8 in the accompaniment needs an E, the shared pitch class between P-10 and R-5. Dallapiccola puts the E for I-8 in the *top* staff, stem up, and all three rows come together at this point. The use of I-8 also allows the first half of the piece to end in m. 6 on an inversionally symmetrical sonority, A–D–Gb–F, or [0347], which means that when the first half of the piece is inverted to form the second half, the final sonority will be a (transposed) duplication of this one.

The only remaining row choice to be discussed is the transposition level for the inversion of the melody, which begins with the Cb in the bottom staff at the end of m. 6. The obvious answer is that I-11 is the only inversion that keeps the opening two dyads invariant:

P-10	(A♯ B)	(D♯ F♯)
I-11	(B A♯)	(F♯ D♯)

Another consideration might have been the nice Gb major-7th sonority in m. 7 formed by the end of R-5 and the beginning of I-11.

COMBINATORIALITY

Sometimes the choice of row forms or transpositions is governed by a desire to form aggregates (without duplication of pitch class) between portions of row forms. For example, in the following diagram, the row that Schoenberg used for his *Piano Piece*, Op. 33a (1929), is followed by its RI–3 form. Notice that when the second hexachord of P-10 is combined with the first hexachord of RI-3, they form an aggregate. In effect, we have created a new row, called a **secondary set**, by combining two hexachords from two different row forms.

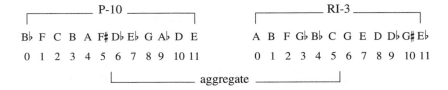

P-10

Bb F C B A F# Db Eb G Ab D E

0 1 2 3 4 5 6 7 8 9 10 11

RI-3

A B F Gb Bb C G E D Db G# Eb

0 1 2 3 4 5 6 7 8 9 10 11

aggregate

This combining of row forms to form aggregates is called **combinatoriality**, and it is an important aspect of some serial compositions. Most often, however, the combining is done *vertically*:

P–10:	Bb	F	C	B	A	F#	Db	Eb	G	Ab	D	E
I–3:	Eb	Ab	Db	D	E	G	C	Bb	Gb	F	B	A
	0	1	2	3	4	5	6	7	8	9	10	11

aggregate   aggregate

This diagram is seen in notation in Example 10-8. The first aggregate occupies m. 14 through the first two notes of m. 16, and the second aggregate occupies the rest of the excerpt. Notice that Schoenberg freely retrogrades or repeats row segments, as in C–B–A–B–C in mm. 14–15.

EXAMPLE 10-8 Schoenberg: *Piano Piece*, Op. 33a (1929), mm. 14–18

Used by permission of Belmont Music Publishers.

Schoenberg's row is so constructed that any pair of row forms that can be combined hexachordally to form twelve-tone aggregates can also be combined tetrachordally to form three sets of eight pitch classes each:

RI-3:	A	B	F	F♯	B♭	C	G	E	D	D♭	A♭	E♭
R-10:	E	D	A♭	G	E♭	D♭	F♯	A	B	C	F	B♭
	0	1	2	3	4	5	6	7	8	9	10	11

└──octachord──┘ └──octachord──┘ └──octachord──┘

Though this does not produce twelve-tone aggregates in the way that the combined hexachords do, the technique is similar. In Example 10-9 each pair of tetrachords occupies approximately one measure.

EXAMPLE 10-9 Schoenberg: *Piano Piece*, Op. 33a (1929), mm. 3–5

Used by permission of Belmont Music Publishers.

Other rows are constructed to produce tetrachord aggregates by combining three rows vertically, or trichord aggregates by combining four rows vertically; however, hexachordal combinatoriality is the approach most commonly used.

Combinatoriality guarantees a more controlled recycling of the 12 pitch classes, and to some it seems a necessary extension of the twelve-tone aesthetic. Schoenberg invented this technique, although he obviously was not using it in his Suite (see the juxtaposed G/D♭ and D♭/G in Example 10-4). Nor was Dallapiccola interested in combinatoriality in his *Notebook* (notice the duplicated G's in m. 3 of Example 10–7). In fact, most rows cannot by their nature be used combinatorially (except with their retrogrades) and must instead be specially constructed for that use. But combinatoriality has been of considerable interest to some composers, and a large number of pieces are combinatorial throughout.

THE ANALYSIS OF SERIAL MUSIC

In analyzing the use of rows in a serial piece, it is often enough to label the row forms (P-0, etc.) without writing the order numbers on the music. If the texture is complex or if some unusual row technique is being employed, it may be necessary to write the order numbers near the noteheads and even to join them with lines. Always work from a matrix. If you get lost, try to find several notes that you suspect occur in the same order in some row form, and scan the matrix for those notes, remembering to read it in all four directions.

It is important to understand that the labeling of row forms and the consideration of the details of their use is only a part of the analysis of a serial composition, somewhat analogous to identifying the various tonalities of a tonal work. Questions regarding form, thematic relationships, texture, rhythm, and other matters are just as relevant here as in the analysis of more traditional music. The music of classical serialism is not especially "mathematical," and it is not composed mechanically or without regard to the resulting sound or the effect on the listener. Probably the best way to appreciate the processes and choices involved in serial composition is to try to compose a good serial piece. The exercises at the end of this chapter will provide some practice at attempting this.

SUMMARY

The pitch materials of a serial work are derived from the 12-note row, so an analysis should begin with the row itself. Two special types of rows are derived rows and all-interval rows. A composition may make use of the prime form of the row, its retrograde, its inversion, and its retrograde inversion, each of which can appear at any of 12 transpositions. This pitch material may be conveniently displayed in the form of a matrix.

Row forms may be used compositionally in a number of ways. For example, a single row form may be distributed among the voices, or more than one row form may be used at the same time. The choice of row forms is often related to invariance or combinatoriality, among other reasons.

Analysis of serial music includes identification of the row forms and consideration of the reasons for choosing a particular row form and transposition, but a thorough analysis cannot be confined only to serial matters.

MUSIC FROM THE CHAPTER IN CHRONOLOGICAL CONTEXT

Year	Composer	Work	Reference
1905	**Charles Ives**	*Three-Page Sonata*	**p. 194**
1912	Schoenberg	*Pierrot Lunaire*	Expressionism
1913	Stravinsky	*Rite of Spring*	Primitivism
1923	**Schoenberg**	**Suite, Op. 25**	**p. 198**
1929	**Schoenberg**	*Piano Piece*, **Op. 33a**	**p. 207**
1930	Stravinsky	*Symphony of Psalms*	Neoclassicism
1933	**Ernst Krenek**	*Karl V*	**p. 203**
1935	Berg	Violin Concerto	Serialism
1952	**Luigi Dallapiccola**	*Musical Notebook for Annalibera*	**p. 205**

Works in **bold** are from the chapter; those not in bold are landmark pieces written around the same time.

NOTES

1. Jan Maegaard, "A Study in the Chronology of Op. 23–26 by Arnold Schoenberg." See the chart on p. 108.

2. Arnold Schoenberg, *Style and Idea*, p. 218.

3. Another approach (and one that was used in previous editions of this book) labels the first appearance of the row as P-0, no matter which pitch class it begins with, and numbers the transpositions chromatically from that pitch class. Also, some authors have employed the letters S or O instead of P for the prime form of the row.

4. Another type of all-interval row contains all of the intervals only if some of them are ascending and others are descending. The Dallapiccola row discussed in this chapter is one example.

5. The so-called "hexachord theorem." See John Rahn, *Basic Atonal Theory*, p. 105.

★

EXERCISES

Part A: Fundamentals

1. Suppose P-7 begins on G and ends on B♭:

Form	Begins on	Ends on	Form	Begins on	Ends on
(a) P-6	_____	_____	(e) I-1	_____	_____
(b) P-11	_____	_____	(f) I-9	_____	_____
(c) R-0	_____	_____	(g) RI-2	_____	_____
(d) R-5	_____	_____	(h) RI-7	_____	_____

2. Analyze the row from Dallapiccola's *Musical Notebook for Annalibera* (p. 205).

3. Analyze the row from Schoenberg's Wind Quintet, Op. 26 (p. 73), and construct a matrix.

4. The following set is P-10 from the first of Milton Babbitt's Three Compositions for Piano (1947). Analyze it and construct a matrix.

   B♭   E♭   F   D   C   D♭   G   B   F♯   A   G♯   E

5. Do the same for the following set, from Webern's Symphony, Op. 21.

   A   F♯   G   G♯   E   F   B   B♭   D   D♭   C   E♭

6. The following row consists of two [014589] hexachords (also referred to in Chapter 2 as the "hexatonic" or "augmented" scale). This row can be used combinatorially

with three transpositions each of the P, I, R, and RI forms of the row. Find the three transpositions of the P form and the three transpositions of the I form that will work combinatorially with P-3. You may find it helpful to construct a matrix before beginning.

Eb   Ab   G   B   C   E   Bb   A   C#   F#   F   D

Part B: Analysis

1. Turn back to Example 6–3 (p. 108). Note that each accidental affects only the note it precedes.

    (a) Analyze the row forms used in the excerpt using the matrix you constructed for Exercise A–4.

    (b) Is the row usage in m. 10 combinatorial? How about m. 11? Explain both of your answers.

    (c) Is a secondary set formed by the last hexachord of m. 9 and the first hexachord in the left hand in m. 10? If so, write out the secondary set. Does something similar happen in the right hand from the end of m. 11 through the beginning of m. 12? Explain.

2. Turn back to Example 2-B-3 (p. 36).

    (a) Analyze the row forms using the matrix you constructed for Exercise A-5. (*Hint:* Four row forms are used simultaneously.)

    (b) Is this excerpt combinatorial? How can you tell?

    (c) Is the excerpt canonic? Explain.

3. Schoenberg. Wind Quintet, Op. 26 (1924), III, mm. 8–15.

    This excerpt is a continuation of Example 4-5 (p. 73). We discussed the use of the row in Example 4-5 in the section titled "Compositional Uses of the Row," and you constructed a matrix for this row in Exercise A-3. This excerpt features a duet between the clarinet and horn, with a secondary duet in the flute and oboe.

    (a) Analyze the row forms in the clarinet and horn. The Eb in the bassoon is part of the first row, but the F# in the horn is not and may be ignored.

    (b) Compare the row usage here with that in Example 4-5. Be sure to review the discussion concerning that example.

    (c) Do you find any other similarities between Example 4-5 and this duet between the clarinet and horn?

    (d) Analyze the row forms in the flute and oboe.

    (e) In what ways is this duet similar to the one in the clarinet and horn? In what ways is it different?

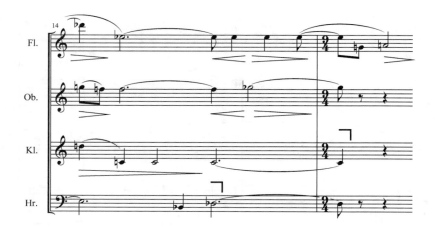

4. In discussing Example 10-4 we identified P-4, P-10, and I-10. What row form ends the excerpt? Remember (a) that this is one of Schoenberg's tetrachord pieces, in which the three tetrachords of a row form may be introduced in any order, and (b) the possibility of common tones linking the row forms. Use the matrix in Example 10-3 for help.

5. Webern: "Das dunkle Herz" (1934), Op. 23, No. 1, mm. 1–11.

    (a) In this song the row begins with the D that is the first note in the piano. Because of the chords that occur in that piano in the first two measures, you will need to do a certain amount of detective work to determine the correct order of the pitch classes. Once you have discovered P-2, construct a matrix.

    (b) Label all of the row forms used in the excerpt. Remember that notes may occasionally serve functions in two row forms, either in the same part (voice or piano) or between parts.

    (c) This piece is more concerned with the unifying effect of invariants than it is with combinatorial aggregates. For example, the vocalist enters on an F that has just been heard in the piano and then sings three of the notes contained in the chord at the end of m. 2 (G–E–E♭). Find similar pitch-class connections that help bring the voice and piano parts together. (Obviously, this technique has much to do with explaining why the various row forms were chosen.)

    (d) Use the pitch-class set terminology you learned in Chapter 9 to study Webern's use of motives. For example, the four-note chord is an important accompanimental motive. In terms of pitch-class set types, how do these chords compare? Consider the other motives in a similar fashion. Do not neglect the voice. Are there any motivic connections between the two?

es   fühlt   ihn   an   dem   dunk - len   Wur - - - - - zel - reich,

das   an   die   To - ten   rührt:

6. Play through and sing the row from Dallapiccola's *Musical Notebook for Annalibera*
   (p. 205) until you are able to sing it without accompaniment, then listen carefully
   to several or all of the movements from that work. In which ones is the unifying
   effect of the row apparent? How is this accomplished? Is there any particular part
   of the row that is more memorable, or perhaps more emphasized by the composer,
   than others?

Part C: Composition

1. *Evocation* (1966), by Hale Smith, uses the following PCs for the first appearance of the prime form of the row: (9 10 4 11 6 2 5 0 7 8 1 3).

    (a) Analyze the ten trichords formed by adjacent PCs trichords (9,10,4), (10,4,11), etc.

    (b) Two trichord types occur three times. Which one would be more useful as a unifying element? Why?

    (c) Compose the first three statements of P-9, emphasizing that trichord type.

2. Compose a twelve-tone row that avoids tonal references and is not predictable in its use of patterns. Be sure to do this at a piano or other instrument, and play (or sing) the row as you compose it.

3. Analyze your row, and construct a matrix. Then compose an unaccompanied melody for some instrument in your class, using three different row forms from your matrix. Label the row forms and transpositions. Try to emphasize in some way any recurrent subsets or other significant features that the row contains, and explain what you are attempting. Include tempo, dynamics, and phrasing.

4. Compose an instrumental duet using a single form of your row distributed between the two instruments in a manner similar to that used by Schoenberg in Example 4-5 (p. 73), discussed under "Compositional Uses of the Row." Try to give the duet a musical shape, with some amount of motivic unity and a climax in the second half of the duet. Analyze your work.

5. Use your row for a simple piano piece in a homophonic (melody-and-accompaniment) texture. Use different row forms in the melody and accompaniment. Label all row forms.

6. Compose a twelve-tone row in which the first hexachord contains the PCs C♯, D, E♭, F, A, and B♭. Put the notes in any order you choose, except that D should be the first note. The second hexachord should contain the remaining notes, in any order. Then compose a duet beginning with P-2 in one part and I-7 in the other. These two forms are combinatorial, so be sure to line up the hexachords to form aggregates. Then continue the duet with two different combinatorial pairs (such as P-4 and I-9). Label the row forms.

FURTHER READING

Antokoletz, Elliott. *Twentieth-Century Music*. See Chapter 3, Vienna Schoenberg Circle: The Twelve-Tone System.

Brindle, Reginald Smith. *Musical Composition*. See Chapter 12, Serialism.

——. *Serial Composition*. See Chapters 1 through 7.

Cope, David. *Techniques of the Contemporary Composer*. See Chapter 6, Serialism.

Dallin, Leon. *Techniques of Twentieth Century Composition*. See Chapter 14, The Twelve-Tone Method.

Fennelly, Brian. "Twelve-Tone Techniques," in John Vinton, Ed., *Dictionary of Contemporary Music*.

Griffiths, Paul. "Serialism," in Stanley Sadie, Ed., *The New Grove Dictionary of Music and Musicians*.

Kostka, Stefan, and Dorothy Payne. *Tonal Harmony with an Introduction to Twentieth-Century Music*. See pp. 552–562.

Krenek, Ernst. *Studies in Counterpoint*.

Lester, Joel. *Analytic Approaches to Twentieth-Century Music*. See Chapters 10 through 13.

Morgan, Robert P. *Twentieth-Century Music*. See Chapter 9, The Twelve-Tone System.

Perle, George, and Paul Lansky. "Twelve-Note Composition," in Stanley Sadie, Ed., *The New Grove Dictionary of Music and Musicians*.

Schoenberg, Arnold. "Composition with Twelve Tones," in *Style and Idea*.

Simms, Bryan R. *Music of the Twentieth Century*. See Chapter 4, Serialism, pp. 68–74 and 78–83.

Straus, Joseph N. *Introduction to Post-Tonal Theory*. See Chapter 5, Basic Twelve-Tone Operations.

Whittall, Arnold. *Serialism*. See Chapters 1 through 7.

Wittlich, Gary. "Sets and Ordering Procedures in Twentieth-Century Music," in Gary Wittlich, Ed., *Aspects of Twentieth-Century Music*. See pp. 388–430.

Wuorinen, Charles. *Simple Composition*. See Chapter 7, The 12-Tone Pitch System: Elements and Operations.

CHAPTER 11

Timbre and Texture: Acoustic

INTRODUCTION

It may be that the way post-tonal music *sounds* sets it apart from earlier styles as much as anything. This seems obvious, since music is about sound, after all, but what "sound" means in this context is a little narrower. Here we are referring especially to timbre and texture, two aspects of music that have received much attention from post-tonal composers. **Timbre** means tone color, and it can refer to the tone color of an individual instrument or of an ensemble. As we will see, the timbral ranges of both have expanded greatly since the Romantic era. **Texture** is a little harder to define, although most of us have a pretty good idea of its meaning. We could say that texture refers to the relationships between the parts (or voices) at any moment in a composition; it especially concerns the relationships between rhythms and contours, but it is also concerned with aspects such as spacing and dynamics. Not infrequently the line between timbre and texture is unclear, especially when a large ensemble is involved.

Some of the exploration of new timbres and textures, especially the former, was partly the result of outside influences—jazz and folk music, Asian and Latin American music. In fact, few really new instruments have been invented and successfully introduced since 1900, most of the exceptions being percussion instruments (the vibraphone, for instance). A very important exception is electronic music, an area significant enough to require its own chapter (see Chapter 12).

NEW TIMBRAL EFFECTS FROM TRADITIONAL INSTRUMENTS

Composers of post-tonal music have required performers to learn many new techniques of producing sound with traditional instruments, so many that we can only hope to provide a good sampling in this discussion.[1] One problem that has not been entirely solved at this point is how to notate many of these new techniques, although progress is being made here as successful approaches become recognized and imitated.

Some techniques have been required of all performers, regardless of instrument, including tapping on the instrument or on some other surface, whistling, and a wide variety of vocal sounds. In these cases the performer is not performing as a clarinetist, for example, but as a percussionist, whistler, or vocalist. In Example 6-10 (p. 114)

13 wind players whistle approximately the same pattern (the exact pitches are unspecified), but beginning at different times and proceeding independently. Notice also in the same example the use of glass crystals, or tuned water glasses. Electronic amplification, distortion, and processing are other timbral devices that can be used with any performing medium.

WIND INSTRUMENTS

Some techniques for winds used in contemporary scores are not entirely new but represent an intensification or development of earlier usages. This would include, for example, the use of mutes and glissandi. The brasses use a wider variety of mutes than previously, many of them of jazz origin, and even the woodwinds have been muted in a number of ways. The "bend," which might be considered a special type of glissando, also derives from jazz. Both the bend and the glissando were seen in Example 8-8 (p. 160), where the horn imitates a jazz trombone solo. Other techniques sometime associated with jazz include the flutter-tongue (see mm. 9–12 of Example 4-1 (p. 70) and the enharmonic trill, in which the performer rapidly alternates between two fingerings for the same pitch.

Removal of the mouthpiece permits performing on the mouthpiece alone, without the rest of the instrument, or performing only on the rest of the instrument without the mouthpiece. Wind players are also required to produce breath sounds through their instruments instead of pitches, and in some cases to sing and play simultaneously. Harmonics, though not practicable on brasses, have been used on woodwinds, especially the flute and the clarinet. Several of these techniques are illustrated in a lighthearted way in Example 11-1.

EXAMPLE 11-1 David Amram: Quintet for Winds (1968), III, mm. 106–111

Copyright © 1971 by C. F. Peters Corporation. Used by permission.

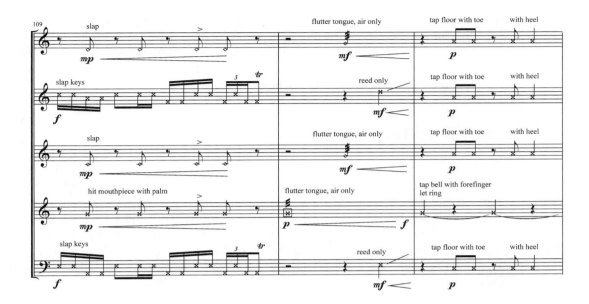

An important development, again available only on woodwinds, is the use of **multi-phonics**, the production on a single instrument of two or more pitches (as many as six are possible) simultaneously. Multiphonics rarely sound like the instrument played in a conventional manner. In Example 11-2 three flutes using multiphonics combine to produce chords of up to six notes. Notice that multiphonics are not simply two harmonics played at once. None of the multiphonics in Example 11-2 are produced as harmonics, and most of them create dissonant intervals, not the consonances associated with the harmonic series. Multiphonics are often difficult to produce, and in a footnote in the score Heiss suggests that the performers "secure the upper note" of each

EXAMPLE 11-2 John Heiss: Four Movements for Three Flutes (1969), III, mm. 40–45

Copyright © Copyright 1977 by Boosey & Hawkes, Inc. Reprinted by permission.

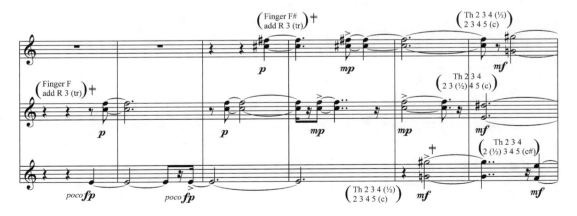

pair and "let the lower one sound more quietly if necessary." Notice also the fingering instructions in the score. Performance instructions such as these are a feature of many works composed since World War II. In his *Moz-Art* (1980), Alfred Schnittke even goes so far as to direct the oboist to certain pages of Heinz Holliger's *Pro musica nova* for instruction on performing the multiphonics.

STRINGED INSTRUMENTS

A large number of special effects are found in the contemporary string repertoire. As with the winds, these devices are in many cases not the invention of post-tonal composers, but they are employed much more frequently in contemporary scores. These would include the use of mutes, open strings, harmonics (both natural and artificial), nonstandard tunings (scordatura), multiple stops, and glissandi. In Example 9-B-14 (p. 190) the lowest string of the contrabass, the E string, is tuned to E♭ instead. The same excerpt also illustrates glissandi and natural harmonics. Remember that the contrabass sounds an octave lower than written.

The traditional pizzicato is still used, but other methods have been developed, including left-hand pizzicato, snap pizzicato, nail pizzicato, buzz pizzicato (the string vibrates against the fingernail), plectrum pizzicato (use of a guitar pick), and strumming. A device that might be considered a kind of pizzicato is silent fingering, in which the player only fingers the notes with the left hand, producing a subtle, semipitched sound. An early use of snap pizzicato is seen in Example 11-3, where the device is indicated by the small circle with a vertical line at the top. All of the instruments are being played pizzicato here, the viola and cello triple-stops being strummed. The arrows in the cello part indicate that the strumming is to be in descending fashion; the "O" specifies that the A3 is to be played on an open string.

EXAMPLE 11-3 Bartók: String Quartet No. 4 (1928), IV, mm. 45–51

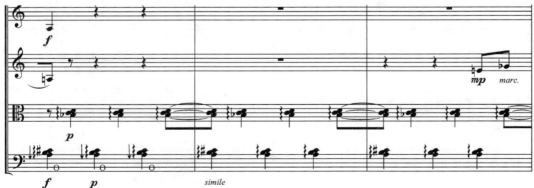

Bowing techniques in common use in post-tonal music include tremolo, bowing with the wood, various kinds of rebounding bow strokes, and nonpitched bowing, in which the idea is to obtain a scratchy sound rather than a pitch. In addition to bowing on the usual part of the string, the player may bow at the bridge, as in Example 9-20 (p. 184), or over the fingerboard, or the two may be combined in circular bowing. Other works call for the performer to bow between the bridge and the tailpiece, or under the strings, or on the body of the instrument. In his *Eight Colors for String Quartet* (1986–1988), Tan Dun asks the performers to produce a growling sound by pressing the bow on the strings and to beat the strings and fingerboard with their palms.

Penderecki's *Threnody: To the Victims of Hiroshima* (1961) is famous for its string techniques, among other things. In Example 11-4 each player performs a series of seven special effects as fast as possible. The wavy lines in some of the parts call for a slow quarter-tone vibrato, performed here on the highest possible note for each instrument. Seven special effects are specified in Example 11-4, and they appear in a different order in each of eight lines in the example. These effects, as seen in the top line of the ten cellos, are (1) strike the upper sounding board, (2) play the highest note on the instrument pizzicato, (3) play a fast tremolo between the bridge and the tailpiece, (4) play an arpeggio on the four strings behind the bridge *legno battuto* (beating with the wood of the bow), (5) strike the upper sounding board twice. (6) play the highest note on the instrument arco and tremolo, and (7) play between the bridge and the tailpiece.

New techniques have also been developed for those stringed instruments traditionally played by plucking: the banjo, the guitar, the mandolin, and above all the harp. In fact, according to Gardner Read, "No modern instrument . . . has undergone such a metamorphosis in the twentieth century as the harp,"[2] with many of the new effects being devised by one composer, Carlos Salzedo. These include a wide variety of glissandi and ways of activating the strings, as well as a number of percussive effects.

EXAMPLE 11-4 Penderecki: *Threnody: To the Victims of Hiroshima* (1961), mm. 6–7

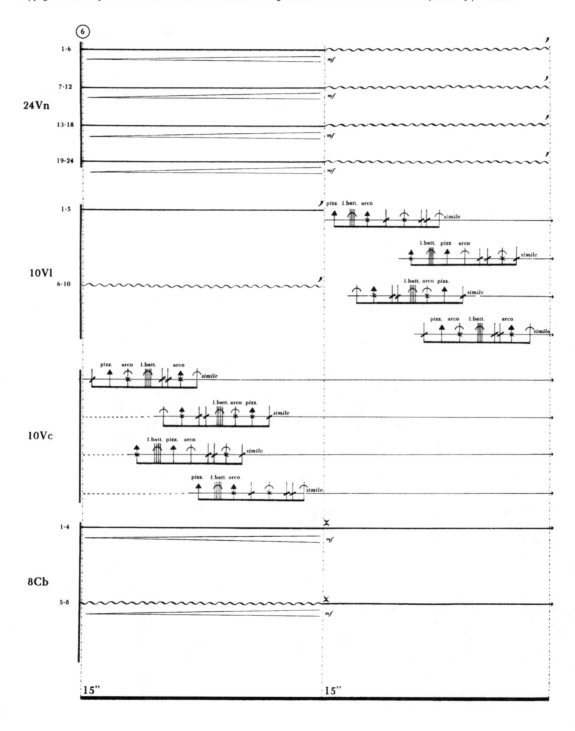

PERCUSSION INSTRUMENTS

One of the most important developments in post-tonal music is the greatly expanded role of percussion. There now exist a great number of percussion concertos, a genre that was unknown before Darius Milhaud composed the first one in 1929–1930. A representative list of more recent examples are the percussion concertos (not always titled as such) by James MacMillan (1992), Joseph Schwantner (1994), John Mackey (2000), Joan Tower (2001), Avner Dorman (2003, 2006, 2007), Jennifer Higdon (2005), Kevin Puts (2006), John Corigliano (2007), and Einojuhani Rautavaara (2008).

The percussion section of the orchestra, to be discussed in more detail below, has been expanded from the classical norm of one timpanist to a varying number of performers playing an ever-expanding array of instruments. Some of these instruments are newly invented, but most are instruments that already existed in Western music (in bands or folk music, for example) or in the music of other cultures. An incomplete but representative list of instruments that are now commonly employed would include the following:[3]

Pitched Instruments	Unpitched Instruments	
Almglocken	Anvil	Snare drum
Antique cymbals	Bass drum	Tam-tam
Brake drums	Bell tree	Tambourine
Chimes	Bongos	Temple blocks
Crotales	Castanets	Tenor drum
Flexatone	Claves	Timbales
Glockenspiel	Congas	Tom-toms
Marimba	Cymbals	Triangle
Musical saw	Field drum	Vibraslap
Roto-toms	Gong	Wind chimes
Timpani	Maracas	Wood block
Vibraphone		
Xylophone		

As if this were not enough, composers freely introduce sounds produced by everyday materials. Examples include a resonant piece of furniture to be struck with a club, silk and sheets of paper to be torn apart, a metal tray filled with dishes to smash, a wooden bowl filled with marbles to rattle, a tree stump to be hit with an ax,[4] and, in Tan Dun's *Paper Concerto* (2003), a large collection of instruments made out of paper.

The more traditional percussion instruments are now played in new ways. Most of these basically consist of unconventional methods of striking the instrument (rim shots, dead-stick strokes), unconventional beaters (wire brushes, knuckles), and striking the instrument in unconventional places (the casing, tuning screws). Dead stick strokes were illustrated in Example 9-B-14 (p. 190). Another interesting technique is the use of a bow to produce sounds from cymbals, gongs, and vibraphones.

The percussion ensemble is one of the more important new ensemble types created in the twentieth century. Example 11-5 is an excerpt from a famous early work for percussion ensemble, in this case an ensemble of 13 players, each player being responsible for at least three instruments:

EXAMPLE 11-5 Edgard Varèse: Ionisation (1931), mm. 75–81

Player	Instruments
1	Crash cymbal, bass drum, cowbell, high tam-tam
2	Gong, high tam-tam, low tam-tam, cowbell
3	Bongos, tenor drum, two bass drums
4	Snare drum, tenor drum
5	High siren, string drum
6	Low siren, slapstick, güiro
7	Three wood blocks (high, medium, and low registers)
8	Snare drum, high and low maracas
9	Thin snare drum, snare drum, suspended cymbals
10	Cymbals, sleigh bells, tubular chimes
11	Güiro, castanets, glockenspiel
12	Tambourine, two anvils, very deep tam-tam
13	Slapstick, triangle, sleigh bells, piano

The passage quoted in Example 11-5 features the pitched instruments, including the piano, which we do not always think of as a percussion instrument. Notice the clusters on the bottom staff. The use of sirens (performers 5 and 6) was innovative at the time, but perhaps is more amusing than novel to today's audiences.

THE PIANO

The piano has been a particularly fertile field for those interested in experimenting with new sounds. Clusters, introduced in Chapter 3, were at first only a keyboard device; early examples included Henry Cowell's *The Tides of Manaunaun* (1912) and Charles Ives's Piano Sonata No. 2 (*Concord*) (1915), which calls for the use of a board to produce the cluster. Piano clusters are typically either diatonic (white keys), pentatonic (black keys), or chromatic. The clusters in Example 11-5 are chromatic clusters, played with the forearm.

A much more extreme alteration of the piano's timbre is accomplished by means of a **prepared piano**, in which objects are placed on and between the strings before the performance. Although predecessors date back at least to Ravel, John Cage's *Bacchanale* (1938) is usually considered the first work for prepared piano. Cage's most famous composition for prepared piano is probably his Sonatas and Interludes (1948), a set of 16 "sonatas," each in two-reprise form, with four interludes. A detailed set of instructions explains how bolts, screws, and pieces of hard rubber and plastic are to be used to prepare 45 of the 88 available notes. For example, C4 is to be modified by (1) putting one bolt 14.5 inches from the damper between strings 1 and 2, (2) putting another bolt seven eighths of an inch from the damper between strings 2 and 3, and (3) inserting pieces of rubber between strings 1 and 2 and 2 and 3 at a distance of six and a half inches from the damper. The resulting sounds are difficult to describe, some of them percussive, others tinny, still others sounding like the gongs of a gamelan orchestra (an early example of the oriental influence in Cage's music). The score itself gives little impression of the actual sound of these pieces, so there is no point in reproducing a musical example here, but the student is urged to listen to this intriguing work at the earliest opportunity.

Clusters and prepared notes are both played by the pianist at the keyboard, but a large array of other techniques call for the performer to reach inside the piano. These include plucking, striking, and scraping the strings using the fingers, fingernails, drumsticks, and so forth. Henry Cowell was an innovator in this area as well, in pieces such as *Aeolian Harp* (1923) and *The Banshee* (1925). Piano harmonics are also possible, as is hand muting, and it is possible to create interesting sounds by pulling threads through the strings. Yet another way to produce sounds from the piano is to have another instrument played into the piano while the damper pedal is depressed, causing the sympathetic vibration of some of the strings.

THE VOICE

The best-known vocal technique that originated in the twentieth century is **Sprechstimme**, a method that lies somewhere between speech and singing. Schoenberg first used it in *Pierrot Lunaire* (1912), an excerpt from which appears in Example 5-8 (p. 98). The small "x" on each stem of the vocal part is the symbol commonly employed to specify *Sprechstimme*. Notice that the voice part is labeled "Recitation."

Singers are also required to make any number of vocal "noises"—grunts, shouts, and so forth—and even to perform multiphonics, as in Example 8-3 (p. 154). The computer part for Charles Dodge's *The Waves* (1985), a work for voice and computer, was derived in part from recorded vocal multiphonics and "reinforced harmonics," which Dodge explains as "intoning in such a way that arpeggiating among adjacent harmonics can be clearly heard above the fundamental frequency."[5] All of these are part of a general tendency to treat the voice as another instrument and not only as a means of presenting a text. Another illustration can be seen in Example 9-B-14 (p. 190) where the "text" is not language at all, but sounds specified by means of the International Phonetic System.

INSTRUMENTATION AND ORCHESTRATION

Music of the nineteenth century tended to be composed for several standard ensembles: orchestra, string quartet, piano trio, and so forth. Though all of these combinations still exist, their dominance of the compositional scene has diminished. For one thing, it is commonplace today to add or omit instruments as demanded by the composer's conception of the way a piece should sound. The instruments added to an orchestra, for instance, might consist of anything from saxophones to wind machines to a toy piano. A number of new "standard" ensembles have attracted the attention of composers. One of these, the percussion ensemble, has already been discussed; others would include chamber orchestra, the concert band, and the woodwind ensemble. A special case is the "Pierrot ensemble," consisting of flute, clarinet, violin, cello, and piano, named for Schoenberg's *Pierrot Lunaire* (1912) and frequently replicated by later chamber ensembles devoted to new music. In addition, numerous works call for an ad hoc ensemble—one that is unique, or almost unique, to the particular composition. Examples would include Debussy's Sonata for Flute, Viola, and Harp (1916) and Crumb's Madrigals, Book I, for soprano, vibraphone, and contrabass (1965), among many, many others. There are even a number of works that leave the instrumentation unspecified, such as Stockhausen's *Sternklang* (Star-Sound) (1971), for five groups of performers, each one consisting of four instrumentalists and/or singers and a percussionist. Nevertheless, a fair proportion of post-tonal works are for the symphony orchestra, and the next few paragraphs will outline some of the new approaches to orchestration.

An important development has been the expansion of the percussion section both in numbers of performers and, especially, in variety of instruments employed (see the section on percussion above). The more traditional orchestral instruments are expected to play in a much wider range than previously; the typical orchestral range has been expanded from about five and a half octaves to seven and a half octaves and more.[6] The conventional spacing of a sonority, with wide intervals at the bottom and fairly even distribution in the middle and high registers, is now treated as only one of countless possibilities. The opening chord of Stravinsky's *Symphony of Psalms* is a famous example of unconventional spacing (see Example 11-6).

EXAMPLE 11-6 Stravinsky: *Symphony of Psalms* (1930), I, mm. 1–4 (piano reduction)

Excerpted from the International Music Co. edition, New York, NY 10018.

The use of multiple divisi in the strings (see, for instance, Example 11-4) illustrates the greater reliance on orchestral performers as potential soloists, while the nineteenth-century preference for heterogeneous doublings—that is, doublings involving two or more of the three main instrumental choirs—has been discarded in many works in favor of pure colors. Doubling frequently involves unconventional pairings or spacing, as in mm. 2–3 of Example 11-6, where the melody is played by bassoon and flute two octaves apart.

Octave doublings were, of course, a necessary part of conventional orchestration. One could hardly score a triad effectively for full orchestra without a number of octave doublings, and bass and melody lines were frequently doubled at the octave. But octave doublings were generally avoided in atonal and serial music, especially by Schoenberg and his followers, no matter what the medium, giving their orchestral music a distinctive sound. Perhaps a more far-reaching contribution by Schoenberg was his notion of **Klangfarbenmelodie**, or "tone-color melody," in which progressions of timbres

EXAMPLE 11-7 Schoenberg: Five Pieces for Orchestra, Op. 16 (1909, 1949) III, "Summer Morning by a Lake (Colors),"
mm. 1–4 (reduced score)

would be equivalent in function to successions of pitches in a melody.[7] Schoenberg used
tone-color melody most systematically in the work from which Example 11-7 is
excerpted. In this example a single chord is sustained throughout the four measures in
two alternating timbres. An even more concentrated example of *Klangfarbenmelodie* is
"Etude No. 7" of Elliott Carter's Eight Etudes and a Fantasy for Woodwind Quartet
(1950), which consists of a single pitch (G4) heard in varying instrumental combinations,
dynamics, and articulations. Other famous examples of *Klangfarbenmelodie* include the
third movement of Ruth Crawford Seeger's String Quartet (1931) and Ligeti's *Lontano*
(1967), but these works also include sound-mass, to be discussed below.

To some people, *Klangfarbenmelodie* has come to stand for simply "the principle
of maximum variety of color,"[8] and as such is applied to music like that in Example
2-B-3 (p. 36). In the first six measures of that excerpt, the following solo timbres are
heard:

Clarinet (low and middle registers)
Horn (low to moderately high registers)
Harp
Violin
Viola (pizzicato)
Cello (pizzicato and arco)

Perhaps a satisfactory definition of tone-color melody would be "the constant
re-orchestration of a line or sonority as it proceeds through time." In Example 11-8 the
violas (not the solo viola), muted and (in mm. 4–7) bowing over the fingerboard, are

doubled at various points by clarinet, bassoon, and bass clarinet, creating a subtle sort of timbral modulation that might well be characterized as *Klangfarbenmelodie*.

Spatial effects, such as separating the performers into two distinct groups, are not unique to post-tonal music, but they are an important feature of many such works. This might involve multiple ensembles, as in Carter's Symphony of Three Orchestras (1977); offstage performers, such as the strings in Ives's *The Unanswered Question* (1906); or even performers located among the audience, as in Iannis Xenakis's *Polytope* (1967). Ideally, *Polytope* is performed as in Example 11-9, where the letters "A" through "D" represent the audience, the numerals "I" through "IV" represent the four small orchestras that perform the piece, and "X" represents the conductor. Space is equally important for small ensembles, and it is not uncommon for the score of a small ensemble to include a seating plan.

EXAMPLE 11-8 William Walton: Concerto for Viola and Orchestra (1929, 1962), I, mm. 1–7

EXAMPLE 11-9 Xenakis: *Polytope* (1967), Seating Arrangement

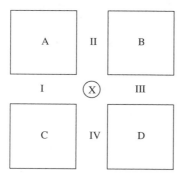

TRADITIONAL TEXTURES AND COMPOUND TEXTURES

Discussions of traditional musical textures generally sort them into three main categories:

1. Monophonic—a single line, perhaps doubled at the octave

2. Homophonic, meaning either
    (a) melody with accompaniment or
    (b) chordal texture

3. Contrapuntal—relatively independent lines, either
    (a) imitative or
    (b) free.

The traditional musical textures still exist, of course, and the vast majority of post-tonal music probably can be analyzed texturally using those categories. Sometimes textures are complicated by harmonizing the individual lines, and we will refer to these as **compound textures**. Debussy's music is especially rich in compound textures, although they certainly can be found elsewhere. One instance was seen in Example 3-B-2 (p. 63), where a three-part texture is thickened into 11 voices:

> Part 1: three voices on the immobile D–G–D in the highest register
> Part 2: five voices in similar motion in the middle register
> Part 3: three voices descending in parallel motion in the lowest register.

A more involved example is seen in Example 11-10, the final 17 measures of one of Debussy's preludes. A three-part texture is found in mm. 48–53:

EXAMPLE 11-10 Debussy: Preludes, Book I, "Sails" ("Voiles"), mm. 48–64

Très apaisé et très atténué jusqu'à la fin

(1), a B♭ ostinato/pedal point;
(2), a glissando/ostinato in the middle register;
(3), a melody in mm. 50–53 in the highest register.

The texture changes in mm. 54–57:

(1) and (2), continuing;
(4), a figure, G♯–E–G♯–G♯, harmonized with secundal chords;
(5), a figure, C–E–F♯, harmonized with whole-tone chords.

In mm. 58–61:

(1) and (5), continuing;
(4), shortened to two chords;
(6), a melody harmonized in parallel major 3rds.

In mm. 62–64 only two elements remain: the glissando (2) and the remnants of the last melody (6).

POINTILLISM, STRATIFICATION, AND SOUND-MASS

Pointillism, stratification, and sound-mass are approaches to texture that were developed in the twentieth century (although not without historical precedent). **Pointillism** gets its name from a technique used by some French painters in the nineteenth century that represented scenes by means of dots of color rather than lines. A pointillistic texture in music is one that features rests and wide leaps, a technique that isolates the sounds into "points."

A good example can be seen in the piano accompaniment in Example 10-B-5 (p. 213). Pointillistic textures for an ensemble frequently also involve *Klangfarbenmelodie*, because the changes in timbre cause the points of sound to seem even further isolated from each other. The texture of Example 2-B-3 (p. 36), discussed earlier in connection with tone-color melody, is an example of a pointillistic texture combined with tone-color melody.

Stratification is a term that has been used in musical discourse in at least two ways. One usage, perhaps better called "block juxtaposition," refers to abrupt successive changes in texture or in the basic sound of a passage. The other usage refers to very contrasting elements happening at the same time but in different registers—a sort of extreme example of a compound texture.

The term **sound-mass** is sometimes used for a chord in which the pitch content is irrelevant compared to the psychological and physical impact of the sound. The most characteristic examples of sound-mass (this term seems never to be used in its plural form) are large clusters, such as the ones in Example 3-24 (p. 56) or in the piano part in Example 11-5. But sound-mass can be created by other means as well—the brutal chords at the beginning of the "Dance of the Adolescents" in Stravinsky's *Rite of Spring* (1913) are actually polychords (E♭7 over F♭), but the effect created by the *fortissimo* successive down-bowed chords is that of sound-mass. Yet another kind of sound-mass can be created by extreme activity in a large ensemble, as in the hair-raising climax to Toru Takemitsu's *Asterism* (1968), where the effect is of every instrumentalist playing both loudly and randomly.

SPECTRALISM

In the early 1970s some composers, many of them working in Paris or Cologne, began to experiment with the notion of composing music in which sound—timbre, or tone color—would not be just a prominent element, but would instead be the main focus of the composition. Although many of its practitioners object to the term (just as Schoenberg objected to "atonality"), this approach became known as spectral music, or **spectralism**. Among the better known composers of spectral music are two of its originators, Gérard Grisey and Tristan Murail.

The term comes from "spectrogram," an image produced by a device called a spectrograph that allows the study of the relative amplitudes (volumes) of the harmonics (or partials) of a musical sound. Any pitched musical tone other than a sine tone consists of a fundamental pitch and a large number of harmonics above the fundamental, each one having a frequency that is a multiple of that of the fundamental. The relative amplitudes of the various harmonics largely determine the tone quality of a musical pitch. The

EXAMPLE 11-11 First sixteen partials of harmonic series above A1

beginning of a harmonic series with A1 as the fundamental is seen in Example 11-11. In actuality, the series continues upward to the limits of human hearing and beyond.

The only pitches in Example 11-11 that conform exactly to the equal-tempered scale are the A1, A2, A3, A4, and A5. This means that spectral composers, if they are going to use the fundamentals of musical sound as their materials, have to require the performers to play microtones. The offsets given above Example 11-11 show the direction and amount of offset (measured in cents) relative to the closest pitch in an equal-tempered scale. In Example 11-12, from a composition for two horns, one can see how the microtones that are native to the harmonic series might be realized in a musical score. In this work, microtones as small as an eighth of a whole step are indicated by nonstandard accidentals and arrows.

EXAMPLE 11-12 Grisey: *Accords perdus* (1987), II, mm. 17–18

Spectral composers typically reject the use of melodic motives as the source of organic unity in a musical work and instead look to the overtone series to provide that unity. The structure of the overtone series can be developed dramatically over the course of a work in many different ways. In Grisey's "Partiels" (1975), for example, the entire composition is based on partials of the same fundamental, and the dramatic shape of the work is formed by beginning with the consonances inherent in the lower partials and gradually replacing those with the dissonances found naturally in the upper partials, some of them shifted down one or more octaves, and many of them related microtonally to the lower partials. In Grisey's "Périodes" (1974), the overtone series is the source of its formal structure, as is shown in Example 11-13.[9] The relative durations of its eight sections measured in seconds are directly proportional to the size of the intervals between odd numbered partials in the overtone series measured in quarter tones. Example 11-13 measures the size of these intervals in quarter tones, and what follows the example shows how these quarter-tone intervals are translated into seconds to form the lengths of the eight different sections, A–H, as well as how these sections are ordered in the work.

EXAMPLE 11-13 The overtone series used in Grisey's "Périodes"

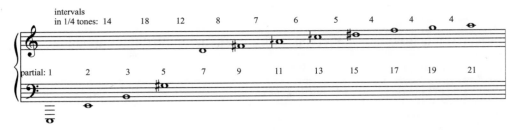

The intervals between partials in quarter-tones multiplied by 8 and their corresponding sections in "Périodes" (quarter-tone intervals are converted to time intervals in seconds):

intervals:	14	18	12	8	7	6	5	4	4	4
(× 8 =)	112	144	96	64	56	48	40	32	32	32
sections:	D	A	F	B	G	C	E	H1	H2	H3

. . . as realized in "Périodes":

A	B	C	D	E	F	G	H1	H2	H3
144″	64″	48″	122″	40″	96″	56″	32″	32″	32″

Elsewhere in the work Grisey creates some spectacular effects by employing an acoustical approximation of ring modulation, a technique used in traditional electronic music studios. Other spectral works borrow additional techniques, such as additive synthesis, from electronic music.

SUMMARY

Musical timbre has been greatly altered by post-tonal composers. The means of producing sounds with conventional instruments have been expanded to the extent that entire books are devoted to the new techniques for a single instrument. Ensemble timbre has been changed by these new techniques, as well as by the expanded role of the percussion section. Several new techniques of orchestral writing have been developed, among them *Klangfarbenmelodie*, or tone-color melody. Other important developments include the tendency to compose for ad hoc combinations instead of the standard ensembles, and the creative use of space. Traditional textures—monophonic, homophonic, and contrapuntal—continue to be important in post-tonal music. Other aspects of texture include compound textures, pointillism, stratification, and sound-mass. Spectralism is an approach to composition that uses timbre as the central element.

MUSIC FROM THE CHAPTER IN CHRONOLOGICAL CONTEXT

Year	Composer	Work	Reference
1909	**Schoenberg**	**Five Pieces for Orchestra**	**p. 228**
1910	**Debussy**	**Preludes, Book I**	**p. 231**
1912	Schoenberg	*Pierrot Lunaire*	Expressionism
1913	Stravinsky	*Rite of Spring*	Primitivism
1928	**Bartók**	**String Quartet No. 4**	**p. 220**
1929	**William Walton**	**Concerto for Viola and Orchestra**	**p. 229**
1930	Stravinsky	*Symphony of Psalms*	Neoclassicism, p. 227
1931	**Edgard Varèse**	*Ionisation*	**p. 224**
1935	Berg	Violin Concerto	Serialism
1952	John Cage	*4'33"*	Chance Music
1954	Edgard Varèse	*Poème Electronique*	Electronic Music
1961	**Penderecki**	*Threnody: To the Victims of Hiroshima*	**Aleatoric Music, p. 222**
1964	Terry Riley	*In C*	Minimalism
1968	**David Amram**	**Quintet for Winds**	**p. 218**
1969	**John Heiss**	**Four Movements for Three Flutes**	**p. 219**
1987	**Gérard Grisey**	*Accords perdus*	**p. 234**

Works in **bold** are from the chapter; those not in bold are landmark pieces written around the same time.

NOTES

1. An excellent survey, with references to a large number of scores, is provided by Gardner Read's *Contemporary Instrumental Techniques*.

2. Read, *Contemporary Instrumental Techniques*, p. 185.

3. A more comprehensive list is provided in Reginald Smith Brindle's *Contemporary Percussion*.

4. Read, *Contemporary Instrumental Techniques*, pp. 183–184.

5. Charles Dodge, liner notes to *Perspectives of New Music*, compact disc PNM 27.

6. Henry Brant, "Orchestration," in John Vinton, Ed., *Dictionary of Contemporary Music*, p. 543.

7. In his "Schoenberg's *Klangfarbenmelodie*," Alfred Cramer writes that our conventional understanding of the term is not what Schoenberg had in mind. Instead, Schoenberg thought of *Klangfarbenmelodie* as a kind of harmonic progression.

8. Reginald Smith Brindle, *Serial Composition*, p. 127.

9. Thanks to Mei-Fang Lin for bringing this example to our attention; it is published in Jérôme Baillet's book *Gérard Grisey: Fondements d'une écriture* (Paris: Editions L'Harmattan, 2000).

★

EXERCISES

Part A: Fundamentals

1. There is a pattern in the string techniques used in Example 11-4. Discover that pattern and the departure from that pattern that is apparently an error.

2. What scale (missing its D♭) seems to be the basis of Example 11-6?

3. Provide the prime form of the five-note chord in Example 11-7.

4. What scale is being used in Example 11-10?

5. Prepare a C4 on a grand piano according to John Cage's instructions given on p. 225. For the pieces of rubber you could use pencil erasers. How would you characterize the resulting sound?

Part B: Analysis

1. Debussy: Preludes, Book II, "Dead Leaves" ("Feuilles mortes"), mm. 19–35. In your analysis, consider the excerpt to be in three phrases: (1) mm. 21–24, (2) mm. 25–30, and (3) mm. 31–35.

    (a) Analyze each phrase separately in terms of texture and compositional techniques. That is, separate and identify each element of the texture and discuss the compositional techniques involved with that element. Be sure to include voice leading in our discussion where appropriate.

    (b) What scale predominates in phrase 1, even if it doesn't account for every note? And in phrase 2?

    (c) What is the tonal center of each phrase? How is it established? What elements are in conflict with it?

    (d) An F♯ major triad is the basis of phrase 3. What is the relationship between that triad and the other two triads in that phrase?

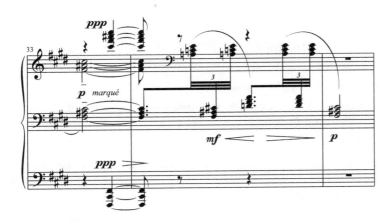

2. Carry out a textural analysis of Example 7-1 (p. 131). Use an approach similar to that in Exercise 11-B-1.

3. Listen several times to a recording of Ligeti's *Ramifications* (1969), for string orchestra. Then write out an analysis similar in format to that of Penderecki's *Threnody* (p. 222).

4. Listen to Grisey's "Partiels," discussed briefly on p. 234. Try to decide how many sections there are to the work and what creates the impression that a new section is beginning. Then write out an analysis as above.

5. The theme that is heard in mm. 1–2 of the "Fantasy" from Carter's Eight Etudes and a Fantasy for Woodwind Quartet (1950) returns in mm. 121–140, augmented and in a *Klangfarbenmelodie* setting. Devise a method to show through color-coding how the timbres vary in those final measures of the piece. The clarinet is in B♭.

Part C: Performance

Be prepared to demonstrate for the class a number of the new playing techniques that have been developed in this century for your instrument. You may find the following readings helpful in completing this assignment.

FURTHER READING

Bartolozzi, Bruno. *New Sounds for Woodwind.*

Brant, Henry. "Orchestration," in John Vinton, Ed., *Dictionary of Contemporary Music.*

Brindle, Reginald Smith. *Contemporary Percussion.*

————. *The New Music.* See Chapter 15, Colour—New Instrumental Usages, and Chapter 16, Vocal Music—The New Choralism.

————. *Serial Composition.* See Chapter 12, Orchestration, Texture, and Tone Color.

Brooks, William. "Instrumental and Vocal Resources," in John Vinton, Ed., *Dictionary of Contemporary Music.*

Bunger, Richard. *The Well-Prepared Piano.*

Cope, David H. *New Directions in Music.* See the section titled "Sound Mass Evolution" in Chapter 3, and Chapter 4, Instrument Exploration.

————. *Techniques of the Contemporary Composer.* See Chapter 11, Percussion and the Prepared Piano, and Chapter 12, New Techniques and Instruments.

Cramer, Alfred. "Schoenberg's *Klangfarbenmelodie*: A Principle of Early Atonal Harmony."

DeLone, Richard P. "Timbre and Texture in Twentieth-Century Music," in Gary Wittlich, Ed., *Aspects of Twentieth-Century Music*, pp. 66–207.

Dempster, Stuart. *The Modern Trombone.*

Dick, Robert. *The Other Flute: A Performance Manual of Contemporary Techniques.*

Erickson, Robert. *Sound Structure in Music.*

Fineburg, Joshua. "Guide to the Basic Concepts and Techniques of Spectral Music."

Heiss, John C. "Some Multiple-Sonorities for Flute, Oboe, Clarinet, and Bassoon."

Howell, Thomas. *The Avant-Garde Flute.*

Kennan, Kent, and Donald Grantham. *The Technique of Orchestration.* See Chapter 17, Special Devices.

Lansky, Paul, and Malcolm Goldstein. "Texture," in John Vinton, Ed., *Dictionary of Contemporary Music.*

Morgan, Robert P. *Twentieth-Century Music.* See Chapter 18, Innovations in Form and Texture.

Read, Gardner. *Contemporary Instrumental Techniques.*

Rehfeldt, Phillip. *New Directions for Clarinet.*

Salzedo, Carlos. *Modern Study of the Harp.*

Simms, Bryan R. *Music of the Twentieth Century.* See Chapter 6, Orchestration, Tone Color, and Texture.

Turetzky, Bertram. *The Contemporary Contrabass.*

CHAPTER 12

Timbre and Texture: Electronic

INTRODUCTION

The rise of electronic music is responsible for the most important development in musical timbre since 1900. In the course of less than two decades, music progressed from an almost total dependence on traditional musical instruments, some of which had not changed appreciably for centuries, to one that allowed the use of any sound that could be imagined or defined in acoustical terms. The effect of all of this development has been considerable in the area of concert and popular music.

The beginnings of electronic music go back at least to 1906, when Thaddeus Cahill installed his 200-ton Telharmonium in Telharmonic Hall in New York City, an experiment that was not a complete success. More significant in the history of electronic music was the development of the Theremin (1920) and the Ondes Martenot (1928), both of which were true electronic instruments. These instruments did make an impact, especially the Ondes Martenot, which was used in Messiaen's *Turangalîla-symphonie* (1948), as well as in works by Honegger, Milhaud, Boulez, and others.

But it was not until the first studies by Pierre Schaeffer and Pierre Henry in France (1948–1949) and the development of the tape recorder that the modern history of electronic music really got started. The technological innovations that followed during the next half-century had enormous consequences. For composers these developments opened a new and exhilarating soundscape never before available. As technology has become more powerful and more affordable, activities that were once the domain of government and academic institutions have become available to people working with personal computers. Radical notions of sound and music have become part of the sonic fabric of everyday life, stretching from mainstream popular music, to film, to alternative forms of rock and dance music, to continued explorations by contemporary concert composers.

CONCRETE MUSIC

Most electronic music is assembled in some way by the composer and stored on some medium for later playback. Originally, recording tape was used for both editing and storage. Over time, computers gradually replaced tape as an editing and storage medium.

Eventually, the computer became responsible for generating and processing sound as well. Two primary sound sources are available for electronic music. One of these is electronically or computer synthesized sound, to be discussed in the next section. The other is simply all of the sounds available in the "natural" world, including musical instruments, voices, steam engines, dripping water, burning charcoal, or whatever the composer might wish to use. Electronic music that uses natural sounds as a sound source is referred to as **concrete music** (or *musique concrète*).

Although the computer has taken over the means for manipulating sound (and has greatly expanded these means), early concrete music relied entirely on manipulation of the tape on which the sound had been recorded. Initial discussions of concrete music will focus on tape manipulation and the works that grew out of this early period. The process of tape manipulation typically involved several stages of recording, rerecording, and mixing. The alterations were basically carried out in five different ways, each of which can be combined with the others:

1. Change of tape speed
2. Change of tape direction
3. Tape loops
4. Cutting and splicing
5. Tape delay.

Change of tape speed. Playing a tape at a speed other than the speed at which it was recorded changes the pitch of the material recorded on the tape. Playing it at a speed greater than the original raises the pitch, while playing it at a slower speed lowers it. Tape speed on professional reel-to-reel decks is measured in **inches-per-second (ips)**. Playing a 15-ips tape at 7½-ips, exactly one-half the recorded speed, multiplies each frequency by one-half, lowering all of the pitches by exactly one octave. Playing a 33-rpm phonograph record at 45 rpm multiplies each frequency by 45/33, approximately 4/3, raising the pitch by a P4. When speed change is employed on a tape recorder that allows a wider range of speeds, a larger number of ratios can be produced, allowing more subtle graduations of pitch as well as glissandos. Change of speed also alters the timbre of a sound, because harmonics that were above the audible range in the original may become audible, or the reverse. Also, harmonics of sounds are related by multiples of the fundamental frequency. When the tape playback speed is changed, all frequencies change by the same ratio, changing the relationship between fundamental and harmonics. An entertaining work that uses prerecorded sounds played at various speeds is Kenneth Gaburo's *Exit Music II: Fat Millie's Lament* (1965), briefly described in Chapter 7 (p. 130).[1] Other examples include Otto Luening's *Low Speed* (1952) and Iannis Xenakis's *Concret P.H.* (1958).

Change of tape direction. Playing a recorded sound backward reverses its **amplitude** (loudness) envelope, so that a sound that normally "decays," like a note played on the piano, will instead increase in amplitude. An early tape piece employing change of direction as well as speed is *Incantation* (1952), which was composed in tandem by Otto Luening and Vladimir Ussachevsky.

Tape loops. A piece of tape on which a sound has been recorded can be cut out and the ends spliced together to make a loop. Obviously, the longer the sound, the longer the loop. When the loop is played on a tape player, the sound is repeated over and over, creating an ostinato. The tape loop in Steve Reich's *Come Out* (1966) is simply a recording of the words "come out to show them." Two copies of the loop were played on machines that ran at slightly different speeds, the loops beginning together and moving slowly out of phase with each other; the result was recorded and made into two loops that were played again on the same machines, and so on, the process being repeated until an extremely dense texture developed.

Cutting and splicing. By cutting and splicing, the composer can juxtapose sounds that are normally unrelated, or the envelopes of recorded sounds can be altered by cutting out and discarding the unwanted portions, a process that can disguise the source of the original sound more than one might expect. Juxtaposition of unrelated sounds can also lead to new rhythmic patterns. An example of a piece that uses cutting and splicing extensively is Cage's *Williams Mix* (1952), discussed briefly in Chapter 7 (p. 144). While most electronic compositions from this period emerged from the composer's studio as tape recordings ready for performance, *Williams Mix* is a detailed set of instructions for splicing together six different categories of prerecorded sounds, and every "realization" of the piece will be unique.

Tape delay. Echo effects can be achieved by playing a prerecorded sound on a tape recorder and simultaneously rerecording the sound on the same tape. Using either one or two tape recorders, the sound is channeled from the playback head back to a record head, usually with a reduction in amplitude, creating the echo effect. For this process to work, the erase head of the tape recorder has to be disabled so that the recording process does not erase whatever sounds already exist on the tape. A work that features tape delay is *I of IV* (1966) by Pauline Oliveros. Tape delay also can be done "live" in a concert performance, as in Jacob Druckman's *Animus II* (1969) for clarinet and tape and James Tenney's *Saxony* (1978) for solo saxophone.

THE CLASSICAL ELECTRONIC MUSIC STUDIO

The first studio for electronically synthesized music was established in Cologne, West Germany, in 1951, only a few years after the first experiments with concrete music. Although many people have designated concrete music a French tradition and electronically synthesized music a German tradition, the distinctions were hardly ever absolute. One of the early synthesizers, the Ondes Martenot, was a French development. Stockhausen, one of the leading composers associated with the development of the electronic studio in Germany, studied in Paris. Composers today feel free to employ any sounds, concrete or electronic, in their music. Stockhausen's *Song of the Youths* (*Gesang der Jünglinge*) (1956) and *Hymns* (*Hymnen*) (1967) stand as notable examples of works that employ both electronic and concrete sounds.

The "classical studios" of the 1950s and later all had their own configurations that reflected such things as the interests of the people who designed the studio, the state of the art at the time that the equipment was purchased, and constraints related to budget and space. The configurations of some studios were so distinctive that a connoisseur could sometimes identify where a composition had been realized just by the kinds of sounds that were used. The works composed at the Columbia–Princeton Studios in the 1960s and 1970s, particularly by Mario Davidovsky, epitomized such a recognizable sound that it led to widespread imitation. Davidovsky's *Synchronisms*, composed for different combinations of acoustic instruments and electronic tape, collectively and individually represent milestones of achievement from this period, particularly his "Synchronism No. 6" (1970) for piano and tape.

In general, most of the equipment found in a classical studio falls into one of four categories: sound-producing equipment, sound-processing equipment, controllers, and sound storage equipment. Oscillators, including noise generators, are the primary components for sound production. Sound processing was typically handled by envelope generators, filters, equalizers, reverberation units, and ring modulators. Sequencers and keyboards were typically used as controllers, so named because they allowed a composer to control a variety of sound parameters with one touch, or sequence of keys pressed. Keyboards were often modeled after acoustic piano keyboards, but in some cases the typical piano key layout was avoided so that a piano performance paradigm would not dominate compositional practice. Reel-to-reel tape recorders were an essential part of any classical electronic studio, providing a means for storing and editing electronically produced sound.

An **oscillator** is an electronic device that produces a fluctuating electrical signal, a **waveform**, at a controllable frequency. Different types of waveforms, named after the shape of the wave over time, produce different sounding timbres. Oscillators in a classical electronic studio could generally produce **sine waves** (a fundamental pitch with no additional partials); **sawtooth waves** (a fundamental pitch with all harmonics in the series); **square waves** (a fundamental pitch with odd-numbered harmonics); **triangle waves** (same as a square wave but with less energy in the upper harmonics); and **pulse waves** (a positive-amplitude-only type of square wave that had a variable number and energy level of harmonics based on the relative width of the positive pulse to the overall length of the wave). **Noise generators** are special types of oscillators that produce randomly varying waveforms, theoretically with all frequencies present. Different types of noise (white, pink, yellow) have different relative amplitude levels for the frequencies present. For example, the frequencies in white noise are all at relatively equal amplitudes to one another, but pink noise has equal energy per octave band of frequencies. Since frequency doubles with every octave, there are many more frequencies within higher octaves than lower octaves, giving white noise a higher sound.

Mixers combine multiple audio signals at varying amplitudes. Used not only to combine multiple musical passages, mixers are an essential component of **additive synthesis**, where harmonically simple sounds are combined to produce more complex sounds. Filters and equalizers reduce or increase the amplitude of some portion of the spectrum of a sound (for instance, the portion between 440 and 660 cps—A4 and E5— or above 1,000 cps). Filters are an essential component of **subtractive synthesis**. Conceptually the opposite of additive synthesis, subtractive synthesis starts with a harmonically rich waveform (usually noise, sawtooth wave, or pulse wave) and eliminates, or filters away, parts of the spectrum to produce the final sound.

Events such as a change in frequency or amplitude can be controlled manually by various means, including knobs (or **potentiometers**) and the **keyboard**, which could be used as a tunable electronic-organ keyboard or an arbitrary collection of switches. Events can also be controlled automatically by **voltage control**, an important aspect of electronic music since the development of the voltage-controlled synthesizer in the 1960s. A voltage-controlled oscillator will usually double its frequency (a change of one musical octave) when one volt is added to its control voltage input. One method of voltage control uses the fluctuating current of one oscillator to change or "modulate" the amplitude or frequency of another. For example, a very low-frequency sine wave, say at 5 cps, could be used as the *modulating signal* to control changes in frequency of another oscillator, perhaps one generating a sawtooth wave at 440 cps. The frequency of the sawtooth oscillator would change, positively and negatively, five times per second. How much the frequency would change depends on the amplitude of the modulating signal. The greater the modulating signal amplitude, the greater the change in frequency would be. If the frequency of the modulating signal is high enough, the change in amplitudes or frequencies occurs so fast that it produces new audible sound of its own, called **sidebands**, which may also be used compositionally. Another way to control the amplitude of a sound automatically is by the use of an **envelope generator**, a device that produces a signal that can be used to change a sound parameter over time. The kind of **sequencer** found in the classical electronic studio is a voltage-control device that produces one or more series of voltages that can be used to control frequencies, amplitudes, filter settings, or the speed of the sequencer itself. Often the series produced by the sequencer are used repetitively, resulting in a sound like that of a tape loop.

The **tape recorder** was an essential part of any classical electronic studio, for it is here that sounds are stored, either temporarily while a composition is under way, or permanently when the work is completed. Although cassette tape machines were sometimes used for producing copies in a convenient format, the professional-quality reel-to-reel tape recorder was the workhorse of the classical studio. These machines came in various configurations, with anywhere from 2 to 24 "tracks" (paths on the tape on which sound is recorded independently of other paths) using tapes ranging from ¼ inch to 2 inches wide at speeds of 7.5, 15, or 30 inches per second. Good-quality machines allowed for "overdubbing" (recording one track without erasing the others), and some allowed speed variations in small increments between the usual tape speeds. Today, digital recording has largely replaced analog recording. Digital recorders come in a variety of formats: tape recorders (two-track and multitrack), dedicated hard disk systems, and computer-based systems.

In the late 1960s modular voltage-controlled synthesizers began to replace the one-of-a-kind electronic studio as the standard. These synthesizers were designed to function as musical instruments as well as compositional devices. Their designs varied widely but usually included combinations of a variety of oscillators, filters, envelope generators, and other modules, all designed to work together as part of a single larger unit. Composers created sounds by using "patch cords" to connect the outputs and inputs of the modules to create sounds or even full gestures. Smaller units incorporated internal wiring matrices that allowed for connections to be made with buttons and switches. While the core modules were similar, different composers were able to create a remarkably wide variety of sounds, even on the same instrument. Two widely used voltage-controlled synthesizers were the Moog, used in Wendy Carlos's *Switched-On Bach* (1968), and the Buchla, used in Morton Subotnick's *Silver Apples of the Moon* (1967). Both were also used by rock bands such as the Grateful Dead and Emerson, Lake, and Palmer.

A drawback that these modular synthesizers shared with earlier electronic equipment was that it was often difficult and time consuming to create and later try to re-create patches. This led to synthesizers that combined and routed the modules together internally with simpler buttons and knobs for limited patching and controls. The Minimoog is a good example of this type of prerouted synthesizer, and many software programs available today emulate its operation. As microprocessors became more common (and affordable), they were added to synthesizers, making it possible to store and recall these patch configurations and settings. This allowed composers and performers to recall even complex patches with "a push of the button."

Microprocessors rapidly became more inexpensive and incredibly more powerful. In a relatively short time, commercial synthesizers became entirely digital—with the synthesizer becoming a "dedicated" music-making computer—a computer built only to make music. As personal computers have become even more powerful, they have increasingly taken over synthesis and music-making functions from their "dedicated" predecessors.

DIGITAL SYNTHESIS

Electronic music synthesis has from the beginning made use of *analog* equipment like that described in the preceding section, but since the late 1970s there has been increasing interest in *digital* synthesizers and digital synthesis software running on computers. A basic difference between the two (analog and digital synthesis) is that an analog device allows an infinite number of measurements within its range, whereas digital devices count in a limited number of steps. For example, the old-fashioned analog watch can theoretically display the time more accurately than a digital watch, because it is not limited to a fixed number of increments. With a digital system, measurements that fall between increments must be assigned the value of a nearby step. The reader can easily see the result of this *quantization*, or "rounding," of values by changing the color resolution of a computer monitor while looking at a photograph. Most computer systems display pictures with millions of colors (almost 17 million). Lowering the resolution to "thousands of colors" (around 65,000) makes a somewhat noticeable impact on the picture quality. Setting the resolution to 256 colors changes the picture quality dramatically. For audio, quantizing creates audible noise. For CD-quality and higher, quantization noise is rarely a factor. The advantages of a digital system include its smaller size, the greater ease of "patching" the various components together, and the ability to instantly and accurately recall parameter settings. A more important advantage is its compatibility with digital computers, which has led to the development of computer-driven digital synthesizers, and more recently the widespread development and use of high-quality, complex digital synthesis software on mainstream personal computers.

Computer Music and Digital Sampling

Computers offer an alternative method of sound synthesis. Note that computer sound synthesis is not the same thing as computer composition, in which the computer makes compositional decisions (to be discussed in Chapter 14), although the two can work in tandem.

Computer sound synthesis systems usually fall into one of two categories: premade ("ready-to-use") or open-ended. Premade systems are found in computer-driven synthesizers, as well as most commercial applications for sound synthesis, such as Reason™, which emulates (or copies) the look and functionality of a modular analog rack of hardware synthesis equipment. Open-ended systems, such as Csound and Max/MSP, allow users to program their own synthesis routines and in theory are only limited by the skill of the programmer/composer in specifying the details of the operation. Premade systems have the advantage of providing the composer with a relatively easy path to sound generation by means of default programs and a limited set of possible connections. Open-ended systems generally come with a more significant learning curve, but they offer greater flexibility and power to the composer. As personal computers and microprocessors have become more powerful, many attempts have been made to find a middle ground between the power and complexity of open-ended systems and their simpler premade counterparts.

Early developments in computer music synthesis were done entirely with open-ended systems, and this led to the development of specialized programming languages for sound synthesis. Most of these languages are descended from a series of Music N programs (Music I, Music V, etc.) developed at the Bell Telephone Laboratories. The most popular descendant used today is Csound, developed by Barry Vercoe at the Massachusetts Institute of Technology (MIT). Using these programming languages requires the composer to specify for the computer the details of the desired sound—its frequency, harmonic structure, amplitude envelope, and so on—all of which can be made to change over time. Typically, the composer defines a number of "instruments" in terms that are similar to the techniques used on analog synthesizers. The instruments play a "score" that is also defined by the composer. All of these instructions are specified in text format—not through the use of a standard musical score. The computer then calculates *samples* of the waveform at a specified rate (44,100 times per second for CD-quality audio) and stores these samples as numbers. At some point, the stored numbers are sent at the same specified rate to a **digital-to-analog converter**, which converts the numbers into voltages that can drive a loudspeaker.

In addition to the complexity of specifying synthesis instructions, the "turnaround time" from the specification of a sound to its actual production was a significant drawback to composers working with these open-ended systems. In the early days of computer music, it could take a computer working all night to produce a minute of sound. Modern computers can now usually do all but the most complex forms of synthesis in *real time*, meaning that the computer can compute and output the required samples at the same rate or faster than they are required for playback. The development of graphic audio mixing programs (such as Pro Tools, Digital Performer, Cakewalk, etc.) has also made the process of using open-ended systems easier. Before the advent of mixing programs, a computer composition had to be realized in one operation from start to finish. Naturally, a long and complex composition required the input of a large amount of data, although that data in stages could be retained, edited, and reused at will. Graphic mixing programs allow for the gathering and precise placement of a number of files, with their amplitude controlled over time by the mixing program.

One example among many of a work using a Music *N* language prior to the advent of graphic mixing programs is Charles Dodge's *Changes* (1970), which makes extensive use of digital filtering.

As with many areas of study, early research in computer music has trickled down to the consumer in a variety of ways. For example, pioneering computer music work in frequency modulation (FM) synthesis by John Chowning at Stanford University, which was used in works such as *Turenas* (1972), was later adapted by Yamaha Corporation to produce a line of synthesizers, including the popular DX-7 keyboard. More recently, granular synthesis, phase vocoding, and convolution techniques have made their way from the research center to commercial applications.

Granular synthesis, originally developed for the computer by Curtis Roads working at the University of California, San Diego, and later at MIT, builds sound by combining many short moments of audio, called *grains*. A sound grain usually has a duration between 1 and 100 ms. The technique can be applied to synthesized waveforms or sampled sounds. When applied to sampled sounds, granular synthesis can be used to change the pitch of a sound without changing its length, and vice versa—something not possible to do with an analog tape recorder. Granular synthesis is used by a large number of composers, often in conjunction with other synthesis techniques. Barry Truax has used the technique extensively in his music, developing his own system for generating and modifying grains. His composition *Riverrun* (1986) makes use of sampled river and water sounds, broken into sonic grains and reassembled to make more abstract sonic images of rushing water.

Phase vocoding and convolution are sound synthesis techniques that rely on computer analysis of existing recorded sounds. The analysis technique most often used is the **Fourier transform**, named after the nineteenth-century French engineer and aristocrat Jean Baptiste Joseph, Baron de Fourier (1768–1830). Fourier developed a theory that any sound, no matter how complex, could be re-created through the combination of many simple sine waves. Sound recordings consist of changing loudness values over time. Fourier analysis takes slices of time and determines what frequencies are present in a sound. That information can then be manipulated, and then through a reverse analysis process be used to "resynthesize" the sound.

Phase vocoding changes how fast the slices of time are resynthesized, allowing the sound to be dramatically lengthened or shortened in time without changing its pitch, similar to granular synthesis. Phase vocoding can be compared to playing back a film at a different speed than it was recorded. Film usually consists of 24 frames, or pictures, per second. Play the film back at 12 frames per second and you get slow motion—in this case, half the original speed of movement captured on the film—without altering the individual pictures. A Fourier transform takes "pictures" of the sound at a regular rate. Phase vocoding changes the playback rate of these "frames" of sound. Roger Reynold's *Transfigured Wind IV* (1985) for flute and digital audio uses phase vocoding to alter recordings of flute gestures that are then played back as accompaniment to a live flutist.

Convolution is a type of **cross synthesis** that takes the frequency characteristics of one sound and applies them to the frequency characteristics of another sound. The mathematical process involves multiplication of frequencies, which means that frequencies present in both sounds will be enhanced, and frequencies present in only one sound will be eliminated. In one respect, it can be thought of as using one sound to *filter* another sound.

Other analysis/resynthesis techniques exist and have been used to good musical effect. Jonathan Harvey's *Mortuos Plango, Vivos Voco* (1981) uses an analysis of a large church bell applied to the recording of a boy's voice. The effect is one of a merged boy and bell that produces unique and haunting textures. Paul Lansky's *Idle Chatter* (1985) takes analyzed vocal sounds and separates the more static portions from the fast-changing transients (the vowels from the consonants, plosives, and sibilants) to create a rhythmic chorus of nonsense vocal sounds.

The affordability, power, and versatility of this technology have led to a resurgence of interest and compositional activity in the area of concrete music. Composers are able to alter concrete sound sources digitally to create rich textures more easily and quickly than with tape, and there is no loss of signal quality (or added noise) like that associated with analog techniques.

THE DEVELOPMENT OF MIDI

Early programming languages required massive mainframe computers to synthesize sound (making access to them very limited), but many composers today work with a variety of open-ended systems and premade systems on personal computers that provide far greater processing power than those earlier mainframes.

Most premade applications trace their history to the development of the **MIDI** (Musical Instrument Digital Interface) specification in the early 1980s. MIDI is a digital communication standard (or language) designed originally to allow the synthesizers of one manufacturer to transmit performance instructions (such as "now play a C4, now stop playing that C4") to synthesizers made by another manufacturer. MIDI made it easily possible for computers to store and communicate performance instructions and led to the development of *sequencing* programs that allowed composers to organize and edit computer music scores in more musically intuitive ways than afforded by early programming languages.

Despite MIDI's weaknesses (slow communication speed between devices, limited resolution of control values, and control parameters defined by keyboard performance only), the specification has remained largely unchanged since its inception. Even today, almost all new computer music synthesis programs (premade or open-ended) use MIDI as the basis for controlling parameters and communicating between applications. MIDI breaks down most of the common keyboard-based performance actions into a stream of bits (the smallest unit of binary data, 1 or 0—on or off) arranged in groups of eight to form a byte. Usually two to three bytes are arranged to form a single MIDI message, with seven bits of each byte being used to represent a value from 0 to 127. When a key is pressed on a MIDI keyboard, a message is sent that tells what key was pressed and usually how fast (or hard) the key was pressed. Since MIDI is a performance language that only transmits information when something changes, a separate message is sent when the key is released. Various MIDI messages allow one to transmit a variety of performance information. The most common messages include the following:

Note on/off messages—transmit information about what key is pressed or released, and how it was pressed or released;

Continuous controllers—transmit information about loudness, vibrato, position in stereo field (left/right), sustain pedals, and a variety of similar information through the use of knobs, sliders, pedals, and aftertouch (pressing harder on a key that is already being held down);

Pitch bend—allows inflection of pitch;

Program (patch) changes—selects a program to be used to produce a sound or effect, allowing one to change the sound of an instrument playing.

Whereas MIDI was designed to allow communication between synthesizers in a live performance situation, many composers use MIDI to organize communication with synthesizers and software as part of the composition process. The most common application used for this purpose is a MIDI sequencer. Although MIDI does not transmit digital audio, most sequencer applications are modeled after a multitrack tape recorder, with performance information separated into tracks based on the synthesizer or software chosen to receive the information. What is more significant than the ability to organize information into tracks is the ability to edit stored MIDI data much like a word processor does. A sequencer allows a composer to cut, copy, paste, and rearrange MIDI data, change or transpose notes, change the durations of notes, change loudness, change instruments, and record new information, as well as a variety of other such transformations. MIDI sequencing programs are now almost always combined with graphic audio mixing programs, and this combination forms the centerpiece of much computer music composition. Although the programs are oriented in both layout and editing commands toward more traditional (and tonal) forms of music, experienced composers have adapted them for use in more modern and abstract ways.

SAMPLERS, PERSONAL COMPUTERS, AND RECENT TRENDS IN DIGITAL SYNTHESIS

The same principles that allow a computer to generate and record sound found their way first into dedicated devices called **samplers** and later to personal computers through the use of software. Samplers (either hardware or software) are devices that record sound digitally into memory that can then be played back, either as recorded or after being manipulated in some fashion. Early samplers were usually limited in their manipulations to transposition, looping portions of sound, applying different loudness envelopes, and playing limited portions of a recording. Samplers can also be used to substitute for actual acoustic instruments, or to expand the sound of a small number of instruments. In this capacity digital samplers have become an important tool for commercial and film music composers, both as a tool for "sketching" ideas during the compositional process as well as playing a part in the final recorded product. Hans Zimmer (*The Lion King*, 1994) and other film composers make extensive use of samplers during composition and recording of their scores.

As personal computers became more powerful and adopted *graphical user interfaces* (*GUI*, pronounced like "gooey"), the computer with specialized software took over much of the task of recording, editing, and playing back sound. The use of the computer

EXAMPLE 12-1 Sampled Speech

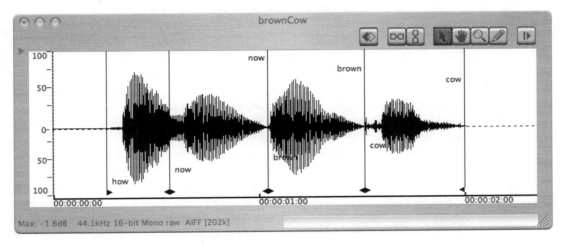

for sampling, editing, mixing, and playing back digital sound has numerous advantages over the use of hardware systems. Most of the advantages come from the more advanced GUIs available on personal computers that allow the user to "see" the recorded sound, quickly finding edit points in one or many sounds. Example 12-1 shows how a recording of the words "how now, brown cow" would look displayed on a computer monitor, with graphic "markers" indicating the start of each word.

As samplers and computers have become more complex, it has become possible to subject the recorded sound to extensive digital synthesis and processing techniques, such as the previously discussed granular synthesis, phase vocoding, and convolution techniques. With recent software developments focusing on virtual instruments, or re-creating different types of analog synthesizers in the digital domain, a vast array of synthesis, sampling, and digital signal processing is available to the contemporary computer music composer.

TAPE AND INSTRUMENT, LIVE PERFORMANCE, AND INTERACTIVE COMPUTER MUSIC

The performance of an electronic composition in the concert hall is a somewhat eerie experience for the uninitiated. Because there is no parade of performers onto the stage, the audience is usually alerted to the fact that the piece is about to begin by dimming the lights. Then someone (seen or unseen) starts the playback device, and the audience listens, facing an empty stage. The applause at the end of the piece is not for the performer, who is, after all, only a tape recorder or CD player, but instead for the composer, who may or may not even be there to hear it. Though the experience may seem a bit strange to those who are new to it, there is at least an advantage in hearing the music over a sound system that is probably superior to most home systems.

Whether or not large audiences will ever warm to a concert format of this kind remains to be seen. Certainly the proliferation of CD recordings has made electronic music more widely available to the public, but the typical electronic music concert still exists outside of the mainstream of concert life. Composers have developed several responses to the situation. One response has been to design more elaborate playback systems comprised of many loudspeakers (8, 16, 32, or more), and to focus the concert on the act of distributing, or *diffusing*, the prerecorded sound throughout the available speakers. Some composers work in multichannel formats, going beyond the two channels of stereo to compose works that take advantage of special speaker installations. Initially limited to concert halls, multichannel works are finding their way into the home through the increasing popularity of DVD players and their accompanying 5.1 audio channels.[2]

Combined tape music and live instrument works can be seen as another response to the empty concert stage, but they also were developed for their own aesthetic reasons. Early examples include Edgard Varèse's *Déserts* (1954), for woodwinds, brass, percussion, and tape, and Stockhausen's *Kontakte* (1960), for piano, percussion, and tape (an example of "moment form," discussed in Chapter 7). The tape portions of these works used all of the tools available to the electronic composer—a wide variety of electronically synthesized sounds as well as sampled sounds. Often, these sampled sounds were derived from the acoustic instruments used in the piece, such as in Jacob Druckman's *Animus II* (1968). Davidovsky's *Synchronisms* is a series of compositions that explores ideas of ensemble between acoustic performers and tightly integrated electronic parts.

The term **live electronics** can refer to various techniques, from simple amplification of conventional instruments—George Crumb's *Black Angels* (1970) for amplified string quartet—to live performance using electronic instruments, such as keyboard synthesizers. Philip Glass created his own keyboard synthesizer ensemble to perform his early minimalist compositions, such as "Floe" found on the *Glassworks* CD (1984). More recently, the term *live electronics* has come to mean the use of live, computer-generated synthesis and/or interactive computer processing of acoustic instruments.

Because MIDI is primarily a set of performance instructions, it was (and is) an important tool for composers interested in creating works of highly interactive electroacoustic music. *Eight Sketches: Duet for One Pianist* (1989) by Jean-Claude Risset has the pianist playing on a special acoustic piano that sends and responds to MIDI data (such as a Yamaha Disklavier). The performance information is sent to a computer, processed, and sent back to the piano to be played while the performer plays new material. Other musicians use pitch-to-MIDI converters, devices that listen to an acoustic instrument and determine the pitch being played, so that MIDI systems can interact with live acoustic performers. The *Voyager* series of pieces by George Lewis uses software of the composer's own design to listen for musical gestures and phrases being played by a live performer. The software responds to the musical input, sometimes with recognizable variations of the acoustic material, and sometimes with new material of its own design.

One of the more important software applications that have fueled the recent boom in interactive computer music is **Max/MSP**, originally developed by Miller Puckette, with additional development by David Zicarelli. Max/MSP was originally designed to handle MIDI information only (because that was all early personal computers could handle), but it grew to handle live audio processing as computers became more powerful. Named after computer music pioneer Max Matthews, Max/MSP is a graphic programming language with a collection of MIDI and sound processing objects and user interface elements (such as sliders and knobs). The composer links simple objects to create complex processing routines. Originally developed in Paris at IRCAM (in English, the Institute for Music/Acoustic Research and Coordination), the audio processing portion of the program originally required large mainframe computers in the 1980s. Pierre Boulez's *Répons* (1981) for clarinet, chamber ensemble, and live computer processing made use of such a large system. Later, a special add-in processing card could perform the live audio processing. Now, the software works without the need for any additional computing hardware on standard Windows and Macintosh computer systems. *Music for Clarinet and ISPW* (1992) by Cort Lippe is another example of this type of live computer processing of acoustic instrumental performance.

The greatest musical impact of electronics, from electrically amplified guitars to computer-based performance systems, has been in the various areas of commercial music. The development of electronic instruments for real-time ("live") performance during the past few decades has been phenomenal, to the point that sales of electronic instruments today exceed those of acoustic instruments. Although most live electronics are used by popular-style commercial groups, there are a number of artists who combine serious experimental techniques with a popular musical setting. Artists such as Laurie Anderson, Peter Gabriel, Björk, and Radiohead (who even quote the music of Paul Lansky) have made significant forays into experimental electronic music performance.

NOTATION OF ELECTRONIC MUSIC

There is no standard notation for electronic music[3] and, in fact, most electronic pieces do not exist in notated form at all. A primary purpose of musical notation, after all, is to allow a composition to be performed, and this purpose is not relevant to most electronic pieces that do not involve live performers. There are exceptions, of course, such as Cage's *Williams Mix*, in which the score gives instructions for realizing the piece, and Stockhausen's *Electronic Study II* (1954), which shows detailed frequency, envelope, and durations in a graph form. Although strikingly different from standard musical notation, the Stockhausen score is really quite traditional in that it provides all of the instructions necessary to "realize," or re-create, the work.

When prerecorded electronic music is to be combined with live performers, some method of coordination has to be provided. One method is for one channel of the recording to provide cues to the performer through headphones, while another is to provide the performers with a score that provides some kind of representation of the recorded music. The composition from which Example 12-2 is excerpted is for clarinet (on the bottom staff) and two-channel compact disc. (A prerecorded CD comes with the score.) The score instructs the person operating the CD player to start the CD at the beginning of measure 6, and from that point on it is up to the clarinetist to coordinate the performance with the CD by means of the notation provided. An obvious disadvantage here is that the performer cannot take any liberties with tempo, reducing the possibilities for creative interpretation. An interesting parallel in acoustic music is Steve Reich's *Double Sextet* (2007), which may be performed by two sextets or by one sextet along with a previously made recording of itself.

The lack of scores and written documentation has proven to be a significant hurdle for the analysis and theoretical discussion of electronic music. Trevor Wishart has

EXAMPLE 12-2 Davidovsky: "Synchronisms No. 12" (2006), mm. 5–12

written that musical notation actually creates musical priorities as much as it reflects them.[4] Some researchers have used technology to aid in the creation of alternate forms of documentation for a piece. In his book *New Images of Musical Sound*, Robert Cogan uses spectrum photos of recorded music to study selected electroacoustic works (as well as other genres of music). Such work has continued to evolve under the umbrella term of "spectro-morphology," which focuses on the change of spectral information over time as an important organizing feature of electronic music.

A SAMPLE ANALYSIS: SAARIAHO'S *LONH*

We end this chapter with a sample analysis of Kaija Saariaho's *Lonh* (1996) for soprano, electronics, and pre-recorded sounds.[5] The text of *Lonh* is based on a twelfth-century troubadour song "Lanquand li jorn son lonc en mai" ("When the Days are Long in May") by Jaufré Rudel, but to call Saariaho's composition itself a song would stretch our typical conception of song to its breaking point. For one thing, a song typically sets each line of the poem upon which it is based, whereas in the case of *Lonh*, only about half of the text is actually sung by the soprano. While all but one of the stanzas of the original are seven lines, only the first stanza is set in its entirety; only the last line of the fifth stanza is sung, and only the third line of the seventh stanza. This is not simply an

EXAMPLE 12-3 The first stanza set in *Lonh*; translation by Leo Treitler (1992)

> When the days are long in May
> I like the sweet song of the birds from afar;
> And when I have departed from there,
> I remember a love from afar:
> I go sad and bowed with desire
> So that neither song nor Hawthorn flower
> Please me more than icy winter.

arrangement of the original song, but a radically altered recomposition that only partially depends on the original for its material. An English translation of the first stanza is given as Example 12-3, which is recited in English during the Prologue, and then sung in the original language (Occitan) during Part I. Example 12-4 provides an analysis of its form. It is divided into nine sections, including a prologue and a closing section. Listen to a recording of it while following along (using the timings indicated along the top row) with Example 12-4.

In Example 12-4, shaded boxes indicate whether or not a particular sound or instrument is present or absent in each section, and the dotted vertical lines indicate when the music seems to move seamlessly into the next section as opposed to the solid lines that indicate a stronger sectional division. The sectional divisions in *Lonh* are more often created by changes in texture and timbre than they are by means dependent on pitch and rhythm. Nevertheless, one can see that pitch relations do play an important role in the dramatic shape of *Lonh*. Note how the range of the soprano part and the relative stability of the part's modal collection follow a familiar dramatic arch from a

EXAMPLE 12-4 Formal Diagram of Saariaho's *Lonh* (1996)

	Prologue	I	II	III	IV	V	VI	VII	Closing
start time	0:00	1:20	2:54	5:33	6:11	8:06	9:29	11:53	13:15
soprano first note		D4	E4	A4	D5	E5	D4	A4	D4
soprano last note		F4	E4	E5	G4	C#5	B4	B5	A5
modal collection		stable	stable	stable	changing	only 4 pitches	unstable	stable	stable
range in semitones		12	13	9	12	12	17	14	19
recorded sounds:			"Gamelan music"	stream of hits on cymbal		faster; more active perc. parts	slower sop. and perc. parts	stream of hits on glockenspiel	
voices	unprocessed female voice reading 1st stanza		processed male and female voices						whispered text
birds									
glockenspiel			x						
"vibraphone/chime"									
gong									
windchime									
bell (sustained)									
cymbal									
bass drum									
high electronic sound									
low electronic sound									

more restful state (i.e. more stable and lower in range) to a more restless state (i.e. less stable and higher in range), and though the stability of the collection is regained by the end, the distance between the first and last notes in each section increases to its greatest interval in the closing, effectively painting the text about the strain of loving one who is far away.

SUMMARY

The technology that allowed electronic music to really develop was not available until the late 1940s. Since that time, the medium has developed from concrete music to electronic synthesis, to computer music, and from a studio art to one that allows a variety of live performance and interactive formats. The development of personal computers powerful enough to handle complex audio processing has led to a vast expansion of activity in the field, often crossing stylistic boundaries. The integration of electronic music into the mainstream concert hall has been slow, but attitudes toward new media are slowly changing in even the most traditional of organizations.

MUSIC FROM THE CHAPTER IN CHRONOLOGICAL CONTEXT

Year	Composer	Work	Reference
1952	**John Cage**	***Williams Mix***	**p. 243**
1952	John Cage	*4'33"*	Chance Music
1954	Edgard Varèse	*Poème Electronique*	Electronic Music
1954	**Karlheinz Stockhausen**	***Electronic Study II***	**p. 253**
1961	Krzysztof Penderecki	*Threnody: To the Victims of Hiroshima*	Aleatoric Music
1964	Terry Riley	*In C*	Minimalism
1967	**Morton Subotnick**	***Silver Apples of the Moon***	**p. 246**
1968	**Wendy Carlos**	***Switched-On Bach***	**p. 246**
1970	**Charles Dodge**	***Changes***	**p. 248**
1981	**Pierre Boulez**	***Répons***	**p. 253**
1984	**Philip Glass**	***"Floe"***	**p. 252**
1996	**Kaija Saariaho**	***Lonh***	**p. 255**
2006	**Mario Davidovsky**	***"Synchronisms No. 12"***	**p. 254**

Works in **bold** are from the chapter; those not in bold are landmark pieces written around the same time.

NOTES

1.   A number of the examples in this section were suggested by Barry Schrader's *Introduction to Electro-Acoustic Music*, an excellent and highly recommended text.

2.   "5.1 surround sound" delivers six channels of audio—five channels of full-range audio and one channel of low-frequency effects (the ".1"). In addition to the standard pair of stereo channels for left and right, there is a front center channel, and two rear "surround" channels.

3.   This is not to say that no attempts have been made to develop such a notation. See, for example, Louise Gariépy and Jean Décarie, "A System of Notation for Electro-Acoustic Music: A Proposition."

4.   Trevor Wishart, *On Sonic Art*, p. 11.

5.   For a more detailed analysis, see Judy Lochhead, *Reconceiving Structure in Contemporary Music: New Tools in Music Theory and Analysis*.

★

EXERCISES

Part A: Concrete Music Techniques

Simple concrete music techniques can be performed with a variety of low- and no-cost audio editors. One such free program is *Audacity*, developed by researchers at Carnegie Mellon University and available for free download through Sourceforge (http://sourceforge.net) for Windows, Linux, and Macintosh computer systems. Depending on your computer system and installed software, many people have limited-edition versions of stereo audio editors such as *Peak* (Mac) and *Sound Forge* (Windows). They will have the letters "LE," "DV," or "XP" after their name. They still include many basic editing and processing functions. If you have access to one of these programs, you should try the following techniques both separately and in combination. Not all of the commands may be available on your particular software. They are most successful when done as class projects. The first step is to collect a variety of sounds—musical, text, and natural—to be used as source material. For educational purposes you can use excerpted material from audio CDs.

1.   **Speed (pitch) change**. Change the playback rate of the recorded sounds, which will change both the pitch and the spectra of the sounds. Most programs offer a "pitch change" command, sometimes with the option of maintaining the original duration of the sound. Don't select this particular option. With this operation and all that follow, make sure that you save your edited sound with a new file name so as not to destroy your original sound file.

2.   **Pitch change**. Similar to the previous exercise, but this time select the option of maintaining the duration of the original sound, if available.

3. **Duration change**. Change the duration of the recorded sounds without changing the pitch. Programs usually offer either one or two ways to do this operation— either through granular synthesis or phase vocoding. Try both ways, if available in your program.

4. **Reverse direction**. Change the playback direction of the sound by using the "reverse" command.

5. **Looping**. Select a portion of the sound and choose the "loop" command. By zooming in on the beginning and end points of the loop you can make subtle adjustments to remove audible "clicks," if necessary.

6. **Cutting and splicing (copying and pasting)**. Select different portions of the audio and choose "cut" or "copy." You can "paste" these portions of audio into a new file, changing the order of sounds, splicing sounds together from different segments, etc.

7. **Amplitude change**. Select a portion of the sound (usually after cutting it out of the original audio) and change its amplitude (or gain) envelope. This operation allows you to change the overall amplitude of a sound. You can create **forte-piano-crescendo** and other dynamic effects with otherwise steady-state sounds.

8. **Filtering**. Use a filter or equalizer (EQ) to change the spectral makeup of the sound. You can remove high frequencies or low frequencies or emphasize some frequency range, either alone or in combination.

9. **Effects**. If available, try processing your recorded sound with an audio effect, such as reverberation (reverb), echo, distortion, flanging, or something else available to you.

Part B: Studio Visit/Concert Performance

Computer music studios take many different forms. Many universities have a general-purpose music technology lab that also functions as a computer music lab. Other universities will have a dedicated room, often with more elaborate recording, mixing, and synthesizer systems. Many musicians outside of universities have home studios. If possible, try to arrange a studio demonstration. It would be particularly helpful to hear a demonstration of some of the more advanced sample processing and synthesis techniques, such as convolution, phase vocoding, and physical modeling synthesis.

Attending a concert that involves electronic music performance is especially worthwhile. Many electronic concerts make use of multiple loudspeakers, often eight or more, to provide an immersive listening experience. You may find multimedia combinations, particularly involving video and computer music. It is also possible that you could encounter interactive computer music performance.

Part C: Listening

Many of the works listed below were discussed in this chapter. Works not discussed in the chapter are marked with an asterisk. Select several of them to which you have access and try to create listening guides to them. Using the CD player's counter or a watch, note the timings of what you hear as important events, and jot down brief descriptions of them. There is no right or wrong description, but try to be as musically descriptive as possible without adding external programmatic descriptions. Adding a musical program to a work changes the way it was intended to be heard, and can interfere with understanding the work. If there is definite rhythm or pitch, you may want to include this information. You could also indicate whether the work uses natural or synthesized sounds as its main source material, or some combination.

Using your listening guide, draw the individual events onto a time graph (graph paper works well) at the correct time in order to create a "score." When possible, place high sounds vertically above the lower-pitched sounds, although it may not be possible to do this. If sounds appear at several transpositions, try to represent this by placing the different occurrences at different vertical locations. The graphic score of Ligeti's *Artikulation* done by Rainer Wehinger might provide some inspiration, although it is very detailed. There is also a score to Xenakis's *Mycenae Alpha*, produced by the composer. Xenakis was also a skilled architect, and he created a computer system to translate line drawings into musical compositions.

Once you have finished your score, consider the following questions:

1. Can you recognize any techniques discussed in this chapter? If so, what are the techniques? At what timings do they occur?

2. Does the piece have a form that you are familiar with?

3. Do you perceive a climax? If so, where?

4. Does the composer build tension? If so, how?

5. Does the work juxtapose many different elements, or is a limited amount of material gradually transformed?

6. Is there an overall progression in the timbre of the piece? From noise-based sounds to clear pitches, or from clear pitches to noise-based sounds? From sounds that emphasize low frequencies to sounds that emphasize high frequencies?

7. If the piece is concrete music, can you recognize the sound sources? Does this add some extramusical element to the piece?

8. Could this piece be transcribed and realized by acoustic instruments (perhaps using extended techniques)?

William Albright: *Sphaera

Luciano Berio: *Thema (Omaggio a Joyce)

Pierre Boulez: *Répons; *Dialogue de L'Ombre Double*

John Cage: *Williams Mix*

Wendy Carlos: *Switched-On Bach*

John Chowning: *Turenas*

George Crumb: *Black Angels*

Mario Davidovsky: *Synchronisms No. 6; Synchronisms No. 12*

Charles Dodge: *Changes*

Paul Dresher: **Dark Blue Circumstance*

Jacob Druckman: *Animus II*

Kenneth Gaburo: *Exit Music II: Fat Millie's Lament*

Philip Glass: "Floe"

Jonathan Harvey: *Mortuos Plango, Vivos Voco*

Pierre Henry: **Variations pour une Porte et un Soupir*

Paul Koonce: **Walkabout*

Paul Lansky: *Idle Chatter*

George Lewis: *Voyager*

Cort Lippe: *Music for Clarinet and ISPW*

Otto Luening: *Low Speed*

Otto Luening and Vladimir Ussachevsky: *Incantation*

Thea Musgrave: **Narcissus*

Jon Christopher Nelson: **Waves of Refraction*

Pauline Oliveros: *I of IV*

Steve Reich: *Come Out*

Roger Reynolds: *Transfigured Wind IV*

Jean-Claude Risset: *Duet for One Pianist; *Mutations I*

Karlheinz Stockhausen: *Song of the Youths; Hymns; Contact; Electronic Study II*

Morton Subotnick: *Silver Apples of the Moon*

James Tenney: *Saxony*

Barry Truax: *Riverrun*

Vladimir Ussachevsky: **Sonic Contours*

Edgard Varèse: *Deserts; *Poème Electronique*

FURTHER READING

Anderton, Craig. *MIDI for Musicians.*

Antokoletz, Elliott. *Twentieth-Century Music.* See Chapter 18, Musique Concrète and Electronic Music.

Bateman, Wayne. *Introduction to Computer Music.*

Brindle, Reginald Smith. *The New Music.* See Chapter 10, Concrete Music, and Chapter 11, Electronic Music.

Chadabe, Joel. *Electric Sound: The Past and Promise of Electronic Music.*

Cogan, Robert. *New Images of Musical Sound.*

Cogan, Robert, and Pozzi Escot. *Sonic Design.* See Chapter 4, The Color of Sound.

Collins, Nick, and Julio d'Escriván, Eds., *The Cambridge Companion to Electronic Music.*

Cope, David H. *New Directions in Music.* See Chapter 8, Analog Electronic Music, and Chapter 9, Digital Electronic Music.

———. *Techniques of the Contemporary Composer.* See Chapter 15, Musique Concrète, and Chapter 16, Electronic Music.

Davies, Hugh. "Electronic Music: History and Development," in John Vinton, Ed., *Dictionary of Contemporary Music*, pp. 212–216.

Dodge, Charles, and Thomas A. Jerse. *Computer Music.*

Emmerson, Simon, Ed., *The Language of Electroacoustic Music.*

Fennelly, Brian. "Electronic Music: Notation," in John Vinton, Ed., *Dictionary of Contemporary Music*, pp. 216–220.

Howe, Hubert S. *Electronic Music Synthesis.*

Lochhead, Judy. *Reconceiving Structure in Contemporary Music: New Tools in Music Theory and Analysis.* See Chapter 5, Technê of Radiance: Kaija Saariaho's Lonh.

Luening, Otto. "Origins," in John H. Appleton and Ronald C. Perera, Eds., *The Development and Practice of Electronic Music*, pp. 1–21.

Manning, Peter. *Electronic and Computer Music.*

Pellman, Samuel. *An Introduction to the Creation of Electroacoustic Music.*

Pressing, Jeff. *Synthesizer Performance and Real-Time Techniques.*

Roads, Curtis. *The Computer Music Tutorial.*

Schrader, Barry. *Introduction to Electro-Acoustic Music.*

Schwartz, Elliott. *Electronic Music: A Listeners Guide.*

Simms, Bryan R. *Music of the Twentieth Century.* See Chapter 14, Electronic Music.

Slawson, Wayne. *Sound Color.*

Wishart, Trevor. *On Sonic Art.*

CHAPTER 13

Serialism after 1945

INTRODUCTION

The end of World War II in 1945 was followed by two major developments in music. One of these was the beginnings of electronic music, the subject of Chapter 12. The other development, the subject of this chapter, was the dissemination of the serial technique and the extension of its principles into all facets of musical composition.

Although Schoenberg composed his first twelve-tone work in 1921, serialism did not appeal at once to a large number of composers outside of his immediate circle. But when World War II ended, interest in serialism spread rapidly, and the technique was taken up with enthusiasm by the younger generation of composers as well as by established composers as diverse as Copland and Stravinsky. It may be that serialism represented to some composers a rationality that was welcome after the irrational horrors of the war, and the fact that Hitler's regime had tried to suppress serialism certainly did nothing to harm its postwar reputation. In the United States, considerably less affected by the war, interest in twelve-tone music was due in part to Schoenberg's tenure from 1936 on as a professor at the University of California at Los Angeles.

But many of the new adherents to serialism felt that Schoenberg had not taken the technique far enough. Instead of restricting serialism to the domain of pitch class, these composers felt that other aspects of composition should also be controlled by some kind of precompositional plan. This approach, inspired to a certain degree by the works of Webern, has been given various labels, among them "total serialization," "total control," "generalized serialism," and the one we will use, **integral serialism**.

INTEGRAL SERIALISM

In classical serial technique, the composer constructs the pitch series before beginning the actual composition. The compositional process is thereby restricted to the extent that, once having begun the presentation of some form of the row, the notes of the row must be used in order; however, everything else is left up to the creativity and skill of the composer. As anyone who has ever composed a twelve-tone piece knows, composition using the techniques of classical serialism is far from a mechanical or automatic procedure.

Some of the areas in which the composer has complete freedom are:

    rhythm
    dynamics
    register
    articulation
    row form.

It is these areas that the proponents of integral serialism looked at most closely (though others, such as timbre, were not ignored). Many examples of integral serialism apply serial techniques to only a few of these aspects, but others are so thoroughly preplanned that they truly are automatic, in the sense that all of the composer's decisions were made before the actual notation of the piece was begun. In the next several paragraphs, we will examine approaches to integral serialism in three very different works by composers from the United States, France, and Italy.

Milton Babbitt: Three Compositions for Piano (1947), No. 1

In this composition, evidently the very first to employ integral serialism, Babbitt "serialized" the dynamics by associating a particular dynamic level with each row form:

    P   =   *mp* (*pp* in mm. 49–56)
    R   =   *mf* (*p*)
    I   =   *f* (*mp*)
    RI =   *p* (*ppp*)

There is obviously no true dynamic series here, no parallel to the series of 12 pitch classes. (The prime form of the row appears on p. 195.) Nevertheless, the dynamic levels are controlled precompositionally, which is the only requirement for integral serialism. Turn back to Example 6-3 (p. 108) to see an excerpt from this work. You can tell from the dynamic levels in the excerpt that the row forms used are:

	m. 9	m. 10	m. 11	m. 12
Top staff:		R	I	I
Bottom staff:	P	RI	RI	

The rhythm in this composition is organized around the number series 5–1–4–2, which sums to 12. This series of numbers is always associated in some way with the P form of the pitch set. To invert the number series, Babbitt subtracts each number from 6:

6	6	6	6
−5	−1	−4	−2
—	—	—	—
1	5	2	4

Six is chosen here because it is the only value that can be used if the resulting differences are going to sum to 12 (as they must, in order to be associated with the inversion of the twelve-tone pitch series).

The resulting durational set is:

P = 5   1   4   2   R = 2   4   1   5

I   = 1   5   2   4   RI = 4   2   5   1

Each member of the durational set is always associated with its corresponding row form. The durational set is expressed in a variety of ways (rests, phrase marks, and so on). In Example 13-1 groups of notes are formed by making the last note of a group longer than the others and/or by following the last note with a rest. The series being stated in the excerpt are:

	mm. 49–50	mm. 51–52
Top staff:	P (5–1–4–2)	RI (4–2–5–1)
Bottom staff:	RI (4–2–5–1)	I (1–5–2–4)

Notice that the rhythms of the two RI forms in the excerpt are similar but not identical.

EXAMPLE 13-1 Babbitt: Three Compositions for Piano (1947), No. 1, mm. 49–52

The rhythm series is expressed in Example 6-3 (p. 108) in different ways. In the left hand in mm. 9–10, the P and RI rhythm series is stated by means of phrase marks and accents. The I form in the right hand, m. 12, is presented the same way. The other measures in the excerpt are organized rhythmically by using the 16th note as the unit of measure. For example, in m. 10 the right hand states 2–4–1–5 by durations of two 16ths (one 8th), four 16ths (two 8ths tied), one 16th, and five 16ths (a 16th tied to a quarter note).

Register appears to be left open, except in the voicing of trichords. When Babbitt segments the pitch series into vertical trichords, as in mm. 10–11 of Example 6-3 (p. 108), he voices the trichords in relation to the row in this way:

		1–3	4–6	7–9	10–12
P	=	Up	Down	Up	Down
I	=	Down	Up	Down	Up
R	=	Up	Up	Down	Down
RI	=	Down	Down	Up	Up

That is, the members of a prime form of the row would be voiced in trichords as:

3	4	9	10
2	5	8	11
1	6	7	12

The three row forms in Example 6-3 that are used trichordally are:

m. 10, R.H.: R–10   (E G♯ A)   (F♯ B G)   (D♭ C D)   (F E♭ B♭)

m. 11, R.H.: I–11   (B F♯ E)   (G A G♯)   (D B♭ E♭)   (C D♭ F)

m. 11, L.H.: RI–11   (F D♭ C)   (E♭ B♭ D)   (G♯ A G)   (E F♯ B)

Pierre Boulez: *Structures Ia* (1952)

European composers, unaware of Babbitt's work in the United States, developed a different approach to integral serialism. In some works each note has its own duration, dynamic level, and articulation, all precompositionally assigned. The multiplicity of dynamic levels was especially troublesome for performers, but the rhythms were also difficult because they were generally ametric.

Structures Ia uses as its primary material the following pitch series, borrowed by Boulez from *Mode de valeurs et d'intensités* (1949), composed by his teacher, Messiaen. (We number the PCs 1–12 instead of 0–11 to facilitate the discussion that follows.)

E♭	D	A	A♭	G	F♯	E	C♯	C	B♭	F	B
1	2	3	4	5	6	7	8	9	10	11	12

As we shall see, the pitch series is made to govern duration, dynamic level, articulation, and row choice.

The first step is to make a matrix of prime forms of the series. The second row of the matrix transposes the row and begins it with the second note of the original series; the next transposition of the row begins with the third note of the original series, and so on:

Eb	D	A	Ab	G	F♯	E	C♯	C	Bb	F	B
D	C♯	G♯	G	F♯	F	Eb	C	B	A	E	Bb
A	Ab	Eb	D	C♯	C	Bb	G	F♯	E	B	F
Ab	G	D	etc.								

Notice that this is not the kind of twelve-note matrix discussed in Chapter 10.

Next, each note name is replaced with the position number (from 1 to 12) that the note had in the original series. That is, every Eb is replaced with 1, every D with 2, every A with 3, and so on:

1	2	3	4	5	6	7	8	9	10	11	12
2	8	4	5	6	11	1	9	12	3	7	10
3	4	1	2	8	9	10	5	6	7	12	11
4	5	2	8	9	12	3	6	11	1	10	7
5	6	8	9	12	10	4	11	7	2	3	1
6	11	9	12	10	3	5	7	1	8	4	2
7	1	10	3	4	5	11	2	8	12	6	9
8	9	5	6	11	7	2	12	10	4	1	3
9	12	6	11	7	1	8	10	3	5	2	4
10	3	7	1	2	8	12	4	5	11	9	6
11	7	12	10	3	4	6	1	2	9	5	8
12	10	11	7	1	2	9	3	4	6	8	5

A similar matrix of inversions must then be constructed:

Eb	E	A	Bb	B	C	D	F	F♯	G♯	C♯	G
E	F	Bb	B	C	C♯	D♯	F♯	G	A	D	G♯
A	Bb	Eb	E	F	F♯	G♯	B	C	D	G	C♯
Bb	B	E	etc.								

This matrix in turn is converted to numbers using the position numbers associated with the prime form of the row. That is, Every Eb becomes a 1, every D is replaced with a 2, and so on.

1	7	3	10	12	9	2	11	6	4	8	5
7	11	10	12	9	8	1	6	5	3	2	4
3	10	1	7	11	6	4	12	9	2	5	8
10	12	7	11	6	5	3	9	8	1	4	2
12	9	11	6	5	4	10	8	2	7	3	1
9	8	6	5	4	3	12	2	1	11	10	7
2	1	4	3	10	12	8	7	11	5	9	6
11	6	12	9	8	2	7	5	4	10	1	3
6	5	9	8	2	1	11	4	3	12	7	10
4	3	2	1	7	11	5	10	12	8	6	9
8	2	5	4	3	10	9	1	7	6	12	11
5	4	8	2	1	7	6	3	10	9	11	12

Structures Ia is a work for two pianos, and the two pianos between them state all 48 forms of the row: Piano I states the 12 P forms and the 12 RI forms, and Piano II states the 12 I forms and the 12 R forms. The transposition levels for the row forms are selected by using the position numbers in the two matrices. For example, the 12 P forms in Piano I are governed by the first row of the inversion matrix (1, 7, 3, etc.); thus, the prime beginning with position number 1 would be first, the prime beginning with position number 7 would be second, and so on. (Note that these are not the same as P-1 and P-7.) In Example 13-2, Piano I states the prime beginning with position number 1, while Piano II states the inversion beginning with position number 1.

The duration of each note is also dictated by the two matrices. All 12 rows of each matrix are worked through both forwards and backwards to provide durations for the 576 notes in the piece (12 notes × 48 row forms). The numbers are used as multiples of 32nd notes, so that the position number 1 represents one 32nd note, 2 represents a 16th note, 3 a dotted 16th note, and so on. The duration series in Example 13-2 are:

Piano I:	12	11	9	10	3	6	7	1	2	8	4	5
Piano II:	5	8	6	4	3	9	2	1	7	11	10	12

If you compare these duration series with the number matrices, you will see that Piano I is taken from the last row of the I matrix, whereas Piano II is taken from the last row of the P matrix, both in retrograde order. Boulez's rhythmic structure, with 48 rhythmic patterns, is obviously more complicated than Babbitt's, with only four.

Dynamics and articulation are serialized by making a list of 12 dynamic levels (*pppp* to *ffff*) and ten "modes of attack." A single dynamic level and a single articulation are used with each row form, the particular one to be used being again dictated by the number matrices. In this case, instead of rows, diagonals of the matrices are used, some for the dynamics and others for articulation. Because the numbers 4 and 10 do not appear in the articulation diagonals, the 4th and 10th modes of attack are not needed. In Example 13-2, Piano I uses the 12th dynamic level and the 12th mode of attack, while Piano II uses the 5th dynamic level and the 5th mode of attack.

EXAMPLE 13-2 Boulez: *Structures Ia* (1952), mm. 1–7

Once all of these procedures have been established, the actual notation of the composition can begin; however, by now there are few decisions left to be made. One of them is the choice of time signatures, which do not seem to follow any particular pattern; another is the choice of register. Octave register appears to be controlled only to the extent that a pitch class occurring in two row forms simultaneously must be used in the same register.

Luigi Nono: *Il canto sospeso* (1956), II

The pitch material of this composition derives from a series that is usually characterized as a "wedge" row (Example 13-3a); it can also be viewed as a hexachord followed by its retrograde at the tritone (Example 13-3b). In view of the structure of the duration set, the second interpretation is probably more appropriate. Only P-9 is used in this movement.

EXAMPLE 13-3 Series from Nono's *Il canto sospeso*

The duration set is a palindrome[1] based on a Fibonacci series. This series, discussed in Chapter 7 in connection with musical form and the golden mean (see p. 140), is an infinite one in which each number (after the first two) is the sum of the previous two numbers:

$$1 \quad 2 \quad 3 \quad 5 \quad 8 \quad 13 \quad 21 \quad 34 \quad \text{etc.}$$

Nono uses the first six numbers and their retrograde for his duration set:

$$1 \quad 2 \quad 3 \quad 5 \quad 8 \quad 13 \quad 13 \quad 8 \quad 5 \quad 3 \quad 2 \quad 1$$

In mm. 108–142 of this movement (the movement begins with m. 108), these values are distributed as needed among four rhythmic strands. Each strand uses its assigned values as multiples of some basic duration:

Strand A: 8th note
Strand B: triplet 8th note
Strand C: 16th note
Strand D: quintuplet 16th note.

All four strands begin simultaneously and proceed at their own rates without pause, except that the four strands are distributed among eight voice parts, which allows the singers to breathe. Example 13-4, which shows the first presentation of the rhythmic series, may help to clarify how this works. All four strands start simultaneously at the beginning of the excerpt, with the first four durational values—1, 2, 3, and 5— distributed from the top down. As the duration of each strand is exhausted, the next durational value is assigned to it: 8 for strand A; 13 for strands B and C; 8, 5, and 3 for strand D; 2 for strand C; and 1 for strand D.

EXAMPLE 13-4 Nono: *Il canto sospeso* (1956), II, mm. 108–10 (rhythm only)

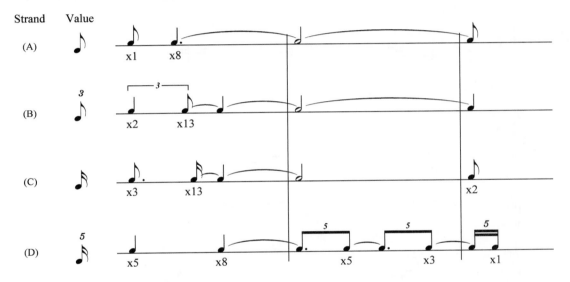

Pitch classes from P-9 are distributed among the four strands as needed. In Example 13-4, strand A would get order numbers 0 and 4 (A and G), strand B would receive 1 and 5 (B♭ and C), strand C would receive 2, 6, and 10 (A♭, F♯, and E), and strand D would use order numbers 3, 7, 8, 9, and 11 (B, C♯, F, D, and E♭).

In the score, Example 13-4 appears as in Example 13-5. The strands are distributed as follows:

Strand A: Alto 2
Strand B: Soprano 2–Basso 1
Strand C: Soprano 1–Soprano 1 + Tenor 2–Tenor 2
Strand D: Alto 1–Basso 2–Soprano 1

The first note in m. 110, Basso 2, is evidently an error and should be a 16th-note quintuplet.[2]

EXAMPLE 13-5 Nono: *Il canto sospeso* (1956), II, mm. 108–110

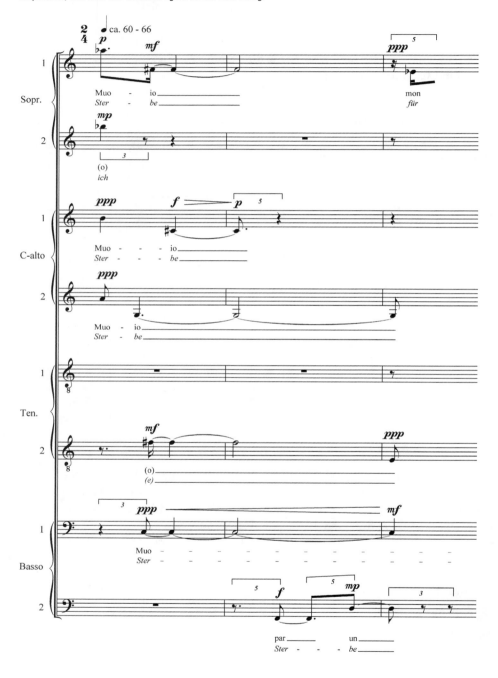

Because the pitch and duration sets are of equal length, if the composition were continued in this manner, each member of the row would always be assigned to the same number from the duration series. To avoid this, the duration set is rotated for each statement of the row:

Statement 1:	1	2	3	5	8	13	13	8	5	3	2	1
Statement 2:	2	3	5	8	13	13	8	5	3	2	1	1
Statement 3:	3	5	8	13	13	8	5	3	2	1	1	2
etc.												

In the coda (mm. 142–157) each strand presents the entire duration series independently. The entrances are staggered, with strand A beginning, followed by strands B, C, and D. This allows all four strands to reach their maximum level of activity simultaneously for the climax of the movement in m. 150.

INTEGRAL SERIALISM IN PERSPECTIVE

The three works that have been surveyed here demonstrate just three of many possible approaches to integral serialism. None of them serialize register or timbre, but all three serialize rhythm, and it is interesting to compare them in that regard. Babbitt's rhythmic series is apparently not derived from his pitch series at all, which might seem a weakness because there is no single organizing force at work. There is a connection between Nono's pitch series and his rhythmic series, in that both are symmetrically designed, but there is not a direct one-to-one correspondence between the two. Boulez probably comes closest to the ideal of having a pitch series control all elements of a work, but the listener could never recognize the relationship between a pitch series and a duration series derived from *position numbers* of transpositions and transposed inversions of the pitch series.

Babbitt later devised other methods that linked the durations more closely with the original pitch series. One method, used in his String Quartet No. 2 (1967), derives the duration set from the original row by numbering the notes chromatically, using the first note as 0:

G	Bb	F#	B	G#	A	Eb	F	C	E	D	C#
0	3	11	4	1	2	8	10	5	9	7	6

By substituting 12 for the 0 that begins the row, a durational set is established. The numbers in the set can serve as multiples of any constant value. In Example 13-6 the constant value is the 8th note.

Alternatively, a series can be interpreted as **time points** within a measure. That is, the series 0, 3, 11, 4, etc., can be interpreted as the zeroth 8th note in a measure, the third 8th note in a measure, the eleventh 8th note in a measure, the fourth 8th note in a measure, and so on, as in Example 13-7. The twelve 8th notes in each measure are numbered 0 through 11 instead of 1 through 12, in order to correspond with the range of values in the duration series.

The durations in Example 13–7 closely reflect the intervals between the adjacent notes of the series. To illustrate this, calculate the pitch-class intervals between each note and the next one:

P–0:   G   Bb   F#   B   G#   A   Eb   F   C   E   D   C#   (G)
        3   8   5   9   1   6   2   7   4   10   11.   (6)

These numbers, it turns out, are the same as the durations in Example 13-7. That is, the first note is three 8th notes in duration, the second is eight 8th notes, and so on.

Although Examples 13-6 and 13-7 were derived from the same pitch series, each is unique, and each could be subjected to transposition, inversion, and retrograde operations.

The composers of integral serialism faced a number of problems, not the least of which was the resistance of performers who found that the difficulty of the music outweighed its rewards. Imagine the problems experienced by performers of the Boulez and Nono examples in this chapter, and you will understand their concern. Also discouraging was the lack of enthusiasm on the part of the musical public. The compositional method was ultimately irrelevant to the listener, because few of the relationships were audible. In fact, some of the most tightly controlled works give the listener the impression that they are completely random and disorganized (*Structures Ia* is a good example of this).

EXAMPLE 13-6 A Durational Series

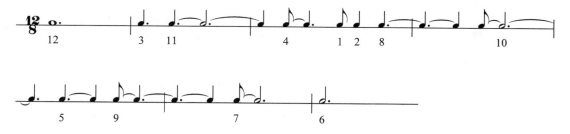

EXAMPLE 13-7 A Time-Point Series

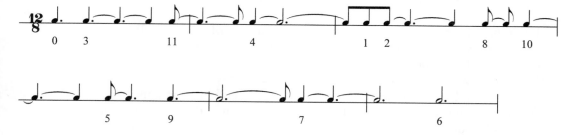

OTHER ASPECTS OF SERIALISM

Our two chapters on serialism have by no means exhausted the subject. A really thorough discussion of this topic would require many chapters. We should not leave the subject, however, without briefly mentioning a few other aspects of serialism.

Although most serial works use a pitch series of 12 pitch classes, some use more or fewer than 12. Stravinsky used the following four-note set in *Three Songs from William Shakespeare* (1953):

   B   G   A   Bb

and this five-note row in his *In Memoriam Dylan Thomas* (1954):

   E   Eb   C   C#   D

Berio used a 13-note set in *Nones* (1954). Notice that this set is symmetrical around its central PC, A:

  C Eb B Ab F E A D C# Bb G Eb F#

    ←————————   ————————→

Also, Example 6-12 (p. 116), although not taken from a strictly serial composition, does employ a 16-note pitch series.

Rotation of sets or of portions of sets is another possibility that composers have explored. Stravinsky used two methods of hexachordal rotation for *Abraham and Isaac* (1963).[3] In the first, the pitch classes are rotated in a circular fashion, right to left:

G	G#	A#	C	C#	A
G#	A#	C	C#	A	G
A#	C	C#	A	G	G#
C	C#	A	G	G#	A#
C#	A	G	G#	A#	C
A	G	G#	A#	C	C#

The second method of rotation works just like the first, but all are transposed to begin with the same pitch class:

G	G#	A#	C	C#	A
G	A	B	C	G#	F#
G	A	A#	F#	E	F
G	G#	E	D	D#	F
G	D#	C#	D	E	F#
G	F	F#	G#	A#	B

Less systematic reordering of rows also occurs. George Rochberg's *Twelve Bagatelles* (1952) uses a single row in only a few transpositions, but the row is frequently reordered. Example 13-8 employs the following row forms:

RI-8:	B	C	F	D	F♯	B♭	E	E♭	A	C♯	G	A♭
I-8:	A♭	G	C♯	A	E♭	E	B♭	F♯	D	F	C	B
	0	1	2	3	4	5	6	7	8	9	10	11

EXAMPLE 13-8 Rochberg: *Twelve Bagatelles* (1952), No. 8, mm. 1–8

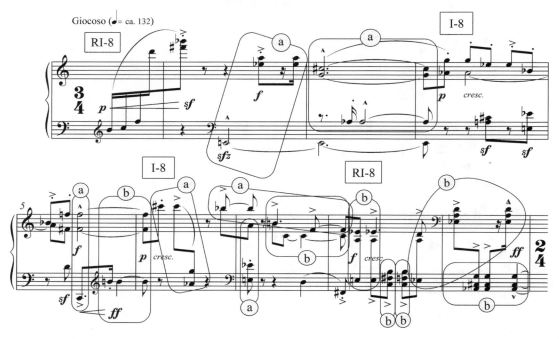

The rows in mm. 1–4 are presented in the correct order, but those in mm. 5–8 are not; the final RI-8 is particularly reordered. Rochberg's purpose may have been to emphasize two particular arrangements of a [0,1,6] set type, labeled here as "a" and "b."

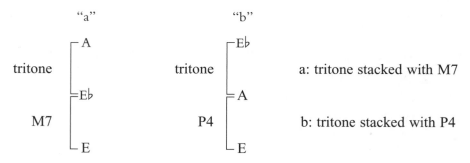

Occurrences of these two arrangements (or their inversions) are shown in the example. Notice particularly how many of them occur in mm. 5–8, where the rows are reordered.

Serialism has also been employed in electronic and microtonal music, an example of the latter being Ben Johnston's String Quartet No. 2 (1964).

MUSIC AFTER SERIALISM

For the most part, serialism as a movement, as a compositional aesthetic, died out in the 1960s, but that is not to say that serial music is no longer being written. Instead, serial techniques have joined all of the other techniques, from free atonality to pitch centricity to traditional harmony, that composers have at their command. It is not uncommon, for example, to find a twelve-tone theme supported by pitch-centric, nonserial harmonies.

There are several reasons for the decline of serialism, especially integral serialism, as a movement. One is the insistence on originality that robbed post-tonal music of any chance of developing a "style" in the way that there are Baroque and Classical styles. Also, the demands that integral serialism made on listener and performer proved intolerable to both. In the words of one writer and composer who was active throughout this period:

> And so integral serialism quickly reached an impasse, through its own limitations and the burdens it laid on performers. But its importance, in both aesthetic and historical contexts, must not be denied, for it forged a completely new musical language, as different from anything that had gone before (except Webern) as chalk from cheese, and paved the way to a new, more spontaneous music which is still the most potent means of emotive expression today.[4]

The same writer goes on to summarize the movement from free atonality in the early 1900s to serialism in the 1920s, then to integral serialism in the 1950s, and finally back to free atonality in the 1960s: "The cycle was then complete and serialism had come and gone, but leaving decisive and lasting traces of its sojourn."[5]

SUMMARY

Integral serialism refers to the precompositional control not only of pitch, as in classical serialism, but of other elements of a composition as well. Rhythm, dynamics, articulation, register, row form, and timbre have all been subjected to precompositional ordering. In some cases these orderings are independent of each other, but often the composer attempts to relate all of the musical materials to a single series.

Other aspects of serialism discussed in this chapter included the use of tone rows with fewer or more than 12 pitch classes, the use of rotation, and the reordering of rows.

Though serialism has declined as a compositional technique, its influence on later styles has been substantial.

MUSIC FROM THE CHAPTER IN CHRONOLOGICAL CONTEXT

Year	Composer	Work	Reference
1935	Alban Berg	Violin Concerto	Serialism
1947	**Milton Babbitt**	**Three Compositions for Piano**	**p. 265**
1952	John Cage	*4'33"*	Chance Music
1952	**Pierre Boulez**	***Structures Ia***	**p. 269**
1954	Edgard Varèse	*Poème Electronique*	Electronic Music
1956	**Luigi Nono**	***Il canto sospeso***	**p. 270**
1961	Krzysztof Penderecki	*Threnody: To the Victims of Hiroshima*	Aleatoric Music
1964	Terry Riley	*In C*	Minimalism

Works in **bold** are from the chapter; those not in bold are landmark pieces written around the same time.

NOTES

1. A palindrome is a structure that reads the same backwards as it does forwards. Examples are the word "noon" and Messiaen's nonretrogradable rhythms (see p. 116).

2. There are apparently at least two other errors, in mm. 125 and 135, both being occasions when the last note of the row is articulated slightly after the first note of the next statement. The second of these makes little difference, but "correcting" m. 125 significantly alters mm. 125–42.

3. George Perle and Paul Lansky, "Twelve-Note Composition," in Stanley Sadie, Ed., *The New Grove Dictionary of Music and Musicians.*

4. Reginald Smith Brindle, *The New Music,* p. 52.

5. Ibid., p. 53.

★

EXERCISES

Part A: Fundamentals

1. Suppose that P-2 of some row begins on D and ends on B♭. Fill in the missing information below.

	Row Form	First Note	Last Note
(a)	P-2	D	B♭
(b)	P-___	___	A♭
(c)	R-2	___	___
(d)	R-___	___	F
(e)	I-2	___	___
(f)	I-___	E	___
(g)	RI-2		___
(h)	RI-___	E♭	___

2. Identify any rows discussed in this chapter that are all-interval rows.

3. Identify any rows discussed in this chapter that are derived sets, and explain your answer.

4. Is combinatoriality employed in Example 13-1? Explain how you can tell whether it is or is not.

5. Same question for Example 13-2.

Part B: Analysis

1. Boulez: *Structures Ia* (1982), mm. 8–15. This excerpt is a continuation of Example 13-2. When doing the following exercises, consider both excerpts, as well as the discussion of *Structures Ia* in the text.

   (a) Identify the P forms in Piano I, and explain how they are derived from the matrices.

   (b) Do the same for the I forms in Piano II.

   (c) Study the durations used in Piano I, and explain how they are derived from the matrices. A rest should be counted as part of the duration of the note that precedes it.

   (d) Do the same for Piano II.

(e) Try to determine what the dynamic "scale" must be, if 1 = *pppp* and 12 = *ffff*.
    Hint: Boulez inserts *quasi p* between *p* and *mp* and *quasi f* between *mf* and *f*.

(f) Use the dynamic scale to determine which matrix diagonals are being used
    for Piano I and Piano II. Note that the dynamics in Example 13-B-1 count twice
    for each piano because they apply to two row forms.

2. Analyze Stravinsky's use of his five-note row in the "Dirge-Canons (Prelude)" from *In Memoriam Dylan Thomas* (discussed on p. 275). In addition to labeling the row forms, comment on the relative consonance and dissonance of the vertical sonorities used.

Part C: Composition

1. Compose an excerpt that will be similar to Nono's *Il canto sospeso* (discussed earlier). Instead of four strands use three—8th note, triplet 8th note, and 16th note—or choose three durations of your own. Notate each strand on a separate staff. Use Nono's pitch set, but instead of using Nono's 12-element duration series, use this 11-element series: 1, 2, 3, 5, 8, 13, 8, 5, 3, 2, 1. Continue through at least three statements of the durational series (33 notes). If possible, this should be composed for instruments in your class. Make the rhythms as easy to read as you can, and include an analysis.

FURTHER READING

Antokoletz, Elliott. *Twentieth-Century Music.* See Chapter 15, Total Serialization in Europe, and pp. 387–396.

Brindle, Reginald Smith. *The New Music.* See Chapter 5, Integral Serialism, and Chapter 6, Numbers.

———. *Serial Composition.* See Chapter 14, Permutations and Other Variants of a Series, and the section titled "Integral Serialism" in Chapter 15.

Dallin, Leon. *Techniques of Twentieth Century Composition.* See Chapter 15, Total Organization.

Griffiths, Paul. *Modern Music and After.* See "Europe 2: Total Organization, 1949–1954" and pp. 59–69.

———. "Serialism," in Stanley Sadie, Ed., *The New Grove Dictionary of Music and Musicians.*

Lester, Joel. *Analytic Approaches to Twentieth-Century Music.* See Chapter 15, Other Aspects of Serialism, and pp. 277–285.

Morgan, Robert P. *Twentieth-Century Music.* See Chapter 16, Integral Serialism.

Simms, Bryan R. *Music of the Twentieth Century.* See pp. 84–90, 108–112, 348–352.

Straus, Joseph N. *Introduction to Post-Tonal Theory.* See pp. 231–245.

———. *Stravinsky's Late Music.*

———. *Twelve-Tone Music in America.*

Whittall, Arnold. *Serialism.* See Chapters 8 through 14.

Wittlich, Gary. "Sets and Ordering Procedures in Twentieth-Century Music," in Gary Wittlich, Ed., *Aspects of Twentieth-Century Music.* See pp. 430–444.

CHAPTER 14

The Roles of Chance and Choice in Post-Tonal Music

INTRODUCTION

There has been a general tendency in Western music to restrict the performer's options ever more closely, and at the same time an increasing dedication to honoring the composer's intentions at the expense of the performer's interpretive freedom. Compare Bach's *Well-Tempered Clavier* (1722, 1742), which lacks any indications of tempo, dynamics, or articulation, with Debussy's Preludes (1910, 1913), which are full of detailed and descriptive instructions, and compare them both with the examples of integral serialism in which every note has its own dynamic marking and articulation. Though elements of chance are present in any live musical performance (after all, there is always the possibility of a mistake), the emphasis has usually been on more control, not on improvisation.

Nevertheless, an important force in music in the second half of the twentieth century moved in just the opposite direction, toward less control by the composer and more creative responsibility for the performer. As we shall see, this new responsibility can range from making an insignificant decision to shaping all aspects of the piece. In either case, the composer deliberately leaves something unspecified, up to chance or to the whim of the performer. Two terms used for music of this sort are **indeterminacy** and **aleatory**. The distinction between these two terms, when one is made, is philosophical: "indeterminacy" refers to a desire to distance the composer from the process of making music, whereas "aleatory" refers to allowing performers a certain amount of latitude in order to achieve an effect that would be difficult or impossible to notate.

A related movement has made use of chance in the compositional process itself. If it is a good thing for the composer to be less involved in the way a piece is to be performed, then it might follow that the composer should also be less involved in the way that it is composed, and this can be accomplished by introducing elements of chance into the compositional process.

These two approaches—chance in composition and choice in performance—form the two related branches of **experimental music**, a term that is appropriate for any music in which the final product is deliberately kept beyond the control of the composer.

CHANCE IN COMPOSITION

To allow chance to play a part in composition, the composer must decide what aspects of the work are to be decided by chance and what the range of probabilities of each aspect should be. For example, we could compose a piece for piano without dynamics and then apply the dynamics randomly by flipping coins or rolling dice. We would still have to decide on the range of the dynamics (perhaps *ppp* to *fff*) and how often they were to change. In general, however, composers who make use of chance apply it much more broadly than this.

The most influential composer to make extensive use of chance in composition was an American, John Cage, who was mentioned in Chapter 8 in connection with Eastern philosophy (see p. 164). In a number of his chance compositions, Cage made use of procedures drawn from the *I-Ching*, a Chinese treatise on probabilities, making each decision by tossing a coin six times and looking up the result on a table of "hexagrams" that symbolically represent the 64 possible outcomes (that is, 2 to the 6th power) for six coin tosses.

Imaginary Landscape No. 4 (1951) provides an early example of Cage's use of chance and an example of his originality as well. Presumably Cage decided without the help of chance the instrumentation of this piece (12 radios) and the number of performers (two for each radio). The *I-Ching* was employed to help determine the changing dynamic levels and frequencies to which each radio would be set. All of this is notated on a 12-stave score employing both traditional musical symbols and numbers. Even though the score is precisely notated, chance has a role in the performance as well, because the signals that the radios pick up are unpredictable and will vary with each performance. The *I-Ching* was also used by Cage for *Williams Mix* (see pp. 144 and 243), as well as in other works.

Composers have employed other random decision-making techniques of course. Cage used imperfections in paper to determine the placement of notes in *Music for Piano* (1952–56) and astronomical maps for *Atlas Eclipticalis* (1962). The arias for his opera *Europera 1* (1987) are selected by the 19 singers from any out-of-copyright operas, although the singers do not know until the last minute whether or when they will actually get to sing. The orchestra parts are photocopies of instrumental parts selected at random by the composer, also from out-of-copyright operas. The parts may be distributed to the players at random. Perhaps the most outlandish use of chance is *The Thousand Symphonies* (1968) by Dick Higgins, in which the "score" was produced by firing a machine gun at manuscript paper.

Computers have been used to some extent in chance composition, since they can be programmed to produce an apparently random series of numbers within a specified range and to use those numbers in decision-making processes. The speed of a computer makes practical the use of much more complex probabilistic procedures. Conditional probabilities, for example, can vary according to one or more conditions that have been decided on previously. As a very simple example, suppose we want to generate a melody that will conform to the following rules:

1.   Use only the notes C, E, and G.
2.   Allow no repeated notes.
3.   Use fewer Gs than Cs or Es.
4.   Distribute the Cs and Es evenly.

The following table would tend to produce such a melody, although we still must specify its length and the first note. To use the table, find the most recent note on the left border. Then use the percentages shown in that row to generate some note on the top border. For instance, if C is the most recent note generated, then the next note will probably be E (75 percent) but might be G (25 percent).

	C (%)	E (%)	G (%)
G	50	50	0
E	75	0	25
C	0	75	25

Conditional probabilities can be nested to any depth, with the result that the selection of a particular event may depend on the results of the last several decisions.

Lejaren Hiller is a composer whose name is often associated with computer composition.[1] Together with Leonard Isaacson, he composed the first serious computer piece, the *Illiac Suite for String Quartet*, in 1957. Though the *Illiac Suite* was somewhat tentative creatively, the *Computer Cantata* (1963), by Hiller and Robert Baker, is a more substantial composition and explores conditional probabilities systematically. Other composers associated with this technique include Iannis Xenakis, who calls his computer music "stochastic music," Larry Austin, whose *Canadian Coastlines* (1981) is a complex eight-part canon for instruments and tape, and Barry Vercoe, whose *Synapse for Viola and Computer-Synthesized Tape* (1976) is a serial work in which many of the details were decided by a computer.

A great deal of work in computer-synthesized sound and in computer-assisted composition has been carried out in Paris at IRCAM, which opened in 1977 and was for many years directed by Pierre Boulez. Software packages developed at IRCAM to assist in composition include Formes, Crime, and, more recently, PatchWork.

Computers have also been used for many years in an attempt to create new music in the style of some composer of the past, such studies typically concentrating either on the compositional process or on how a musical style is defined. Important work in the latter area has been done in recent years by the composer David Cope.

CHOICE IN PERFORMANCE

Aleatory in performance can range all the way from the most insignificant detail to the entire shape of the piece. On the one hand are works in which the indeterminate elements may be so unimportant that any two performances of the piece will be very similar; on the other hand are pieces that are totally improvised and will vary greatly from one performance to the next. The elements of composition that may be left up to the performer include the following:

medium (instrumentation)
expression (dynamics, etc.)
duration (rhythm and tempo)
pitch
form.

In practice, these categories often appear in combination, but it is useful to discuss them briefly individually, after which we will consider some examples from the literature.

Leaving the performing medium unspecified is not a practice unique to post-tonal music—Bach's *Art of Fugue* (1750) is a famous eighteenth-century example—but it is a practice that had been largely abandoned for some time. Nevertheless, a number of post-tonal works leave open either the performing medium or the number of performers, or both.

Expression, including everything from dynamics and articulation to the most subtle nuance, has been of increasing concern to most composers. Even from Mozart to Beethoven we see development in this area, and much more from Beethoven to Debussy. However, composers interested in allowing the performer to have more freedom frequently omit expression marks, although the usual practice is not to do so unless other aspects of the piece are also indeterminate.

Indeterminacy in duration can be handled in a number of ways. Tempos can be "as fast as possible" or "as slow as possible." Rhythm can be left open by providing note heads on the staff while leaving the durations completely up to the performer. The composer can exercise more control by the use of **proportional notation**, in which the spacing of the notes on the page indicates their approximate durations, as in Example 6-9 (p. 113).

A simple example of pitch indeterminacy is the instruction "as high as possible." More extended examples often show the general contour, while leaving the precise pitches up to the performer. An instance of this was encountered in Example 6–10 on p. 114. Here the flutes are given contours to follow repetitively for 18 seconds, after which all are to begin at a fairly low pitch and work their way upward. A composer may choose not to provide even a contour, in which case the choice of pitch and register is entirely up to the performer.

The usual method of leaving the form of a work unspecified, short of total improvisation, is to allow the performer or conductor to choose the order in which the sections of a piece will be performed, how often they will be performed, and even whether they will be performed at all. This approach to form is sometimes called **open form** or **mobile form**.

Free improvisation, where nothing is specified, can be exhilarating for the performer, but it never seemed to catch on and was largely a phenomenon of the 1970s. More structured improvisation has had followers since at least the 1960s, and it is still flourishing under the guidance of composer-performers such as John Zorn.

SOME EXAMPLES OF PERFORMER INDETERMINACY

Stockhausen's *Piano Piece XI* (*Klavierstück XI*) (1956) was one of the first European works to employ open form. The score, a single page roughly 21 (37 inches, consists of 19 precisely notated segments of varying lengths, the proportions being governed by a Fibonacci series.[2] The segments are played in any order, and the performer is instructed to choose the order randomly without intentionally linking one to another. If a segment is played a second time, instructions in parentheses such as *8va* may allow some variation. When a segment is "arrived at for the third time," the piece is over, even though some segments may not have been played at all. Each segment is followed by symbols that specify tempo, dynamics, and mode of attack, and these are to be applied to the *next* segment in each case (the performer chooses the tempo, dynamics, and mode of attack for the first segment that is performed).

Cornelius Cardew's *Octet '61 for Jasper Johns* (1961) is a free-form composition "not necessarily for piano." The score consists of 60 "signs" that are to be interpreted cyclically—that is, sign 60 is followed by sign 1. The performer may begin anywhere and end anywhere, and the signs may be taken in reverse order if desired. An additional wild-card sign is provided for use "anywhere and as often as desired." The first six signs are shown in Example 14-1. Notice that sign 1 includes the Arabic numerals 6 and 7, sign 3 contains 3 and 5, and sign 6 contains 1, 6, and 7. Cardew provides hints for interpreting some of the symbols used in the signs, but the instructions emphasize creativity and interpretation rather than conformity. As an illustration of one of the many ways of interpreting signs 1 through 6, Cardew provides the illustration seen in Example 14-2. His key to the illustration follows the example.

EXAMPLE 14-1 Cardew: *Octet '61 for Jasper Johns* (1961), signs 1–6

Used by permission of C. F. Peters Corporation, on behalf of Hinrichsen Edition, Ltd., London. © 1962 by Hinrichsen Edition, Ltd.

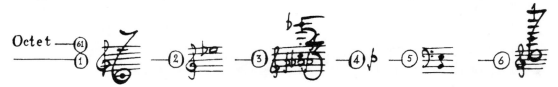

EXAMPLE 14-2 Cardew: *Octet '61 for Jasper Johns* (1961), illustration and key from instructions to score

Used by permission of C. F. Peters Corporation, on behalf of Hinrichsen Edition, Ltd., London. © 1962 by Hinrichsen Edition, Ltd.

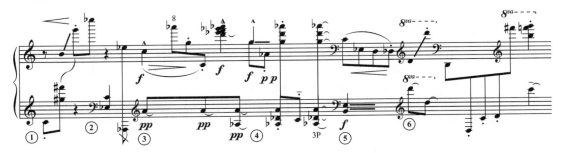

1. Seven taken literally as a configuration in musical space. Six Cs, one added to each of the first six signs.
2. Add E flats.
3. Three As. Five A flats. Three sustained notes *forte:* the others *piano* or *pianissimo.* Five-note cluster-type chord.
4. Two chords *piano* following the dot-dash rhythm of the Gs in 3.
5. Slide from E down towards B.
6. Six different registers for D (colour pitch). Seven described as in 1. One described as subsequent cluster. One C at given pitch—longer duration.

Stockhausen's *Piano Piece X* (*Klavierstück X*) (1961) calls for a tempo "as fast as possible." Macro-durations are indicated above the staff, as in Example 14-3. Here the durations above the staff are a quarter note, a double whole note tied to an 8th note, an 8th note, and so on. The pitches on the staff are to be played within the given duration, with ascending and descending beams indicating *accelerando* and *ritardando*. The long slurs that join some stems (for instance, the F#4–G4 in the right hand near the beginning) call for the first note to be sustained until the second one is reached. The visual attractiveness of *Piano Piece X* is part of its appeal, and the same is true of many works composed in the second half of the twentieth century. Perhaps more than in any other period, it is helpful for the contemporary composer to be competent at drafting or in the use of notational software.

EXAMPLE 14-3 Stockhausen: *Piano Piece X* (1961), first system

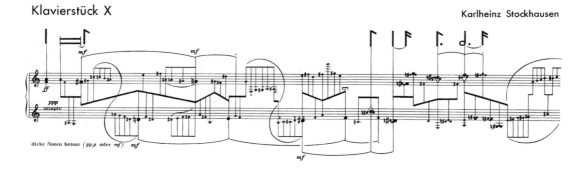

Morton Feldman's *The Straits of Magellan* (1962), for seven instruments, is a good example of controlled ensemble improvisation. Each box in Example 14-4 represents a unit of the basic tempo, MM88. An empty box stands for silence. The other boxes are to be realized by improvisation, except that the symbol in each box restricts what the performer can do:

> *Arabic numeral:* Play that many notes in succession, except for the pianist, who should play them as a chord.
> *Roman numeral:* Play that many notes as a chord.
> *F:* Flutter-tongue one tone.
> *T:* Double-tongue one tone.
> *Diamond:* Play as a harmonic.

The dynamics are specified as "very low throughout," and "all sounds are to be played with a minimum of attack."

EXAMPLE 14-4 Feldman: *The Straits of Magellan* (1962), first 20 boxes on p. I

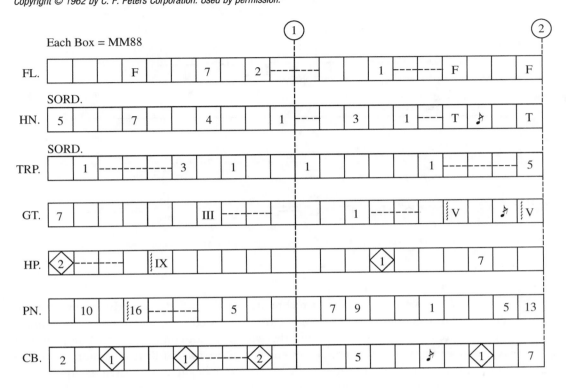

The third movement of Lukas Foss's *Baroque Variations* (1967) is titled "On a Bach Prelude (Phorion)" and is based on the Prelude to Bach's Partita in E Major for solo violin (an example of quotation music—see Chapter 8). This orchestral work requires a number of choices on the part of both the conductor and the performers. For example, at rehearsal no. 2 in the score, a section that "should last circa 2 minutes," the conductor chooses from four groups of instrumentalists, cuing first one, then another, with only general instructions in the score concerning which groups to favor and which to neglect. At 3, five soloists play passages they have selected independently from the "Bach sheet" provided with the score, while at 5 the woodwinds are provided with note heads and the instruction to "place anywhere within bar, unevenly. Vary placement." Similar techniques are used throughout the movement, with nearly all of the pitch material being derived from the Bach work.

Foss's *Thirteen Ways of Looking at a Blackbird* (1978) uses a number of interesting techniques, including tape delay and pitch indeterminacy. The tenth song begins with a 30-second improvised duet for flute and percussion, the percussionist playing on the strings of a piano with tape-covered triangle beaters. Example 14-5 shows the composer's instructions for this duet along with a sample beginning. Note especially the instruction to "Use all twelve notes." The effect desired here, as in most improvisations, is one of free atonality, not serialism, and certainly not diatonicism.

EXAMPLE 14-5 Foss: *Thirteen Ways of Looking at a Blackbird* (1978), X, instructions and first system

Witold Lutoslawski devised a technique that he called **aleatoric counterpoint**, illustrated in Example 14-6. The conductor provides cues at nine points in the example (see the arrows above the score), but otherwise does not conduct. The winds play their repeated patterns at a fast tempo, essentially in an uncoordinated fashion, until the conductor cues a change of pattern (the last arrow) or begins a conducted section. Notice that each group (piccolo/flutes, oboes, and horns) has its own pitch material and that the patterns within each choir are somewhat similar, resulting in uncontrolled imitation within each group. (In this excerpt, all of the instruments except the piccolo sound as written, and an accidental applies only to the note it precedes.) Other composers have sought simpler solutions to this problem. Einojuhani Rautavaara in his Symphony No. 5 (1985) uses a performance direction of "independently," while John Corigliano in his Symphony No. 1 (1988) specifies "nonaligned," both of which result in a similar kind of uncontrolled imitation. The 13 whistlers in Example 6-10 (p. 114) provide yet another example.

GRAPHIC SCORES AND TEXT SCORES

A **graphic score** is one in which conventional musical notation has been abandoned in favor of geometric shapes and designs that suggest more or less clearly how the music is to be performed. The Feldman excerpt (Example 14-4) is an example of one approach to graphic notation. Whereas Feldman provides fairly specific guidance for his performers, Martin Bartlett provides much less for the unspecified ensemble that is to perform the second movement of *Lines from Chuang-Tzu* (1973). In this movement, shown in its entirety in Example 14-7, dynamics are indicated by the size of the dots. Nothing else is specified.

EXAMPLE 14-6 Lutoslawski: Symphony No. 3 (1983), pp. 1–2 (winds only)

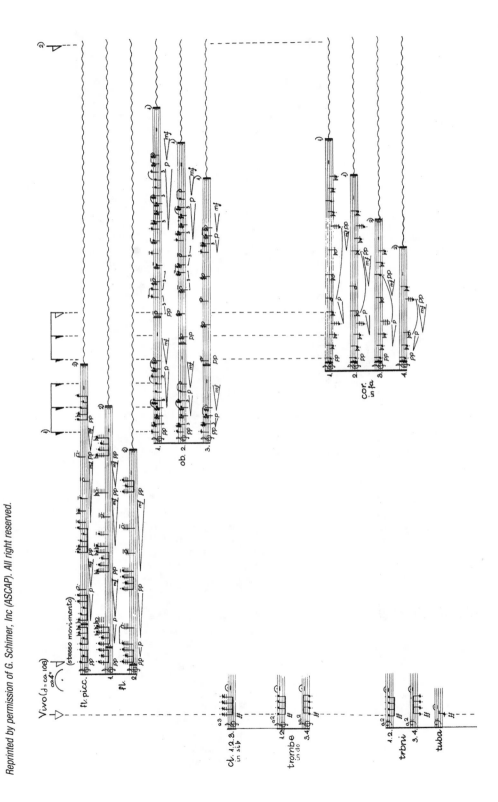

EXAMPLE 14-7 Bartlett: *Lines from Chuang-Tzu* (1973), II

Reprinted from SOURCE: Music of the Avant Garde, Issue 11, 1972, with permission from Composer/Performer Edition, 2109 Woodbrook, Denton, TX 76205.

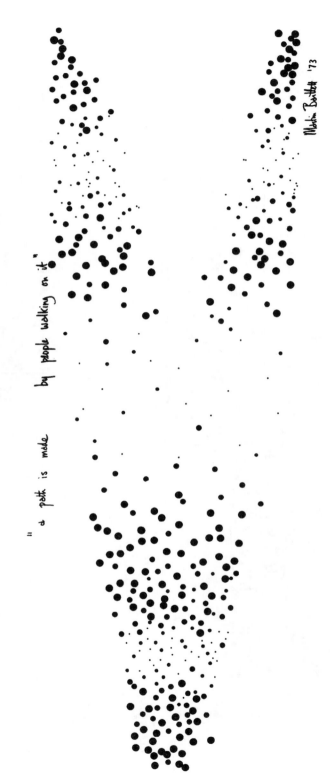

Even less information is given by Robin Mortimore for *Very Circular Pieces* (1970). In the movement shown in Example 14-8, "Repeat" is the only performance instruction.

EXAMPLE 14-8 Mortimore: *Very Circular Pieces* (1970), "Circular Piece"

Reprinted from SOURCE: Music of the Avant Garde, Issue 10, 1971, with permission from Composer/Performer Edition, 2109 Woodbrook, Denton, TX 76205.

A **text score** (also called an event score) is one that consists only of words. The text usually provides instructions for an improvisation, but it may do little more than set a mood. Three examples will suffice as models. Christian Wolff's "Play," from the *Prose Collection* (1969), is fairly specific in its instructions. The beginning is shown in Example 14-9.

EXAMPLE 14-9 Wolff: *Prose Collection* (1969), "Play," first 46 words

Copyright © G. Schirmer, Inc. (ASCAP). International copyright secured. All rights reserved. Used by permission.

> Play, make sounds, in short bursts,
> Clear in outline for the most part;
> quiet; two or three times more towards
> as loud as possible, but as soon as you
> cannot hear yourself or another player
> stop directly. Allow various spaces
> between playing (2, 5 seconds, indefinite) . . .

The second example, Stockhausen's *For Times to Come* (1970) (Example 14-10), is a composition for an unspecified ensemble, and it illustrates what Stockhausen calls "intuitive music."

EXAMPLE 14-10 Stockhausen: *For Times to Come* (1970), "Waves"

Reprinted with permission of Stockhausen-Verlag, 5067 Kuerten, West Germany.

> Overtake the others
> Hold the lead
> Allow yourself to be overtaken
> Less often

The third example, Stephen Montague's *Quintet* (1978), instructs the performer to record four interpretations of "a famous work" on the four tracks of a tape. The tape is then to be played while the musician performs live yet another interpretation, so that the audience hears the five versions simultaneously, each with its own tempos, dynamics, and so forth.

MUSIC ON THE FRINGE

Graphic scores and text scores were typical of the **Fluxus** movement that began in New York City in the early 1960s. Fluxus composers and artists were anti–Art (with a capital A), in much the same way as were the Dada artists of the 1920s, rejecting the notion that art was accessible only by the elite. Some composers in the 1960s and 1970s, especially, whether associated with the Fluxus movement or not, wrote pieces that seemed to many musicians to push the limits of what can be called "music." Traditional definitions of music often include references to organized sound and to the expression of ideas and emotions, but some works challenge these notions. One example is the last movement of Dick Higgins's *Constellations for the Theatre (Number X)* (1965), a text score given in its entirety as Example 14-11.

EXAMPLE 14-11 Higgins: *Constellations for the Theatre (Number X)* (1965), "A Winter Carol"

From Constellations and Contributions by Dick Higgins. Copyright © 1961 by Richard C. Higgins. All rights reserved. Reprinted by permission.

Any number of people may perform this composition. They do so by agreeing in advance on a duration for the composition, then by going out to listen in the falling snow.

This is not the only work to concentrate the attention of the audience on the natural sounds that exist in the environment. Pauline Oliveros's *Bonn Feier* (1976) is an environmental theater piece that uses an entire city or university as its performance stage. All of the normal activities that take place in the environment are part of the performance, but there are also a large number of specialized performers—actors, groups of musicians, picketers carrying blank signs, and so on. In addition, there are a number of "costumed guardians" who stand near the sources of everyday environmental sounds (motors, practice rooms, traffic) and point them out to people who pass by. The piece ends with a "final ritual" in which the performers move in a circle around a bonfire chanting "Feier" (the German word for celebration or festival) "until each person can no longer participate."[3]

A famous work that often outrages audiences new to it is Cage's *4'33"* (1952), for any instrument or combination of instruments. It consists of three movements, each of which consists only of the direction "Tacet," the durations of the three movements adding up to *4'33"*. While usually performed at the piano, it can be equally effective as an ensemble piece.

Other works seem at first to be hopelessly absurd, but the underlying purpose may still be serious. A movement of Mortimore's *Very Circular Pieces* (1970) contains the performance instruction "Play until 2000 a.d." What was an audience in 1970 supposed to do with this? Was the piece not meant to be performed at all? Or were they to keep it in their minds until the year 2000? Or was the purpose to encourage us to meditate on the coming millennium? And what about Paul Ignace's *Symphonie Fantastique No. 2*, a duplication of the Berlioz work sprung on an unsuspecting concert audience, many of whom had heard the Berlioz the previous night? Is the purpose here humor, surprise, or, as the composer suggests, to get people to listen to the music in a new way?[4]

The list of types of music "on the fringe" goes on and on. There is, for example, "biofeedback music," in which the performers control the sounds by means of changing the alpha-wave output from their brains. More sinister is a category that David Cope calls "danger music."[5] Some of it suggests self-directed violence, as in Takehisa Kosugi's *Music for a Revolution*, which begins, "Scoop out one of your eyes five years from now,"[6] while others, such as Philip Corner's *One Antipersonnel-Type CBU Bomb Will Be Thrown into the Audience*, are more threatening to the audience.

Lively accounts of these and other "fringe" movements can be found in the books by Cope and Michael Nyman listed at the end of this chapter.

SUMMARY

Experimental music, in which the composer consciously abdicates control over the compositional process or the performance, or both, has been an important element of music in the second half of the twentieth century. Chance in composition has involved the use of a number of decision-making techniques, including the *I-Ching*, while the computer has made practicable aleatoric compositions that are much more complex.

The element of chance (or, from the performer's viewpoint, choice) has been even more influential in the performance of music than in composition. The improvised portions of a score may be insignificant, or improvisation may be the major element of interest in the work. New notations have been devised for indeterminate music, including proportional and graphic notation; text scores dispense with notation entirely. Finally, a number of "fringe" movements have ranged from the absurd to the violent, calling into question our notion of what music really is.

MUSIC FROM THE CHAPTER IN CHRONOLOGICAL CONTEXT

Year	Composer	Work	Reference
1952	John Cage	*4'33"*	Chance Music
1954	Edgard Varèse	*Poème Electronique*	Electronic Music
1961	Krzysztof Penderecki	*Threnody: To the Victims of Hiroshima*	Aleatoric Music
1961	**Cornelius Cardew**	*Octet '61 for Jasper Johns*	**p. 287**
1961	**Karlheinz Stockhausen**	*Piano Piece X*	**p. 288**
1962	**Morton Feldman**	*The Straits of Magellan*	**p. 289**
1964	Terry Riley	*In C*	Minimalism
1965	**Dick Higgins**	*Constellations for the Theatre*	**p. 294**
1969	**Christian Wolff**	*Prose Collection*	**p. 293**
1970	**Robin Mortimore**	*Very Circular Pieces*	**p. 293**
1973	**Martin Bartlett**	*Lines from Chuang-Tzu*	**p. 292**
1983	**Witold Lutoslawski**	*Symphony No. 3*	**p. 291**

Works in **bold** are from the chapter; those not in bold are landmark pieces written around the same time.

NOTES

1. Do not make the all-too-common error of confusing computer sound synthesis (see Chapter 12) with computer composition. Either or both may be employed in a particular composition.

2. Robin Maconie, *The Works of Karlheinz Stockhausen*, p. 101.

3. Oliveros, *Bonn Feier*.

4. Cope, *New Directions in Music*, pp. 166–167.

5. Ibid., pp. 168–171.

6. Michael Nyman, *Experimental Music*, p. 68.

★

EXERCISES

Part A: Analysis

1. Study the pitch material in each of the three choirs in Example 14-6, remembering that the score is written at concert pitch and that an accidental applies only to the note it precedes.

    (a) What is similar about the pitch material in the three choirs?

    (b) Analyze the pitch-class set types found in each choir.

    (c) Do the pitch classes used in the winds complete an aggregate?

    (d) How does the pitch material in the three choirs relate to the Es that open the movement?

2. Look up the word "music" in at least two dictionaries, and copy out the main (first) definitions. Then relate those definitions to the kinds of works discussed in this chapter. Do some of the works lie outside the definitions and, if so, should the definitions be changed? Are the definitions even too restrictive for more con-servative post-tonal music? Can you suggest a better definition for "music," or a term for the kinds of pieces that you feel are not really music?

Part B: Composition and Performance

1. Compose and rehearse an improvisatory piece for ensemble. Try to restrict the choices of the performers so that the piece will have the same basic shape each time it is performed. Explain how your controls will satisfy the assignment. Then perform it twice for the class.

2. Compose a graphic score to be performed by a soloist (unspecified medium), with few instructions. Explain (to your instructor) how you decided on the arrangement of the graphic symbols and how they might be interpreted. Have it performed by a volunteer from your class.

3. Compose a short piece for some instrument in your class in which some of the compositional decisions are made by random choice (flipping coins, etc.), and explain how you composed it. Make two versions of the piece, and have both performed for the class.

FURTHER READING

Antokoletz, Elliott. *Twentieth-Century Music.* See pp. 474–497.

Bateman, Wayne. *Introduction to Computer Music.* See Chapter 11, Composition with the Computer.

Brindle, Reginald Smith. *The New Music.* See Chapter 8, Indeterminacy, Chance, and Aleatory Music; Chapter 9, Improvisation—Graphic Scores—Text Scores; and Chapter 12, Cage and Other Americans.

Childs, Barney. "Indeterminacy," in John Vinton, Ed., *Dictionary of Contemporary Music.*

Cope, David H. *Computers and Musical Style.*

——. *Experiments in Musical Intelligence.*

——. *New Directions in Music.* See Chapter 5, Indeterminacy; Chapter 6, Experimentalism; and Chapter 10, Automated Music.

——. *Techniques of the Contemporary Composer.* See Chapter 14, Indeterminancy, and Chapter 17, Algorithmic Composition.

Dallin, Leon. *Techniques of Twentieth Century Composition.* See Chapter 18, Indeterminate Procedures.

Dodge, Charles, and Thomas A. Jerse. *Computer Music.* See Chapter 8, Composition with Computers.

Griffiths, Paul. "Aleatory," in Stanley Sadie, Ed., *The New Grove Dictionary of Music and Musicians.*

Heussenstamm, George. *The Norton Manual of Music Notation.*

Karkoschka, Erhard. *Notation in New Music.*

Kostelanetz, Richard, Ed., *John Cage.*

Morgan, Robert P. *Twentieth-Century Music.* See Chapter 17, Indeterminacy.

Nyman, Michael. *Experimental Music.* See Chapter 3, Inauguration 1950–60: Feldman, Brown, Wolff, Cage; Chapter 4, Seeing, Hearing: Flexus; Chapter 5, Electronic Systems; and Chapter 6, Indeterminacy 1960–70: Ichiyanagi, Ashley, Wolff, Caldew, Scratch Orchestra.

Read, Gardner. *Modern Rhythmic Notation.*

Simms, Bryan. *Music of the Twentieth Century.* See Chapter 13, Indeterminacy.

Stone, Kurt. *Music Notation in the Twentieth Century.*

CHAPTER 15

Minimalism and Beyond

INTRODUCTION

This chapter is concerned with minimalism and with other trends that came to the fore even later. These later trends are known by an array of labels such as postminimalism, the new romanticism, the new tonality, totalism, eclecticism, and polystylistics. All of these categories, which are for the most part fuzzily defined and overlapping, share at least one characteristic with each other as well as with minimalism: to some extent, at least, the music that they represent is pitch-centric and occasionally even tonal in the traditional sense of the term.

MINIMALISM

Minimal music, also called **process music, phase music, pulse music, systemic music**, and **repetitive music**, may have had its roots in some of the works that Cage, Wolff, and Feldman composed in the 1950s, but the first important example of what has become known as minimalism was Terry Riley's *In C* (1964). This composition, still well known today, exemplifies most of the characteristics of the minimalist style, and we will discuss it in some detail.

In C is a composition of unspecified duration to be performed by an unspecified ensemble. The score consists of 53 figures—most of them quite short—that are to be performed in order. Each motive is repeated as often as the individual performer desires, except that the performer has an obligation to contribute to the overall ensemble effect. This means that the performers more or less randomly follow each other through the score, sometimes leading the rest of the ensemble, at other times lagging behind, so that several motives may be heard simultaneously, even though gradual progress is being made toward ending the piece. This process, sometimes called **phasing**, resembles that of a traditional canon, which is why *In C* was discussed in Chapter 7 under the heading "Canon and Fugue" (see p. 139).

The pitch material of the figures is extremely limited, very different from the complex motivic material of the serial composers of the same period. They begin by establishing C major (see figures 1 and 2 in Example 15-1). A half-cadence on the dominant is reached at figure 15 (see figures 14 and 15), followed by an E minor section in figures

18 to 28 (see figure 22). After a return to C in 29 to 34 (see figure 29), a tonally ambiguous climax is reached at 35 (see figure 35). The remainder of the piece seems to return to C for a while but ends in G minor (see figures 52 and 53). Superimposed over this modulating canon is a constant pulse, or ostinato, provided by a pianist playing the two highest Cs on the instrument in steady 8th notes.

In all, the work employs only nine of the 12 pitch classes, and the nine are introduced gradually:

Figure	New Pitch Class
1	C, E
2	F
4	G
9	B
14	F♯
22	A
35	B♭
45	D

EXAMPLE 15-1 Riley: *In C* (1964), Figures 1, 2, 14, 15, 22, 29, 35, 52, 53

Used by permission of the composer.

Because it occurs so rarely, the introduction of a new pitch class, or of a new register, becomes a major event in the piece. Even without mentally cataloguing the pitch material used up to that point, the listener is immediately affected, even shocked, by the appearance of a previously unheard pitch class.

Many of the characteristics of minimalism have been encountered in our discussion of *In C*. These characteristics would include the following:

restricted pitch and rhythm materials
pitch-centricity; *Tonic*   *tonal or neotonal language*
~~pan~~diatonicism
use of repetition
phasing
drones or ostinatos
steady pulse
static harmony
indeterminacy
long duration

Many of these aspects are also found in some kinds of Eastern music, as is the meditative quality characteristic of many minimalist works. Riley, Steve Reich, and Philip Glass, the three Americans most closely associated with minimalism, all studied Eastern music, with Glass's study of the improvisations of Ravi Shankar being especially important to the development of his mature style.[1]

Reich's *Come Out* (1966) was mentioned in Chapter 12 in reference to the tape loops that were used to construct the piece (see p. 243). *Come Out* concentrates on the phasing aspect of minimalism, taking it much further than *In C* does. Incidentally, it also illustrates the interest that some post-tonal composers have had in mixing their music with politics. In this case, a victim of police violence during the 1964 Harlem riots wanted to prove that he was injured so that he would be taken to the hospital. He explains, "I had to, like, open the bruise up and let some of the bruise blood come out to show them." The words "come out to show them" were transferred to two loops and played simultaneously, but since no two tape players operate at precisely the same speed, the words move gradually out of phase. A recording of that process was in turn converted into two loops, and so on, building up the texture of the work to a dense and complex level.[2]

Notice that the phasing process in *Come Out* is different from that used in *In C*, because in *Come Out* the part that takes the lead keeps it and pulls ever farther ahead of the follower. Reich used the same approach for live performers in *Piano Phase* (1967). In this work the two pianists repeat in unison the pattern seen in Example 15-2, but soon piano II increases the tempo slightly until the two instruments are one 16th note apart. This process is repeated until piano II completes the "loop" and rejoins piano I in unison.

EXAMPLE 15-2 Reich: *Piano Phase* (1967), m. 1

Gradually moving out of phase as in *Piano Phase* is difficult for performers to accomplish. Reich employs a simpler solution in *Clapping Music* (1972). Here the two performers clap the first measure in unison 12 times. They then move on to the second measure, in which the pattern in the Clap 2 part has been shifted one 8th note to the left. After 12 times through this measure, the performers move on to the next, where Clap 2 is shifted one more 8th note, and so on, until they are once more in unison.

A variation on the phasing technique was introduced by Reich in *Drumming* (1971) and *Six Pianos* (1973) (rescored as *Six Marimbas* in 1986). *Six Pianos* begins with four of the pianists playing a repeated rhythmic pattern in unison (rhythmic unison, not pitch unison). The two "out-of-phase" pianists, in unison with each other, gradually introduce a rhythmic pattern that, when completed, turns out to be the same as the original one, but two beats out of phase with it. Similar techniques are used in Reich's *Sextet* (1985). An important difference between this technique and the earlier phase pieces is that in this case the relationship between the two out-of-phase parts does not change through time.

Reich's *New York Counterpoint* (1985) makes extensive use of pulsing and various kinds of phasing. It is written for 11 clarinets, but ten of the clarinet parts are usually prerecorded by a single clarinetist, who then plays the "Live Cl" part along with the tape. The first movement begins with several minutes of pulsing chords, all diatonic to A♭ major, with the various parts fading in and out. Melodic patterns later appear that are phased as in Example 15-3. The three parts here are in a strict rhythmic canon, but the pitch material, while identical, is slightly reordered in each part. Similar techniques are used throughout the composition. Comparable works are *Vermont Counterpoint* (1982) and *Electric Counterpoint* (1987) for flute and guitar, respectively.

EXAMPLE 15-3 Reich: *New York Counterpoint* (1985), I, rehearsal 17

Another more recent work by Reich, *Different Trains* (1988), recalls his interest in the recorded human voice in *Come Out*, discussed earlier in this chapter. Here, though, the recorded voice is not looped but instead provides the basic motivic material for the string quartet that plays along with the taped voices and train sounds.

Though phasing is important in many of Reich's pieces, this is not true of all minimalist music.[3] Frederic Rzewski's *Coming Together* (1972), for example, another work with political overtones, is for a narrator accompanied by a single musical line, so phasing is impossible. Glass's *Strung Out* (1967) is for a single amplified violin, which begins by stating the central motive of the piece, seen in Example 15-4. Like *In C*, it gradually introduces pitches, in this case all diatonic to C major, until the climax of the piece is reached about 10′ 30″ into the performance, after which the entire piece is repeated. Though the gradual introduction of pitches is important, the listener's attention is also drawn to the variation of the original motive, as well as to the two startling changes of bow technique (at about 2′ 50″ and 6′ 25″).

EXAMPLE 15-4 Glass: *Strung Out* (1967), opening five notes

Nor is phasing a factor in Glass's ensemble works. Instead, the focus is on repetition, pulse, and triadic harmony. His music is insistently pitch–centric, with harmonic progressions that range from banal to surprising. An example on the banal side is *Modern Love Waltz* (1977), where the harmony alternates throughout between an A major triad or an A dominant 7th chord and a B♭ dominant 7th chord.

Glass's *Wichita Vortex Sutra* (1988) consists of 136 measures, almost all of them repeated, in the key of F major. This lack of tonal variety is tiresome to some, but obviously not to all. The excerpt in Example 15-5 is typical of the work.

EXAMPLE 15-5 Glass: *Wichita Vortex Sutra* (1988), mm. 35–37

The usual approach that Glass takes in his more recent music is to establish a tempo through a pulsating background chord, over which various accompanimental figurations are laid. Changes of harmony follow, without disturbing the pulse or the accompanimental figures. After some time, an abrupt shift of tonal center, while maintaining the original pulse, announces a new section with new accompanimental figures. Melody in the traditional sense is absent. Glass frequently uses a singer in his works, but the vocalist usually has no text and instead is treated as an instrument.

Glass has achieved substantial popular success, enabling him to embark on larger projects. In fact, as of mid 2010, he has composed five string quartets, eight symphonies, 13 concertos, 24 operas, and 39 film scores.

John Adams's *Short Ride in a Fast Machine* (1986) is a good (and exhilarating) example of minimalism. Example 15-6 illustrates a primary motive of the piece, a motive that is heard unchanged throughout much of the work. Notice that the two clarinet parts (which sound a minor third lower) are phased one 8th note apart. Although the tonal center of the work is clearly D Mixolydian, it contains a good deal of chromaticism, including the final cadence: ♭II–♭V–I. The use of nondiatonic pitch material is one characteristic that distinguishes Adams's minimalist style from that of most other minimalists. In *The Wound Dresser* (1988), for example, the first 19 measures consist of a single hexatonic [014589] pitch-class set that unfolds mostly in triadic patterns. The other six pitch classes enter rather rapidly after that, completing the aggregate (all 12 pitch classes) by m. 27.

EXAMPLE 15-6 Adams: *Short Ride in a Fast Machine* (1986), mm. 1–4

Copyright 1986 by Hendon Music, Inc., a Boosey & Hawkes Company. Reprinted by permission.

Morton Feldman is a composer who is often credited with providing the model for the minimalist movement, although little of his music is truly minimalist as defined in this chapter. However, *Piano and String Quartet* (1985) and *For Samuel Beckett* (1987) are good examples of late minimalism. Both feature slowly changing textures and pitch material and much repetition, but not of the insistent, pulsating variety that led some critics of minimalism to refer to it as "wallpaper music."

EXAMPLE 15-7 Reich: *Double Sextet* (2007), mm. 33–37

Minimalism began to lose its appeal in the 1980s, and most composers have moved on to other things or have at least branched out. For example, while several of the best known minimalist works were composed by John Adams, including *Shaker Loops* (1978) and *Nixon in China* (1987), there is very little even remotely minimalist about Adams's Violin Concerto (1993), and, in fact, much of it is atonal. On the other hand, his minimalist background is much more apparent in *Hoodoo Zephyr*, which dates from the same year, especially in the track titled "Bump." The term **postminimalism** is often used in connection with works that have a minimalist underpinning but that have a more complex surface and in which the compositional process is less transparent than in the minimalist works of the 1960s and 1970s. An excerpt from a more recent postminimal work is seen in Example 15-7. The *Double Sextet* consists of three movements, performed without a pause between them. The outer movements have a tempo of quarter note = 164, the middle movement exactly half that, and there is an attack on virtually every 8th note in the piece. In the first movement, from which Example 15-7 is excerpted, the meter signatures alternate almost every measure between $\frac{6}{8}$, $\frac{2}{4}$, $\frac{5}{8}$, and $\frac{6}{8}$, so the performers have to think in terms of the 8th note = 328 rather than quarter note = 164. Notice in Example 15-7 the constant 8ths, which are typical of minimalism, but also the additive rhythm and the departures from the prevailing D major scale, which are not.

The influence of the minimalists has been considerable. In the United States this can be seen in the music of Laurie Anderson, a performance artist whose work lies somewhere between the traditionally popular and traditionally serious, and in rock music in groups such as Tirez Tirez. In Europe, minimalism has had an influence on the music of a large number of composers and experimental rock groups.[4] Unfortunately, the student of this music will find that much of it is available only in recorded form, although scores are gradually becoming more available.

BEYOND MINIMALISM

The music of the last two decades of the twentieth century and the first decade of the twenty-first presents a dizzying array of compositional approaches and techniques, and this is reflected in the titles of the final chapters of two books on contemporary music: David Cope's *Techniques of the Contemporary Composer* ends with a chapter titled "Decategorization," and Paul Griffiths's *Modern Music and After* ends with a nearly 90-page discussion called "Strings and Knots." Of course, post-tonal music has always been a study in contrasts, and that is one thing that makes the study of it so fascinating—and sometimes frustrating. It has been a period in which very disparate composers such as Rachmaninoff (1873–1943) and Webern (1883–1945) could come out of Europe and one in which Copland (1900–1990) and Cage (1912–1992) were produced in the United States. What is different about the period we are talking about is that so many composers felt free to work in a number of styles, often combining contrasting compositional approaches—tonality and atonality, for example—within the same work and even within the same movement. This is what is meant by the terms totalism, eclecticism, and polystylistics that were mentioned in the introduction to this chapter. You will encounter many instances of eclecticism in the works discussed later.

In Chapter 8 we discussed the use of musical quotations in post-tonal music, especially in music composed in the mid 1960s and later. In most cases these fragments were quoted out of context, superimposed on an atonal, avant-garde background, or swallowed up in a collage of other quotations in a stream-of-consciousness style. Another movement, which paralleled and grew out of quotation music, involved the return of triadic harmony in a style that is sometimes called neoromanticism, or the new tonality. As we shall see, the more recent music we are examining here tends to be more consonant, more conservative, and much more reminiscent of earlier music.

In the music of George Rochberg, quotation technique led eventually to a "real and personal rapprochement with the past"[5] in the form of a traditional tonal style with a distinctive Romantic flavor. His first neoromantic work was String Quartet No. 3 (1972). The beginning of the first movement is devoted to the kind of dissonant and disjunct figure that one might expect at the outset of an atonal work (Example 15-8).

EXAMPLE 15-8 Rochberg: String Quartet No. 3 (1972), I, m. 1

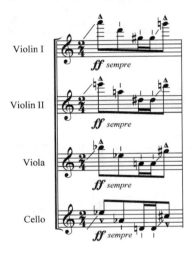

A more lyrical, yet still dissonant, figure interrupts at m. 27, but the dissonant opening motive returns in m. 40. Another lyrical section, related to the one at m. 27, begins at m. 64 and contains elements of polytonality and the whole-tone scale. This leads to the passage shown in Example 15-9. In that excerpt, at m. 87 a B major triad appears beneath the whole-tone/polytonal material. This is followed in mm. 90–102 by a conventional harmonic progression in the key of B major, although we are reminded from time to time of the whole-tone/bitonal material. This B major progression, though not a quotation, is handled in a manner that strongly suggests nineteenth-century music, yet it seems somehow to have a beauty and meaning that it would not possess if it appeared in a nineteenth-century composition. Its purity and the directness of its communication are striking when juxtaposed against the typically dissonant and symmetrical post-tonal structures.[6]

Not all of Rochberg's music since 1972 is neoromantic—his String Quartet No. 7 (1979), for example, is not at all in that style—but much of it is. Often Rochberg will include both tonal and atonal movements in the same work, rather than mixing the two together in a single movement as in Example 15-9. The first movement of his String Quartet No. 6 (1978) is atonal, but the second movement is a tonal scherzo and trio,

EXAMPLE 15-9 Rochberg: String Quartet No. 3 (1972), I, mm. 81–102

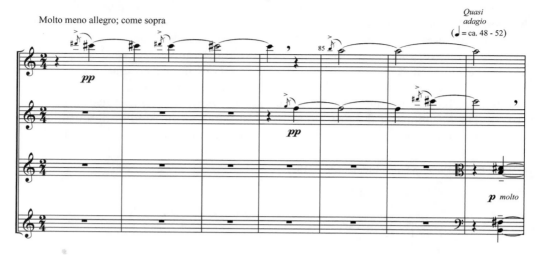

N.B.: Vlns. 1-2 still rubato; loose

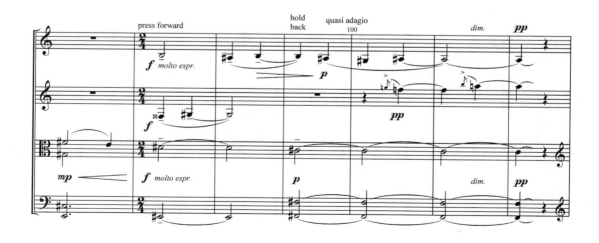

and the third is a set of continuous variations on the tune from Pachelbel's Canon in D. Every movement but the fourth in his String Quartet No. 5 (1978) is in the neoromantic style; the third movement is a scherzo and trio in a familiar nineteenth-century idiom.

Though Rochberg is the composer whose name is most closely associated with neoromanticism in the United States, he is certainly not the only representative of the style. The series of works composed by David Del Tredici on Lewis Carroll's Alice stories are an important example. Some of the music of Frederic Rzewski might be considered neoromantic, although the motivation in his case often seems to be political instead of musical, an example being his piano variations on *The People United Will Never Be Defeated!* (1975). Well-known Europeans associated with neoromanticism or the new tonality include Arvo Pärt, Krzysztof Penderecki, Alfred Schnittke, and John Tavener.

Composers in the late twentieth century found that they were again free to take advantage of the expressive power of the triad, even in an atonal context. An early use of triadic materials is Schnittke's Violin Sonata No. 2 ("quasi una Sonata") (1968), an atonal work that is introduced by a loud, widely spaced G minor triad that reappears frequently in this one-movement work. The effect is reminiscent of the beginning of Stravinsky's *Symphony of Psalms* (see p. 227). Einojuhani Rautavaara's Symphony No. 5 (1986), also an atonal work, begins with a progression that takes nearly three minutes to unfold: C–eb–d–F#. (Notice the two doubly chromatic mediants.) Each chord begins softly, builds in intensity, and then explodes in a dissonance from which the next sonority gradually emerges.

John Tavener's *Celtic Requiem* (1969) is an extraordinary collage of materials from nursery rhymes to noise over an ever-present Eb major triad. His *The Protecting Veil* (1987) is pitch-centric throughout; in fact, the first four minutes of the work are entirely diatonic in F major, although traditional tonal progressions are not used, and the first movement ends over a C#m7 chord. The work does end in F major.

Tavener and others occasionally reach back historically for techniques that even predate tonality. Examples include mensuration canons in Pärt's *Festina Lente* (1988) and Tavener's *The Protecting Veil*. In Example 15-10, the parallel fifths between the solo cello and cello I evoke medieval organum, but the dissonances created by the real inversion in cello II are obviously from a later century.

EXAMPLE 15-10 Tavener: *The Protecting Veil* (1987), first three measures after J

Penderecki's Symphony No. 2 (1980), though chromatic, is clearly in F♯ minor. The beginning of this work, shown in Example 15-11, seems to suggest that key, but it soon shifts to F minor. Especially striking and Romantic in flavor is the B minor to F minor progression in mm. 6–7.

Pärt's *Fratres* (1977), a work that exists in several versions, is based on a Phrygian scale on A with a raised third (C♯), which gives the work a wonderful major/minor quality. (In one version the scale is on G.) It is "tonal" throughout, as are his later works.

EXAMPLE 15-11 Penderecki: Symphony No. 2 (1980), I, mm. 1–8

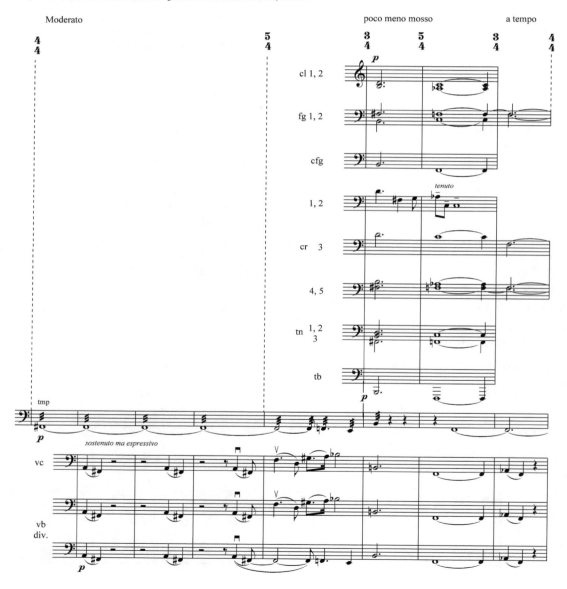

Triadic harmony in the new tonality may or may not conform to traditional tonal progressions. For instance, the nine triads in Example 15-12 contain only one 5th-related progression, the B♭ to E♭ from the second chord to the third one.

EXAMPLE 15-12 Schnittke: Piano Sonata No. 1 (1988), I, page 4

Example 15-13 is from a pitch-centric song that begins and ends in F and in which the harmonic language is largely tertian. Notice the conventional bass line at the beginning of the excerpt (F–G–A♭–B♭–C), although the chords above it are not simple triads.

EXAMPLE 15-13 Libby Larsen: *Sonnets from the Portuguese*, "I thought once how Theocritus had sung" (1991), mm. 7–11

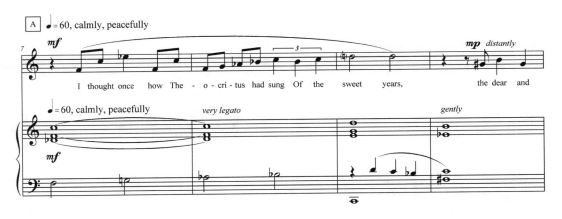

This is not a book about the history of Western art music since 1900, but about the compositional materials and techniques that came into use during that period. Nevertheless, readers naturally want to know what the next big thing is, the new "ism," and we must report at this point that we do not know. Many of the currents covered in this book—and not just in this final chapter—are still flowing through the musical landscape: serialism, improvisation, electronic music, spectralism, postminimalism, and so on.

However, compared to the 1950s, it is apparent that many composers today (but not all, by any means) have adopted a more traditionally accessible, even conservative style. This may be in response to the accessibility and unprecedented popularity of minimalism in its heyday, or it may just be a thoroughly understandable desire on the part of composers to connect with their audiences on a level more emotional than intellectual.

Play through or listen to the excerpt by Lowell Liebermann in Example 15-14. After two measures of introduction on a B minor chord (the Gs are upper neighbors to the F#s), the music unfolds in a very nineteenth-century fashion until it reaches a cadence on the dominant eight measures later. Although some of the harmonic shifts and occasional dissonances may not be clearly nineteenth century in style, the overall effect is Romantic, and the music is immediately accessible to the average listener.

A big question now is this: Do we hear these "traditional" gestures and pieces in the same way we would have had the litany of post-tonal innovations explored in this text never happened? In his famous story, "Pierre Menard, Author of the *Quixote*,"

EXAMPLE 15-14 Liebermann: Nocturne No. 8, Op. 85 (2003), mm. 1–10

Argentinian author Jorge Luis Borges played with the idea that, even if one rewrote *Don Quixote* today exactly, word for word, it would not carry the same meaning as it did when Cervantes wrote it.[7] That is because meaning is contextual. The same is probably true of how we hear music. We simply do not hear neoromantic compositions in the way that listeners did in the nineteenth century, when the style was new, because we are aware now of how they sound against the backdrop of the materials and techniques with which students of this textbook are familiar.

Whatever the future direction of what we consider to be art music, it is clear that the new music scene today is a healthy one, certainly more so than it was in the 1950s. Today nearly every college or university of any size has a new music ensemble, often populated by the very best student musicians and led by a conductor committed to bringing the finest contemporary music to receptive audiences. Writing a few years ago in *The New Yorker*, Alex Ross reported that in 1967 New York City had only two full-time new music ensembles, contrasting that with the situation in 2007, at which time there were more than 40 such organizations.[8] This is good news, and it portends well for new music in the twenty-first century.

SUMMARY

While the postserial avant-garde tradition has not died out, it has certainly met with serious opposition in the forms of indeterminacy, minimalism, and neo-romanticism. Indeterminacy, the subject of Chapter 14, was a reaction against the total control that is the basis for integral serialism. Minimalism opposes the atonal ideals of the incessant recycling of pitch material, of constant variation, and, of course, of atonality itself. Neoromanticism does these things, too, but it also represents a complicated relationship between today's composer (and listener) and the music of the past.

And so twentieth-century music continues into the twenty-first century as it has always been—a maddening but fascinating collage of approaches and materials, a period without a style. It may be, of course, that the differences among composers and techniques that seem so blatant to us now will appear to be only matters of detail to later generations and that post-tonal music will have a characteristic "sound" that will be easily identified, much as the sound of Haydn and Mozart represents a certain portion of the eighteenth century. But those who struggle to understand post-tonal music are generally more impressed by its contrasts than by its consistencies.

One can't help but wonder about Brahms, who died in 1897: What would he think of what has happened to music, and could he have predicted in 1897 what music might be like in our time? Surely none of us can imagine what music will be like at the end of the twenty-first century, when the grandchildren of today's college students will themselves be grandparents, and the newest of today's music will represent a bygone era. It is enough, perhaps, if we can greet each turn in the musical road with an open mind, a receptive ear, and a sense of what has come before.

MUSIC FROM THE CHAPTER IN CHRONOLOGICAL CONTEXT

Year	Composer	Work	Reference
1952	John Cage	*4'33"*	Chance Music
1954	Edgard Varèse	*Poème Electronique*	Electronic Music
1961	Krzysztof Penderecki	*Threnody: To the Victims of Hiroshima*	Aleatoric Musuic
1964	**Terry Riley**	***In C***	**Minimalism, p. 300**
1967	**Steve Reich**	***Piano Phase***	**p. 301**
1967	**Philip Glass**	***Strung Out***	**p. 303**
1972	**George Rochberg**	**String Quartet No. 3**	**pp. 307, 308**
1980	**Krzysztof Penderecki**	**Symphony No. 2**	**p. 310**
1985	**Steve Reich**	***New York Counterpoint***	**p. 302**
1986	**John Adams**	***Short Ride in a Fast Machine***	**p. 304**
1987	**John Tavener**	***The Protecting Veil***	**p. 309**
1988	**Philip Glass**	***Wichita Vortex Sutra***	**p. 303**
1988	**Alfred Schnittke**	**Piano Sonata No. 1**	**p. 311**
1991	**Libby Larsen**	***Sonnets from the Portuguese***	**p. 311**
2003	**Lowell Liebermann**	**Nocturne No. 8**	**p. 312**
2007	**Steve Reich**	***Double Sextet***	**p. 305**

Works in **bold** are from the chapter; those not in bold are landmark pieces written around the same time.

NOTES

1. John Rockwell, *All American Music*, p. 111.
2. Barry Schrader, *Introduction to Electro-Acoustic Music*, pp. 19–20.
3. Some writers prefer to treat phase music as a separate category from minimalism, since minimalist music does not always employ phasing, but they share many of the same characteristics and are often created by the same composers.
4. A representative list is given in Wim Mertens's *American Minimal Music*, p. 11, to which might be added the names of Simon Bainbridge (British) and Wolfgang Rihm (German).
5. Rochberg, in the liner notes for Nonesuch album H-71283, George Rochberg: String Quartet No. 3.
6. An analysis of the first 100 measures of this movement appears in Jay Reese, "Rochberg the Progressive."
7. Borges, *Ficciones*.
8. Alex Ross, "Club Acts: New York's Vital New Music Scene," *The New Yorker*, April 16, 2007, p. 166.

EXERCISES

Part A: Analysis

1. Listen to a recording of Riley's *In C* (1964). Excerpts from this work are given in Example 15-1. Try to notate the other figures that make up the work.

2. Listen to a recording of Glass's *Strung Out* (1967). The opening is given in Example 15-4. Use the track timing to record when exactly new pitches (not pitch classes) are introduced as well as other significant events in the piece, such as changes in articulation. The piece is played twice without pause on the only available recording.

3. Analyze the harmonies and nonchord tones of the B major progression in Example 15-9.

4. Number the chords in Example 15-12, and label them according to root and type. Next, label any chromatic mediant progressions as "<cm>"and any doubly chromatic mediant progressions as "<dcm>." Analyze the other root relationships. Are there any repeated or sequenced progressions involving these chords?

5. Analyze the harmonies and nonchord tones in Example 15-13, being sure to take the vocal line into consideration. Identify the root and quality of the tertian chords in mm. 7, 8, 9, and 11. The nontertian chord in m. 10 will require a different approach.

6. Listen to the entire third movement of Rochberg's String Quartet No. 5. Diagram the form. Identify as many tonal areas and important cadences as you can (the movement begins in A minor).

7. Listen to the entire third movement of Rochberg's String Quartet No. 6. Write down the two lines that constitute the four-measure theme (the key is D major). Then try to follow the theme through the subsequent variations. After several variations (how many?), the theme is augmented into an eight-measure form for one variation— this happens again later. In other variations, the original lines of the theme are almost totally obscured, but the basic four-bar structure is still audible in most cases. Rochberg occasionally ends a variation on I instead of V, and in two variations he inverts the descending contour of the original melody. Try to identify and characterize each variation.

Part B: Composition

1. Compose *In F*, an imitation of Riley's *In C*, for instruments and/or vocalists in your class. See the discussion of *In C* in the text.

2. Compose a phase piece in imitation of Reich's *Clapping Music* for some combination of performers in your class. See the discussion of this work in the text.

3. Try to compose a neoromantic excerpt in imitation of the first movement of Rochberg's String Quartet No. 3. This is a difficult assignment, because the tonal music should not sound silly or mawkish when it enters. Write this for some combination of performers in your class.

FURTHER READING

Bernard, Jonathan W. "Minimalism, Postminimalism, and the Resurgence of Tonality in Recent American Music."

Carl, Robert. *Terry Riley's "In C."*

Cope, David H. *Techniques of the Contemporary Composer.* See Chapter 21, Decategorization.

Gann, Kyle. *American Music in the Twentieth Century.* See Chapter 8, Minimalism, and Chapter 13, Totalism in the 1990s.

———. "A Forest from the Seeds of Minimalism: An Essay on Postminimal and Totalist Music."

Griffiths, Paul. *Modern Music and After.* See "Minimalism and Melody," pp. 209–244, and "Strings and Knots," pp. 239–327.

Mertens, Wim. *American Minimal Music.*

Morgan, Robert P. *Twentieth-Century Music.* See Chapter 20, A Return to Simplicity: Minimalism and the New Tonality.

Nyman, Michael. *Experimental Music.* See Chapter 7, Minimal Music, Determinacy, and the New Tonality.

Reese, Jay. "Rochberg the Progressive."

Schwarz, K. Robert. "Steve Reich: Music as a Gradual Process."

Simms, Bryan R. *Music of the Twentieth Century.* See Chapter 16, Recent Music in Europe and America.

Appendix

PRIME FORMS, FORTE LABELS, AND INTERVAL-CLASS VECTORS

The tables below list all of the possible prime forms (set classes) that contain three to nine pitch classes. Column 1 displays the prime form of the set class (the letter "T" is used, if necessary, to stand for the number 10). Column 2 contains the Forte label for the set class—that is, the name that Allen Forte gave to the set in *The Structure of Atonal Music*, which is the label that is used in all of the current literature. Column 3 contains the interval-class vector of the set class. The next three columns contain the same information, in reverse order, for the **complement** of that set. The complement of any set of pitch classes includes all of the remaining pitch classes out of the total of 12. For example, the complement of the black keys of the piano would be the white keys of the piano.

The set classes are arranged numerically by prime form in order to make it easier to find the Forte labels and the interval-class vectors. Forte's original tables arranged the sets by interval-class vector, which explains why the Forte labels seem to be out of order in some cases.

TRICHORDS

[012]	3–1	<210000>	<876663>	9–1	[012345678]
[013]	3–2	<111000>	<777663>	9–2	[012345679]
[014]	3–3	<101100>	<767763>	9–3	[012345689]
[015]	3–4	<100110>	<766773>	9–4	[012345789]
[016]	3–5	<100011>	<766674>	9–5	[012346789]
[024]	3–6	<020100>	<686763>	9–6	[01234568T]
[025]	3–7	<011010>	<677673>	9–7	[01234578T]
[026]	3–8	<010101>	<676764>	9–8	[01234678T]
[027]	3–9	<010020>	<676683>	9–9	[01235678T]
[036]	3–10	<002001>	<668664>	9–10	[01234679T]
[037]	3–11	<001110>	<667773>	9–11	[01235679T]
[048]	3–12	<000300>	<666963>	9–12	[01245689T]

NONACHORDS

TETRACHORDS

				OCTACHORDS	
[0123]	4–1	<321000>	<765442>	8–1	[01234567]
[0124]	4–2	<221100>	<665542>	8–2	[01234568]
[0125]	4–4	<211110>	<655552>	8–4	[01234578]
[0126]	4–5	<210111>	<654553>	8–5	[01234678]
[0127]	4–6	<210021>	<654463>	8–6	[01235678]
[0134]	4–3	<212100>	<656542>	8–3	[01234569]
[0135]	4–11	<121110>	<565552>	8–11	[01234579]
[0136]	4–13	<112011>	<556453>	8–13	[01234679]
[0137]	4–Z29	<111111>	<555553>	8–Z29	[01235679]
[0145]	4–7	<201210>	<645652>	8–7	[01234589]
[0146]	4–Z15	<111111>	<555553>	8–Z15	[01234689]
[0147]	4–18	<102111>	<546553>	8–18	[01235689]
[0148]	4–19	<101310>	<545752>	8–19	[01245689]
[0156]	4–8	<200121>	<644563>	8–8	[01234789]
[0157]	4–16	<110121>	<554563>	8–16	[01235789]
[0158]	4–20	<101220>	<545662>	8–20	[01245789]
[0167]	4–9	<200022>	<644464>	8–9	[01236789]
[0235]	4–10	<122010>	<566452>	8–10	[02345679]
[0236]	4–12	<112101>	<556543>	8–12	[01345679]
[0237]	4–14	<111120>	<555562>	8–14	[01245679]
[0246]	4–21	<030201>	<474643>	8–21	[0123468T]
[0247]	4–22	<021120>	<465562>	8–22	[0123568T]
[0248]	4–24	<020301>	<464743>	8–24	[0124568T]
[0257]	4–23	<021030>	<465472>	8–23	[0123578T]
[0258]	4–27	<012111>	<456553>	8–27	[0124578T]
[0268]	4–25	<020202>	<464644>	8–25	[0124678T]
[0347]	4–17	<102210>	<546652>	8–17	[01345689]
[0358]	4–26	<012120>	<456562>	8–26	[0134578T]
[0369]	4–28	<004002>	<448444>	8–28	[0134679T]

PENTACHORDS				SEPTACHORDS	
[01234]	5–1	<432100>	<654321>	7–1	[0123456]
[01235]	5–2	<332110>	<554331>	7–2	[0123457]
[01236]	5–4	<322111>	<544332>	7–4	[0123467]
[01237]	5–5	<321121>	<543342>	7–5	[0123567]
[01245]	5–3	<322210>	<544431>	7–3	[0123458]
[01246]	5–9	<231211>	<453432>	7–9	[0123468]
[01247]	5–Z36	<222121>	<444342>	7–Z36	[0123568]
[01248]	5–13	<221311>	<443532>	7–13	[0124568]
[01256]	5–6	<311221>	<533442>	7–6	[0123478]
[01257]	5–14	<221131>	<443352>	7–14	[0123578]
[01258]	5–Z38	<212221>	<434442>	7–Z38	[0124578]
[01267]	5–7	<310132>	<532353>	7–7	[0123678]
[01268]	5–15	<220222>	<442443>	7–15	[0124678]
[01346]	5–10	<223111>	<445332>	7–10	[0123469]
[01347]	5–16	<213211>	<435432>	7–16	[0123569]
[01348]	5–Z17	<212320>	<434541>	7–Z17	[0124569]
[01356]	5–Z12	<222121>	<444342>	7–Z12	[0123479]
[01357]	5–24	<131221>	<353442>	7–24	[0123579]
[01358]	5–27	<122230>	<344451>	7–27	[0124579]
[01367]	5–19	<212122>	<434343>	7–19	[0123679]
[01368]	5–29	<122131>	<344352>	7–29	[0124679]
[01369]	5–31	<114112>	<336333>	7–31	[0134679]
[01457]	5–Z18	<212221>	<434442>	7–Z18	[0145679]
[01458]	5–21	<202420>	<424641>	7–21	[0124589]
[01468]	5–30	<121321>	<343542>	7–30	[0124689]
[01469]	5–32	<113221>	<335442>	7–32	[0134689]
[01478]	5–22	<202321>	<424542>	7–22	[0125689]
[01568]	5–20	<211231>	<433452>	7–20	[0125679]
[02346]	5–8	<232201>	<454422>	7–8	[0234568]
[02347]	5–11	<222220>	<444441>	7–11	[0134568]
[02357]	5–23	<132130>	<354351>	7–23	[0234579]
[02358]	5–25	<123121>	<345342>	7–25	[0234679]
[02368]	5–28	<122212>	<344433>	7–28	[0135679]
[02458]	5–26	<122311>	<344532>	7–26	[0134579]
[02468]	5–33	<040402>	<262623>	7–33	[012468T]
[02469]	5–34	<032221>	<254442>	7–34	[013468T]
[02479]	5–35	<032140>	<254361>	7–35	[013568T]
[03458]	5–Z37	<212320>	<434541>	7–Z37	[0134578]

Hexachords

In this table, Z-related sets are listed across from each other. Because Z-related sets by definition have the same interval-class vector, there is only one column of vectors.

[012345]	6–1	<543210>		
[012346]	6–2	<443211>		
[012347]	6–Z36	<433221>	6–Z3	[012356]
[012348]	6–Z37	<432321>	6–Z4	[012456]
[012357]	6–9	<342231>		
[012358]	6–Z40	<333231>	6–Z11	[012457]
[012367]	6–5	<422232>		
[012368]	6–Z41	<332232>	6–Z12	[012467]
[012369]	6–Z42	<324222>	6–Z13	[013467]
[012378]	6–Z38	<421242>	6–Z6	[012567]
[012458]	6–15	<323421>		
[012468]	6–22	<241422>		
[012469]	6–Z46	<233331>	6–Z24	[013468]
[012478]	6–Z17	<322332>	6–Z43	[012568]
[012479]	6–Z47	<233241>	6–Z25	[013568]
[012569]	6–Z44	<313431>	6–Z19	[013478]
[012578]	6–18	<322242>		
[012579]	6–Z48	<232341>	6–Z26	[013578]
[012678]	6–7	<420243>		
[013457]	6–Z10	<333321>	6–Z39	[023458]
[013458]	6–14	<323430>		
[013469]	6–27	<225222>		
[013479]	6–Z49	<224322>	6–Z28	[013569]
[013579]	6–34	<142422>		
[013679]	6–30	<224223>		
[023679]	6–Z29	<224232>	6–Z50	[014679]
[014568]	6–16	<322431>		
[014579]	6–31	<223431>		
[014589]	6–20	<303630>		
[023457]	6–8	<343230>		
[023468]	6–21	<242412>		
[023469]	6–Z45	<234222>	6–Z23	[023568]
[023579]	6–33	<143241>		
[024579]	6–32	<143250>		
[02468T]	6–35	<060603>		

Straus, Joseph N., *Introduction to Post-Tonal Theory*, 3rd Edition, © 2005, pp. 261–264. Reprinted by permission of Pearson Education, Inc., Upper Saddle River, NJ.

Bibliography

Aldwell, Edward, and Carl Schachter. *Harmony and Voice Leading*. 3rd ed. New York: Schirmer, 2002.

Alegant, Brian. *The Twelve-Tone Music of Luigi Dallapiccola*. Rochester, NY: University of Rochester, 2010.

Anderton, Craig. *MIDI for Musicians*. New York: Amsco, 1986.

Antokoletz, Elliot. *The Music of Béla Bartók: A Study of Tonality and Progression in Twentieth-Century Music*. Berkeley, CA: University of California Press, 1984.

——. *Twentieth-Century Music*. Englewood Cliffs, NJ: Prentice Hall, 1992.

Appleton, John H., and Ronald C. Perera, Eds. *The Development and Practice of Electronic Music*. Englewood Cliffs, NJ: Prentice Hall, 1975.

Austin, William W. *Music in the 20th Century*. New York: W. W. Norton, 1966.

Babbitt, Milton. *Words about Music*. (Eds.). Stephen Dembski and Joseph N. Straus. Madison, WI: University of Wisconsin Press, 1987.

Bailey, Kathryn. *The Twelve-Note Music of Anton Webern*. Cambridge: Cambridge University Press, 1991.

Bartolozzi, Bruno. *New Sounds for Woodwind*. Translated and edited by Reginald Smith Brindle. London: Oxford University Press, 1967.

Bass, Richard. "Sets, Scales, and Symmetries: The Pitch-Structural Basis of George Crumb's Makrokosmos I and II." *Music Theory Spectrum* 13:1 (1991), pp. 1–20.

Bateman, Wayne. *Introduction to Computer Music*. New York: John Wiley, 1980.

Benward, Bruce, and Marilyn Saker. *Music in Theory and Practice*. 8th ed. New York: McGraw-Hill, 2009.

Bernard, Jonathan. *The Music of Edgard Varèse*. New Haven, CT: Yale University Press, 1987.

——. "The Evolution of Elliott Carter's Rhythmic Practice." *Perspectives of New Music* 26:2 (1988), pp. 164–203.

——. "Ligeti's Restoration of Interval and Its Significance for His Later Works." *Music Theory Spectrum* 21:1 (Spring 1999), pp. 1–31.

——. "Minimalism, Postminimalism, and the Resurgence of Tonality in Recent American Music." *American Music* 21:1 (Spring 2003), pp. 112–133.

Berry, Michael. "Sofia Gubaidulina's Serial Music." *Problemy Muzykal'noj Nauki: Rossijskij Naučnyj Specializirovannyj Žurnal/Music Scholarship: Russian Journal of Academic Studies* 2:5 (2009), pp. 53–56.

Berry, Wallace. *Form in Music*. 2nd ed. Englewood Cliffs, NJ: Prentice Hall, 1986.

Borges, Jorge Luis. *Ficciones*. New York: Grove Press, 1994.

Boss, Jack. *Schoenberg's Twelve-Tone Music: Symmetry and the Musical Idea*. Cambridge: Cambridge University Press, 2014.

Brindle, Reginald Smith. *Contemporary Percussion*. London: Oxford University Press, 1970.

——. *Musical Composition*. London: Oxford University Press, 1986.

——. *The New Music*. London: Oxford University Press, 1975.

——. *Serial Composition*. London: Oxford University Press, 1966.

Brown, Stephen C. "Twelve-Tone Rows and Aggregate Melodies in the Music of Shostakovich." *Journal of Music Theory* 59:2 (October 2015), pp. 191–234.

Bunger, Richard. *The Well-Prepared Piano*. Colorado Springs, CO: Colorado College Music Press, 1973.

Burkhart, Charles. *Anthology for Musical Analysis*. 6th ed. Belmont, CA: Schirmer, 2004.

Burkholder, Peter. *All Made of Tunes: Charles Ives and the Uses of Musical Borrowing*. New Haven, CT: Yale University Press, 1995.

Cage, John. *Silence*. Middletown, CT: Wesleyan University Press, 1961.

Capuzzo, Guy. *Elliott Carter's What Next?: Communication, Cooperation, and Separation*. Rochester, NY: University of Rochester, 2012.

Carl, Robert. *Terry Riley's "In C."* Cambridge: Oxford University Press, 2009.

Carr, Ian. *Miles Davis*. New York: William Morrow, 1982.

Chadabe, Joel. *Electric Sound: The Past and Promise of Electronic Music*. Englewood Cliffs, NJ: Prentice Hall, 1996.

Chou, Wen-Chung. "Asian Concepts and Twentieth-Century Western Composers," *Musical Quarterly* 57:2 (April 1971), pp. 211–229.

Cogan, Robert. *New Images of Musical Sound*. Cambridge, MA: Harvard University Press, 1984.

——, and Pozzi Escot. *Sonic Design*. Englewood Cliffs, NJ: Prentice Hall, 1976.

Collins, Nick, and Julio D'Escriván, Eds. *The Cambridge Companion to Electronic Music*. Cambridge: Cambridge University Press, 2008.

Cope, David H. *Computers and Musical Style*. Madison, WI: A-R Editions, 1991.

——. *Experiments in Musical Intelligence*. Madison, WI: A-R Editions, 1996.

——. *New Directions in Music*, 6th ed. Madison, WI: Brown & Benchmark, 1993.

——. *Techniques of the Contemporary Composer*. New York: Schirmer Books, 1997.

Craft, Robert. *Stravinsky: Chronicle of a Friendship, 1948–71*. New York: Alfred A. Knopf, 1972.

Cramer, Alfred. "Schoenberg's *Klangfarbenmelodie*: A Principle of Early Atonal Harmony." *Music Theory Spectrum* 24:1 (2002), pp. 1–34.

Crumb, George. *Ancient Voices of Children*. New York: C. F. Peters, 1970.

Dallin, Leon. *Techniques of Twentieth Century Composition*. 3rd ed. Dubuque, IA: Wm. C. Brown, 1974.

Day-O'Connell, Jeremy. *Pentatonicism from the Eighteenth Century to Debussy*. Rochester, NY: University of Rochester Press, 2007.

De Stwolinski, Gail. *Form and Content in Instrumental Music*. Dubuque, IA: Wm. C. Brown, 1977.

Deem, George. *How to Paint a Vermeer: A Painter's History of Art*. New York: Thames & Hudson, 2004.

Dempster, Stuart. *The Modern Trombone*. Berkeley, CA: University of California Press, 1979.

Dick, Robert. *The Other Flute: A Performance Manual of Contemporary Techniques*. Woodbury, CT: Lauren Keiser, 1989.

Dodge, Charles, and Thomas A. Jerse. *Computer Music*. New York: Schirmer Books, 1985.

Emmerson, Simon, Ed. *The Language of Electroacoustic Music*. Chur, Switzerland: Harwood Academic Publishers, 1987.

Erickson, Robert. *Sound Structure in Music*. Berkeley, CA: University of California Press, 1975.

Fanning, David, and Laurel Fay. "Shostakovich, Dmitry." *Grove Music Online*. Retrieved January 16, 2011, from www.oxfordmusiconline.com.

Ferneyhough, Brian. "Il Tempo della Figura." *Perspectives of New Music* 31:1 (Winter 1993), pp. 10–19.

Fineburg, Joshua. "Guide to the Basic Concepts and Techniques of Spectral Music." *Contemporary Music Review* 19:2 (2000), pp. 81–113.

Fink, Robert, and Robert Ricci. *The Language of Twentieth Century Music*. New York: Schirmer Books, 1975.

Forrest, David. "Prolongation in the Choral Music of Benjamin Britten." *Music Theory Spectrum* 32:1 (2010), pp. 1–25.

Forte, Allen. *The Structure of Atonal Music*. New Haven, CT: Yale University Press, 1973.

Gann, Kyle. *American Music in the Twentieth Century*. New York: Schirmer Books, 1997.

———. "A Forest from the Seeds of Minimalism: An Essay on Postminimal and Totalist Music." Retrieved from http://kylegann.com/postminimalism/html.

———. *The Music of Conlon Nancarrow*. Cambridge: Cambridge University Press, 1995.

Gariépy, Louise, and Jean Décarie. "A System of Notation for Electro-Acoustic Music: A Proposition." *Interface* 13:1 (March 1984), pp. 1–74.

Gauldin, Robert. *Harmonic Practice in Tonal Music*. New York: W. W. Norton, 1997.

Griffiths, Paul. *Modern Music and After*. Oxford: Oxford University Press, 1995.

Grimes, Ev. "Ev Grimes Interviews John Cage." *Music Educators Journal* 73:3 (November 1986), pp. 47–49ff.

Grout, Donald J. *A History of Western Music*. 3rd ed. New York: W. W. Norton, 1980.

Haimo, Ethan. *Schoenberg's Serial Odyssey: The Evolution of His Twelve-Tone Method, 1914–1928*. Oxford: Oxford University Press, 1990.

Hanninen, Dora. "Orientations, Criteria, Segments: A General Theory of Segmentation for Music Analysis." *Journal of Music Theory* 45:2 (Fall 2001), pp. 345–434.

Headlam, Dave. *The Music of Alban Berg*. New Haven, CT: Yale University Press, 1996.

Heiss, John C. "Some Multiple-Sonorities for Flute, Oboe, Clarinet, and Bassoon." *Perspectives of New Music* 7:1 (Fall–Winter 1968). pp. 136–142.

Heussenstamm, George. *The Norton Manual of Music Notation*. New York: W. W. Norton, 1987.

Hicks, Michael. "Text, Music, and Meaning in the Third Movement of Luciano Berio's *Sinfonia*." *Perspectives of New Music* 20 (1981–1982), pp. 199–224.

Hiller, Paul D. "Pärt, Arvo," in *Grove Music Online*, Oxford Music Online. Retrieved April 27, 2010, from www.oxfordmusiconline.com.

Hindemith, Paul. *Craft of Musical Composition*. London: Schott, 1968.

Holland, Bernard. "Alfred Schnittke, Eclectic Composer, Dies at 63." *New York Times*, August 4, 1998.

Howat, Roy. "Bartók, Lendvai, and the Principle of Proportional Analysis." *Music Analysis* 2:1 (March 1983). pp. 69–95.

———. *Debussy in Proportion: A Musical Analysis*. Cambridge: Cambridge University Press, 1984.

Howe, Hubert S. *Electronic Music Synthesis*. New York: W. W. Norton, 1975.

Howell, Thomas. *The Avant-Garde Flute*. Berkeley, CA: University of California Press, 1974.

Howland, Patricia. "Formal Structures in Post-Tonal Music." *Music Theory Spectrum* 37:1 (2015), pp. 71–97.

Johnson, Timothy. "Harmonic Vocabulary in the Music of John Adams: A Hierarchical Approach." *Journal of Music Theory* 37: 1 (1993), pp. 117–156.

Karkoschka, Erhard. *Notation in New Music*. Translated by Ruth Koenig. New York: Praeger, 1972.

Kennan, Kent, and Donald Grantham. *The Technique of Orchestration*. 6th ed. Englewood Cliffs, NJ: Prentice Hall, 2002.

Koozin, Timothy. "Traversing Distances: Pitch Organization, Gesture and Imagery in the Late Works of Tōru Takemitsu." *Contemporary Music* Review 21.4 (2002), pp. 17–34.

Kostelanetz, Richard, Ed. *John Cage*. New York: Praeger, 1970.

Kostka, Stefan, and Roger Graybill. *Anthology of Music for Analysis*. Upper Saddle River, NJ: Prentice Hall, 2004.

———, and Dorothy Payne. *Tonal Harmony with an Introduction to Twentieth-Century Music*. 6th ed. New York: McGraw-Hill, 2009.

Kramer, Jonathan D. "The Fibonacci Series in Twentieth Century Music." *Journal of Music Theory* 17:1 (Spring 1973), pp. 111–148.

——. "Moment Form in Twentieth Century Music." *Musical Quarterly* 64:2 (April 1978), pp. 177–194.

Krebs, Harald. "Some Extensions of the Concept of Metrical Consonance and Dissonance." *Journal of Music Theory* 31:1 (Spring 2009), pp. 99–120.

Krenek, Ernst. *Studies in Counterpoint.* New York: G. Schirmer, 1940.

Lambert, Philip. *The Music of Charles Ives.* New Haven, CT: Yale University Press, 1997.

Lendvai, Ernö. *Béla Bartók: An Analysis of His Music.* London: Kahn & Averill, 1971.

Lester, Joel. *Analytic Approaches to Twentieth-Century Music.* New York: W. W. Norton, 1989.

Ligeti, György. *György Ligeti in Conversation with Péter Várnai, Josef Haüsler, Claude Samuel, and Himself.* London: Eulenberg, 1983.

Lochhead, Judy. *Reconceiving Structure in Contemporary Music: New Tools in Music Theory and Analysis.* New York: Routledge, 2016.

Losada, C. Catherine. "Between Modernism and Postmodernism: Strands of Continuity in Collage Compositions by Rochberg, Berio, and Zimmermann." *Music Theory Spectrum* 31:1 (Spring 2009), 57–100.

——. "Complex Multiplication, Structure, and Process: Harmony and Form in Boulez's Structures II." *Music Theory Spectrum* 36:1 (Spring 2014), pp. 86–120.

Lewin, David. *Musical Form and Transformation: 4 Analytic Essays.* New Haven, CT: Yale University Press, 1983.

Maconie, Robin. *The Works of Karlheinz Stockhausen.* London: Oxford University Press, 1976.

Maegaard, Jan. "A Study in the Chronology of Op. 23–26 by Arnold Schoenberg." *Dansk aarbog for musikforskning* (1962), pp. 93–115.

Manning, Peter. *Electronic and Computer Music.* 2nd ed. Oxford: Clarendon Press, 1993.

Marsh, Roger. "Heroic Motives." *The Musical Times* 135/1812 (Feb. 1994), pp. 83–86.

Marvin, Elizabeth West, and Richard Hermann, Eds. *Concert Music, Rock, And Jazz Since 1945: Essays and Analytical Studies.* Rochester, NY: University of Rochester, 1995.

Mead, Andrew. *An Introduction to the Music of Milton Babbitt.* Princeton, NJ: Princeton University Press, 1994.

Mertens, Wim. *American Minimal Music.* New York: Alexander Broude, 1983.

Messiaen, Olivier. *The Technique of My Musical Language.* Paris: Alphonse Leduc, 1944.

Metzer, David. *Quotation and Cultural Meaning in Twentieth-Century Music.* Cambridge: Cambridge University Press, 2007.

Minturn, Neil. *The Music of Sergei Prokofiev.* New Haven, CT: Yale University Press, 1997.

Mirka, Danuta. "To Cut the Gordian Knot: The Timbre System of Krzyzstof Penderecki." *Journal of Music Theory* 45:2 (Fall 2001), pp. 435–456.

Morgan, Robert P. *Twentieth-Century Music.* New York: W. W. Norton, 1991.

Neumeyer, David. *The Music of Paul Hindemith.* New Haven, CT: Yale University Press, 1986.

Nyman, Michael. *Experimental Music*. New York: Schirmer Books, 1974.

Osmond-Smith, David. *Playing on Words*. London: Royal Music Association, 1985.

Partch, Harry. *Genesis of a Music*. 2nd ed. New York: Da Capo, 1974.

Pearsall, Edward. *Twentieth-Century Music Theory and Practice*. New York: Routledge, 2012.

Pellman, Samuel. *An Introduction to the Creation of Electroacoustic Music*. Belmont, CA: Wadsworth, 1994.

Perle, George. "Berg's Master Array of the Interval Cycles." *The Musical Quarterly* 63:1 (January 1977), pp. 1–30.

———. *Serial Composition and Atonality*. 5th ed. Berkeley, CA: University of California Press, 1981.

Perry, Jeffrey. "Cage's Sonatas and Interludes for Prepared Piano: Performance, Hearing and Analysis." *Music Theory Spectrum* 27:1 (2005), pp. 35–66.

Persichetti, Vincent. *Twentieth-Century Harmony*. New York: W. W. Norton, 1961.

Piston, Walter. *Harmony*. 5th ed. Revised by Mark DeVoto. New York: W. W. Norton, 1987.

Pressing, Jeff. *Synthesizer Performance and Real-Time Techniques*. Madison, WI: A-R Editions, 1992.

Proctor, Gregory. "Technical Bases of Nineteenth-Century Chromatic Harmony: A Study in Chromaticism." Ph.D. Diss., Princeton University, 1978.

Rahn, John. *Basic Atonal Theory*. New York: Longman, 1980.

Randel, Don, Ed. *The New Harvard Dictionary of Music*. Cambridge, MA:Belknap Press, 1986.

Read, Gardner. *Contemporary Instrumental Techniques*. New York: Schirmer Books, 1976.

———. *Modern Rhythmic Notation*. Bloomington, IN: Indiana University Press, 1978.

Reese, Jay. "Rochberg the Progressive." *Perspectives of New Music* 19 (1980–1981), pp. 394–407.

Rehfeldt, Phillip. *New Directions for Clarinet*. Lanham, MD: Scarecrow Press, 1994.

Ringo, James. "The Lure of the Orient." *American Composers Alliance Bulletin* 7:2 (1958), pp. 8–12.

Roads, Curtis. *The Computer Music Tutorial*. Cambridge, MA: MIT Press, 1996.

Rochberg, George. *Music for the Magic Theater*. Bryn Mawr, PA: Theodore Presser, 1972.

Rockwell, John. *All American Music*. New York: Alfred A. Knopf, 1983.

Roeder, John. "Beat-Class Modulation in Steve Reich's Music." *Music Theory Spectrum* 25:2 (2003), pp. 242–267.

Roig-Francoli, Miguel. *Understanding Post-Tonal Music*. New York: McGraw-Hill, 2007.

Rose, François. "Introduction to the Pitch Organization of French Spectral Music." *Perspectives of New Music* 34:2 (Summer 1996), pp. 6–39.

Ross, Alex. "Club Acts: New York's Vital New-Music Scene." *The New Yorker,* April 16, 2007.

Sadie, Stanley, Ed. *The New Grove Dictionary of Music and Musicians*. 2nd ed. London: Oxford University Press, 2001.

Salzedo, Carlos. *Modern Study of the Harp*. New York: G. Schirmer, 1921.

Samson, Jim. *Music in Transition*. New York: W. W. Norton, 1977.

Samuel, Jamuna. "Octatonic Serialism in Luigi Dallapiccola's *Il Prigioniero*." *Rivista di Analisi e Teoria Musicale* 19:2 (2013), pp. 57–81.

Santa, Matthew. "Analysing Post-Tonal Diatonic Music: A Mod7 Perspective." *Music Analysis* 19:2 (2000), pp. 167–201.

——. "Defining Modular Transformations." *Music Theory Spectrum* 21/2 (Fall 2000), pp. 200–229.

Schiff, David. *The Music of Elliott Carter*. New Haven, CT: Yale University Press, 1983.

Schmalfeldt, Janet. *Berg's Wozzeck*. New Haven, CT: Yale University Press, 1983.

Schoenberg, Arnold. *Style and Idea*. Berkeley, CA: University of California Press, 1984.

Schrader, Barry. *Introduction to Electro-Acoustic Music*. Englewood Cliffs, NJ: Prentice Hall, 1982.

Schwartz, Elliott. *Electronic Music: A Listener's Guide*. New York: Praeger, 1975.

Schwarz, K. Robert. "Steve Reich: Music as a Gradual Process." *Perspectives of New Music* 19 (1980–1981), pp. 373–392; 20 (1981–1982), pp. 225–286.

Simms, Bryan R. *Music of the Twentieth Century*. 2nd ed. New York: Schirmer Books, 1996.

Slawson, Wayne. *Sound Color*. Berkeley, CA: University of California Press, 1985.

Slonimsky, Nicholas. *Thesaurus of Scales and Melodic Patterns*. New York: C. Scribner's Sons, 1947.

Smither, Howard E. "The Rhythmic Analysis of Twentieth-Century Music." *Journal of Music Theory* 8:1 (Spring 1964), pp. 54–88.

Smyth, David. "Stravinsky as Serialist: The Sketches for Threni." *Music Theory Spectrum* 22:2 (2000), pp. 205–224.

Steinke, Greg A., and Paul O. Harder. *Bridge to 20th-Century Music*. Rev. ed. Needham Heights, MA:Allyn & Bacon, 1999.

Stoecker, Philip. "Aligned Cycles in Thomas Adès's Piano Quintet." *Music Analysis* 33:1 (2014), pp. 32–64.

Stone, Kurt. *Music Notation in the Twentieth Century*. New York: W. W. Norton, 1980.

Straus, Joseph N. *Remaking the Past*. Cambridge, MA: Harvard University Press, 1990.

——. *The Music of Ruth Crawford Seeger*. Cambridge: Cambridge University Press, 1995.

——. *Stravinsky's Late Music*. Cambridge: Cambridge University Press, 2004.

——. *Twelve-Tone Music in America*. New York: Cambridge University Press, 2009.

——. *Introduction to Post-Tonal Theory*. 4th ed. New York: W. W. Norton, 2016.

Stravinsky, Igor. *Poetics of Music*. Cambridge, MA: Harvard University Press, 1947.

Susanni, Paolo, and Elliott Antokoletz. *Music and Twentieth-Century Tonality: Harmonic Progression Based on Modality and the Interval Cycles*. New York: Routledge, 2016.

Taylor, Timothy D. *Beyond Exoticism: Western Music and the World*. Durham, NC: Duke University Press, 2007.

Turek, Ralph. *Analytical Anthology of Music*. 2nd ed. New York: McGraw-Hill, 1992.

Turetzky, Bertram. *The Contemporary Contrabass*. Berkeley, CA: University of California Press, 1974.

Van den Toorn, Pieter C. *The Music of Igor Stravinsky*. New Haven, CT: Yale University Press, 1983.

Vincent, John. *The Diatonic Modes in Modern Music*. New York: Mills Music, 1951.

Vinton, John, Ed. *Dictionary of Contemporary Music*. New York: E. R. Dutton, 1974.

Webern, Anton. *The Path to the New Music*. Edited by Willi Reich, translated by Leo Black. Bryn Mawr, PA: Theodore Presser, 1963.

Wennerstrom, Mary H. *Anthology of Twentieth-Century Music*, 2nd ed. Englewood Cliffs, NJ: Prentice Hall, 1988.

Whittall, Arnold. *Serialism*. Cambridge: Cambridge University Press, 2008.

Winold, Allen. *Harmony: Patterns and Principles*. Englewood Cliffs, NJ: Prentice Hall, 1986.

Wishart, Trevor. *On Sonic Art*, rev. ed. Amsterdam: Harwood Academic Publishers, 1996.

Wittlich, Gary, Ed. *Aspects of Twentieth-Century Music*. Englewood Cliffs, NJ: Prentice Hall, 1975.

Wuorinen, Charles. *Simple Composition*. New York: Longman, 1979.

Yasser, Joseph. *A Theory of Evolving Tonality*. New York: American Library of Musicology, 1932.

Index

Pages numbered in **boldface** contain musical examples.